NOTHING
RHYMES WITH
ORANGE

PERFECT WORDS FOR POETS, SONGWRITERS, AND RHYMERS

ORIGINALLY PUBLISHED AS
CAPRICORN RHYMING DICTIONARY

BESSIE G. REDFIELD

WITH HOPE VESTERGAARD

A PERIGEE BOOK

A PERIGEE BOOK
Published by the Penguin Group
Penguin Group (USA) Inc.
375 Hudson Street, New York, New York 10014, USA
Penguin Group (Canada), 90 Eglinton Avenue East, Suite 700, Toronto, Ontario
M4P 2Y3, Canada (a division of Pearson Penguin Canada Inc.) · Penguin Books
Ltd., 80 Strand, London WC2R 0RL, England · Penguin Group Ireland, 25 St.
Stephen's Green, Dublin 2, Ireland (a division of Penguin Books Ltd.) · Penguin
Group (Australia), 250 Camberwell Road, Camberwell, Victoria 3124, Australia
(a division of Pearson Australia Group Pty. Ltd.) · Penguin Books India Pvt. Ltd., 11
Community Centre, Panchsheel Park, New Delhi—110 017, India · Penguin Group
(NZ), 67 Apollo Drive, Rosedale, North Shore 0632, New Zealand (a division of
Pearson New Zealand Ltd.) · Penguin Books (South Africa) (Pty.) Ltd., 24 Sturdee
Avenue, Rosebank, Johannesburg 2196, South Africa

Penguin Books Ltd., Registered Offices: 80 Strand, London WC2R 0RL, England

While the author has made every effort to provide accurate telephone numbers and
Internet addresses at the time of publication, neither the publisher nor the author
assumes any responsibility for errors, or for changes that occur after publication.
Further, the publisher does not have any control over and does not assume any
responsibility for author or third-party websites or their content.

NOTHING RHYMES WITH ORANGE
Originally published as *Capricorn Rhyming Dictionary*

Copyright © 1938, 1965, 1986, 2008 by Bessie G. Redfield
Revised and expanded in 2008 by Hope Vestergaard
Cover art by Mike Mitchell
Cover design by Ben Gibson
Text design by Pauline Neuwirth, Neuwirth & Associates

PRINTING HISTORY
Perigee trade paperback edition / January 1965
First revised Perigee trade paperback edition / September 1986
Second revised Perigee trade paperback edition / November 2008

Revised Perigee trade paperback ISBN: 978-0-399-53465-2

The Library of Congress has cataloged the first revised Perigee edition as follows:

Redfield, Bessie Gordon.
    Capricorn rhyming dictionary.
    Reprint. Originally published: 1938.
    1. English language—Rhyme—Dictionaries.   I. Title.
PE1519.R414 1986   423.1   86-16934
ISBN 0-399-51272-1

PRINTED IN THE UNITED STATES OF AMERICA

10 9 8 7 6 5 4 3 2 1

CONTENTS

INTRODUCTION

THERE ARE TWO kinds of reference readers: flippers, who use dictionaries and thesauri merely as tools, and browsers, who enjoy thumbing through the pages, diverted by diphthongs, word origins, and the pure pleasure of the sounds syllables make. I'm definitely a browser, so revising the classic *Capricorn Rhyming Dictionary* was both a thrill and an exercise in staying on task. I revised the book with both kinds of readers in mind.

First, this updated version is designed to be more precise. Longtime *Capricorn* users will notice that many longer entries have been broken down into more accurate divisions—words such as *preface* are no longer listed as rhyming with *place*, for example. This will make the book more useful for nonnative speakers and for writers unwilling to settle for anything less than perfect rhyme. We've included sample phonetic spellings to indicate how each group of words should be pronounced and a rhyming sounds cross-reference to help less "phonetic" folks navigate. We've also added fun (and informative) sidebars about craft: poetic meter, song lyrics, dialects, and more. We hope that *Nothing Rhymes with Orange* will help you hone your craft and inspire you along the way.

—*Hope Vestergaard*

HOW TO USE THIS BOOK

Rʜʏᴍɪɴɢ ᴡᴏʀᴅs ᴀʀᴇ arranged by spelling and sound. At the beginning of each entry, other spellings of the same sound are listed for cross-reference. Spellings that have more than one pronunciation are designated by asterisks: the first pronunciation listed is noted by a single asterisk, the second by two asterisks, and so forth. For example, the letters "AGE" have three entries: AGE* as in *cage*, AGE** as in *garage*, and AGE*** as in *appendage*. Words that have more than one pronunciation will have asterisk(s) designating where to look for the other pronunciations, as in the case of *bow*, which can be pronounced like words found under both OW* and OW**. Please note: single- or two-letter listings such as ER*, OR*, Y*, Y**, and others often list near rhymes rather than true rhymes.

In a few cases, unusual spellings of the sound are not listed alphabetically, but under the expected spelling for that sound, as in A*, which may be spelled AIS, AIT, AY, É, ÉE, EÉ, ET, ER, and UÉ, but never simply A.

With inflected verb endings such as *–ed* or *–ing*, or *–er* or *–est* with adjectives, the alternate entries list will indicate a category of additional rhyming sounds, for example, under ACT*, the entry heading lists ACK+*ed* to show that past tenses of verbs ending in ACK also rhyme with ACT. If an inflected verb ending creates a new noun as with *etching*, *meeting*, or *clearing*, the word will be listed within the regular entries, but the entry heading for ING notes that adding *–ing* to regular verbs will create many additional rhyming words.

PHONETIC SPELLING GUIDE

Each entry in this dictionary includes the phonetic spelling for a word representative of that entry's rhyming sound. In places where it's difficult to discern the difference between two similar sounds, this phonetic spelling will help the reader sort out subtle pronunciation differences and stressed syllables. The following key to phonetic symbols used in this book is based on *Merriam–Webster's Collegiate Dictionary, Eleventh Edition.*

KEY TO SYMBOLS

\\   backslash brackets indicate phonetic spelling within

    phonetic \fə-ˈne-tik\

-    hyphens indicate syllabic breaks

    hyphen \ˈhī-fən\

ˈ   stress marks are placed immediately before the stressed syllable. A single stress mark (ˈ) indicates the primarily stressed syllable and a subscript stress mark (ˌ) indicates a secondary stress, if any.

    precipitate \pri-ˈsi-pə-ˌtāt\

( )   parentheses indicate a sound that is often but not necessarily present.

    sense \ˈsen(t)s\

\a\ as in h*a*t, m*a*d, c*a*rrot
\ā\ as in *a*pe, s*ay*, p*ai*n, th*ey*
\ä\ as in *a*h, f*a*ther, s*e*rgeant, h*ea*rt
\au\ as in p*ou*t, cr*ow*d, h*ou*se, b*ou*gh
\b\ as in *b*ook, cu*b*, ru*bb*er
\ch\ as in *ch*in, pea*ch*, pas*t*ure, ha*tch*, ques*ti*on, righ*te*ous
\d\ as in *d*og, fe*d*, ri*ddl*e
\e\ as in t*e*n, *e*lephant, m*a*ny, s*ai*d, inst*ea*d
\ē\ as in b*e*, t*ee*, pl*ea*, mon*ey*, beli*e*ve

HOW TO USE THIS BOOK

\f\ as in *if*, *puff*, *tough*, *phone*

\g\ as in *goat*, *snug*, *egg*

\h\ as in *hat*, *who*

\hw\ as in *what*, *why*, *whale*

\i\ as in *is*, *milk*, *hymn*

\ī\ as in *ice*, *pie*, *sight*, *height*, *nigh*, *sky*, *guy*

\j\ as in *jam*, *age*, *edge*, *graduate*, *fragile*

\k\ as in *cup*, *kit*, *comic*, *pack*, *acquire*, *chemistry*, *liquor*

\l\ as in *link*, *spell*

\m\ as in *me*, *comma*, *jamb*, *hymn*

\n\ as in *not*, *gnaw*, *inner*, *pneumatic*

\ŋ\ as in *sing*, *think*, *tongue*

\ō\ as in *hope*, *open*, *go*, *beau*, *doe*

\ȯ\ as in *order*, *all*, *law*, *broad*, *octopus*, *watch*

\oi\ as in *noise*, *boy*

\p\ as in *put*, *lip*, *upper*

\r\ as in *run*, *incur*, *ferry*

\s\ as in *seat*, *mess*, *scent*, *decent*

\sh\ as in *shy*, *ocean*, *tissue*, *nation*, *machine*

\t\ as in *top*, *hat*, *bitter*, *stopped*

\th\ as in *thin*, *ether*

\th̲\ as in *then*, *breathe*, *tithe*

\u\ as in *full*, *color*

\u̇\ as in *should*, *good*, *pull*, *wolf*

\ü\ as in *snooze*, *stool*, *dew*, *shoe*, *rude*, *you*

\yü\ as in *use*, *beauty*, *spew*, *view*, *feud*, *cute*

\v\ as in *vital*, *inverse*, *rev*

\w\ as in *wit*, *away*, *quiet*, *choir*

\y\ as in *you*, *onion*, *hallelujah*

\z\ as in *zest*, *fizz*, *size*, *rise*, *scissors*, *has*, *incisor*

\zh\ as in *azure*, *vision*, *garage*, *treasure*

\ə\ as in *alone*, *agent*, *vanity*, *complete*, *bus*, *circus*

\ᵊ\ immediately preceding \l\, \n\, \m\, and \ŋ\: This symbol is not a sound, but indicates that the following consonant is syllabic; the syllable does not contain a vowel, as in *button*, *cuddle*, *mitten*, *table*

RHYMING SOUNDS CROSS-REFERENCE

It's easy to overlook unusual spellings when searching for rhymes. The chart below details multiple spellings for each vowel sound.

A as in *day*	A_E (t<u>a</u>p<u>e</u>), AE (br<u>ae</u>), AG_E (champ<u>agne</u>), AI (<u>ai</u>m), AIG (camp<u>aig</u>n), AIGH (str<u>aigh</u>t), AY (pl<u>ay</u>), É (ol<u>é</u>), EA (br<u>ea</u>k), EE (matin<u>ee</u>), EI (v<u>ei</u>n), EIG (r<u>eig</u>n), ET (duv<u>et</u>), EIGH (w<u>eigh</u>), EY (ob<u>ey</u>), UET (croq<u>uet</u>)
A as in *bat*	A (c<u>a</u>t), AI (pl<u>ai</u>d), AU (<u>au</u>nt, l<u>au</u>gh)
A as in *car*	AR (st<u>ar</u>t), EAR (h<u>ear</u>t), ER (s<u>er</u>geant)
AU as in *fraud*	AU (c<u>au</u>se), AW (cl<u>aw</u>), AWE (<u>awe</u>), OA (br<u>oa</u>d), OU (c<u>ou</u>gh)
E as in *tree*	E (b<u>e</u>), EA (n<u>ea</u>t), EA_E (p<u>ea</u>c<u>e</u>), EE (s<u>ee</u>), EE_E (fl<u>ee</u>c<u>e</u>), EI (prot<u>ei</u>n), I (tax<u>i</u>), I_E (pet<u>i</u>t<u>e</u>), IE (cut<u>ie</u>), IE_E (p<u>ie</u>c<u>e</u>), IS (chass<u>is</u>), UAY (q<u>uay</u>), UI_E (s<u>ui</u>t<u>e</u>), Y (marr<u>y</u>)
E as in *tent*	A (eleph<u>a</u>nt), AI (s<u>ai</u>d), E (<u>e</u>lephant), EA (br<u>ea</u>d), UE (q<u>ue</u>st)

E as in *term*	A (vulg<u>a</u>r), E (butt<u>e</u>r, <u>e</u>rg), EA (l<u>ea</u>rn), EU (chauff<u>eu</u>r), I (b<u>i</u>rd), O (anch<u>o</u>r), U (b<u>u</u>rn), U_E (pleas<u>u</u>re), UO (liq<u>uo</u>r)
I as in *alibi*	AI (Sin<u>ai</u>), AYE (<u>aye</u>), EIGH (h<u>eigh</u>t), EYE, (<u>eye</u>), I (alib<u>i</u>), I_E (s<u>i</u>t<u>e</u>), IE (p<u>ie</u>), IG (s<u>ig</u>n), IGH (h<u>igh</u>), OI (ch<u>oi</u>r), UI (squ<u>i</u>re, qu<u>i</u>et), Y (tr<u>y</u>), YE (d<u>ye</u>) Y_E (st<u>y</u>l<u>e</u>)
I as in *ill*	A_E (us<u>a</u>g<u>e</u>), AI (portr<u>ai</u>t), E (<u>a</u>partment), EA (serge<u>a</u>nt), EIG (sov<u>ei</u>gn), I (s<u>i</u>ck), I_E (eng<u>i</u>n<u>e</u>), O (spig<u>o</u>t), UI (qu<u>i</u>z, circ<u>ui</u>t), Y (h<u>y</u>mn)
O as in *go*	AU (ch<u>au</u>ffeur), AUX (f<u>aux</u>), EAU (b<u>eau</u>), EW (s<u>ew</u>), O (g<u>o</u>), OA (m<u>oa</u>n), O_E (h<u>o</u>s<u>e</u>), OE (t<u>oe</u>), OH (<u>oh</u>), OT (dep<u>o</u>t), OUGH (d<u>ough</u>), OW (t<u>ow</u>), OWE (<u>owe</u>)
O as in *brow*	AU (fr<u>au</u>), OU (<u>ou</u>t), OUGH (b<u>ough</u>), OW (c<u>ow</u>)
O as in *cod*	A (sw<u>a</u>p), O (b<u>o</u>dy, <u>o</u>ctopus, p<u>o</u>nder)
OO as in *good*	OO (b<u>oo</u>k), OU (c<u>ou</u>ld), U (f<u>u</u>ll, octop<u>u</u>s)
OY as in *boy*	OI (h<u>oi</u> poll<u>oi</u>), OY (t<u>oy</u>)

HOW TO USE THIS BOOK

OU as in *out*	AU (fr<u>au</u>), OU (l<u>ou</u>d), OUGH (b<u>ough</u>), OW (h<u>ow</u>)
U as in *gnu*	EAU (b<u>eau</u>ty), EU (f<u>eu</u>d), EW (d<u>ew</u>), IEW (v<u>iew</u>), O (d<u>o</u>), OE (sh<u>oe</u>), OO (tab<u>oo</u>), OU (y<u>ou</u>), OU (carib<u>ou</u>), OUS (rendezv<u>ous</u>), OUT (rag<u>out</u>), OUGH (thr<u>ough</u>), OUX (r<u>oux</u>), U (fl<u>u</u>), U_E (r<u>use</u>), UE (d<u>ue</u>), UG (imp<u>ug</u>n), UI (fr<u>ui</u>t), UT (deb<u>ut</u>)
U as in *bus*	A (bals<u>a</u>m), E (probl<u>e</u>m), IA (nostalg<u>ia</u>), IO (emot<u>io</u>n), O (bott<u>o</u>m, oct<u>o</u>pus, w<u>o</u>nder), OU (r<u>ou</u>gh), U (c<u>u</u>p)
Y as in *pry*	EIGH (h<u>eigh</u>t), I (alib<u>i</u>), IE (p<u>ie</u>), IGH (h<u>igh</u>), Y (tr<u>y</u>), YE (b<u>ye</u>)
Y as in *merry*	E (b<u>e</u>), EE (tr<u>ee</u>), I (wapit<u>i</u>), IE (cook<u>ie</u>), Y (fair<u>y</u>)

GLOSSARY OF POETIC TERMS

accent: a stress of voice on a particular syllable in pronouncing a word. A long mark (´) is used above an accented syllable, while a short mark (˘) is used to indicate an unaccented syllable. *Example:* Hăd wé bŭt wórld ĕnoúgh, ănd time

alexandrine: an iambic hexameter verse, sometimes having an added syllable. *Example:* Thăt, líke | ă woúnd | ĕd snáke, | drăgs íts | slŏw léngth | ălóng.

alliteration: the recurrence of the same consonant sound at the beginning of two or more words. *Example:* What a tale of terror, now, their turbulency tells.

amphibrach: a three-syllable foot consisting of a long syllable between two short ones. *Example:* Thĕ cláns ăre | ĭmpátiĕňt | aňd chíde thў | dĕláy (The last foot is not an amphibrach.)

amphimacer: a three-syllable foot consisting of a short syllable between two long ones. *Example:* Cátch ă stár | fállĭng fást |

anapest: a three-syllable foot consisting of two short syllables preceding one long syllable. *Example:* Nĕvĕr héar | thĕ sweĕt mú | sĭc ŏf spéech |

assonance: the recurrence of vowel sounds in a sequence of words, often as a substitute for rhyme. *Example:* Shrink his thin essence like a riveled flow'r

ballad: a simple lyrical poem, telling a story or legend and often of a romantic nature and adapted for singing.

ballade: a poem commonly consisting of three stanzas of an identical rhyme scheme, followed by an envoy. The last line of each stanza and the envoy is the same refrain.

ballad stanza: a stanza of four lines in which the first and third lines are in iambic tetrameter. The second and fourth lines are in iambic trimeter and also rhyme. In a common variant, the first and third lines also rhyme. *Example:*

> They followed from the snowy bank
> Those footsteps one by one,
> Into the middle of the plank—
> And further there was none.

blank verse: unrhymed blank verse in iambic pentameter, usually not in formal stanza units.

caesura: the main pause in a line of verse, usually near the middle. *Example:* Know then thyself, | | presume not God to scan

cinquain: a stanza consisting of five lines.

closed couplet: a couplet whose sense is completed within its two lines. *Example:*

> True wit is nature to advantage dress'd,
> What oft was thought, but ne'er so well express'd.

consonance: the use of an identical pattern of consonants in different words. *Example:* slow, sly, slew, slay

couplet: two consecutive lines that rhyme.

dactyl: a three-syllable foot consisting of one long syllable followed by two short syllables. *Example:* Cánnŏn tŏ | ríght ŏf thĕm |

dimeter: a line of verse having just two feet.

distich: a couplet, often an epigram or maxim.

elegy: a reflective and meditative poem with a solemn or sorrowful theme, often lamenting the dead.

envoy: I: a short stanza concluding a poem in certain archaic metrical forms; 2: a postscript to a poem, sometimes serving as a dedication.

epic: a long narrative poem celebrating the real or mythical achievements of great personages, heroes, or demigods, and written in stately verse conforming to rigid organization and form.

epigram: a brief and pithy remark, often in verse.

feminine ending: when the final syllable in a word is unaccented. *Example:* sóftnĕss

foot: the metrical unit in poetry, consisting of at least one long syllable and one or more short syllables. The foot is usually set off by a vertical line. *Example:* Ăll clád | ĭn Lín | cŏln gréen, | wĭth cáps | ŏf réd | ănd blúe |

GLOSSARY OF POETIC TERMS

free verse: verse that does not have a fixed pattern of meter, rhyme, or other poetic conventions.

heptameter: a line of verse consisting of seven feet.

heroic couplet: two consecutive rhyming lines in iambic pentameter, as in a Shakespearean sonnet.

hexameter: a line of verse consisting of six feet.

iamb: a foot consisting of one short syllable followed by one long syllable.

internal rhyme: a rhyme that occurs within the same line. *Example:* My <u>fair</u>, dear <u>Clair</u>

Italian sonnet: a sonnet with a rhyme scheme of ABBA ABBA CDE DDE written in iambic pentameter, though occasionally the rhyme scheme varies in the last six lines. The *octave* (the first eight lines) usually poses a theme or premise; the *sestet* (the last six lines) gives the resolution or conclusion.

limerick: a lighthearted poem of five lines with trimeters for the first, second, and fifth lines and dimeters for the third and fourth lines. *Example:*

> There was an old man of Tobago,
> Who lived on rice, gruel, and sago
> Till much to his bliss
> His physician said this,
> To a leg, Sir, of mutton you may go.

lyric: a poem with a particularly songlike quality, which expresses emotions directly and personally.

macaronic verse: a verse in which two or more languages are interlaced.

masculine ending: when the final syllable in a word is accented. *Example:* rĕplý

meter: the basic rhythmic description of a line in terms of its short and long syllables. It describes the sequence and relationship of all syllables in a line of poetry.

monometer: a line of verse consisting of one foot.

nonometer: a line of verse consisting of nine feet.

octave: the first eight lines of an Italian sonnet.

GLOSSARY OF POETIC TERMS

octometer: a line of verse consisting of eight feet.

onomatopoeia: words formed in imitation of the sounds they designate. *Example:* whiz, splash, bang, bowwow

ottava rima: a stanza of iambic pentameter with a rhyme scheme of ABABABCC.

pastoral: a poem dealing with simple rural life.

pentameter: a line of verse consisting of five feet.

Petrarchan sonnet: another name for Italian sonnet.

quatrain: a four-line stanza.

refrain: a phrase or line or group of lines that recurs at certain points in a poem, usually at the end of a stanza.

rhyme royal: a stanza written in iambic pentameter with a rhyme scheme of ABABBCC.

rhyme scheme: the pattern of rhyme used in a poem.

rondeau: a poem consisting of three stanzas of five, three, and five lines, using only two rhymes throughout, and having a refrain at the end of the second and third stanzas.

rondel: a poem usually consisting of fourteen lines on two rhymes, of which four are made up of the initial couplet repeated in the middle and at the end (although the second line of the couplet is sometimes omitted at the end).

rondelet: a poem consisting of five lines on two rhymes with the first word or words being used after the second and fifth lines as an unrhymed refrain.

run-on line: a line that does not end where there would be a normal pause in speech.

scansion: the process of indicating the pattern of long and short syllables in a line of verse.

septet: a stanza consisting of seven lines.

sestet: a group of six lines, especially those at the end of an Italian sonnet.

sestina: a poem consisting of six stanzas of six lines each, with a final triplet, and using the same terminal words in each stanza but in a different order; originally unrhymed but now having usually two or three rhymes.

Shakespearean sonnet: a sonnet written in iambic pentameter with a rhyme scheme of ABAB CDCD EFEF GG. The theme is usually presented in the three quatrains and the poem is concluded by the couplet.

sight rhyme: two or more words that end in identical spelling, but do not rhyme. *Example:* though, bough, through

slant rhyme: an approximate rhyme, usually characterized by assonance or consonance.

song: a short and simple poem, usually suitable for setting to music.

sonnet: a poem consisting of fourteen lines in iambic pentameter. The most common forms are the Shakespearean sonnet and the Italian sonnet.

Spenserian stanza: a stanza consisting of eight iambic pentameter lines and a final iambic hexameter line, with a rhyme scheme of ABABBCBCC.

spondee: a foot consisting of just two long syllables.

stanza: a fixed pattern of lines or rhyme or both.

tercet: three consecutive lines that rhyme together or relate to an adjacent tercet by rhymes.

terza rima: a poem consisting of eleven-syllable lines arranged in tercets, with the middle line of each tercet rhyming with the first and third lines of the following tercet, and written in iambic pentameter.

tetrameter: a line of verse consisting of four feet.

trimeter: a line of verse consisting of three feet.

triolet: an eight-line stanza in which the first line recurs as the fourth and seventh lines, while the second line recurs as the eighth line.

triplet: a stanza consisting of three lines.

trochee: a two-syllable foot consisting of one long syllable followed by a short syllable.

GLOSSARY OF POETIC TERMS

vers de société: a lighthearted and witty poem, usually brief, dealing with some social fashion or foible.

verse: 1: one line of a poem; 2: a group of lines in a poem; 3: any form in which rhythm is regularized.

villanelle: a poem consisting of (usually) five tercets and a final quatrain, and using only two rhymes throughout.

weak rhyme: a rhyme that falls upon the short syllables.

A NOTE ON SONGWRITING

JUST AS POEMS have certain forms or structures, such as a sonnet or limerick, songs also are constructed according to certain patterns. The most popular patterns or song structures are AABA and ABAB. Unlike poetry, these schemes do not refer to rhyme, but to the organization of verses and choruses in a song. Each A is a verse and each B is a chorus. Some songs also have C sections, known as a bridge, which usually comes after a chorus, but may also follow a verse. The bridge adds a new dimension to the dynamics of the song and prevents it from getting monotonous—it is a short melodic and/or rhythmic change. Here are the four most common structures:

1. A (verse)
   A (verse)
   B (chorus)
   A (verse)

2. A (verse)
   B (chorus)
   A (verse)
   B (chorus)

3. A (verse)
   B (chorus)
   A (verse)
   C (bridge)

4. A (verse)
   B (chorus)
   A (verse)
   B (chorus)
   C (bridge)
   B (chorus)

Writing song lyrics with these basic structures in mind makes pairing them with music relatively simple.

· THE ·
RHYMING
ENTRIES

A

SOUNDS

A*
bouquet \bō-ˈkā\
see
AIS, AY, EIGH*, EY**,
UAY, UET**

appliqué, atelier, attaché, au fait, ballet, bébé, béret, bouquet, buffet, cabaret, cabriolet, cachet, café, chalet, Chile, cliché, consommé, coryphée, coupé, crochet, croquet, croupier, curé, décolleté, distrait, dossier, duvet, épée, étouffée, fiancée, foyer, glacé, gourmet, lettre de cachet, lingerie, macramé, maté, matinée, mauvais, mêlée, métier, moiré, naïveté, narghile, née, névé, OK, okay, padre, padrone, pannier, papiermâché, passé, per se, Pompeii, protégée, purée, repoussé, requiescat in pace, résumé, retroussé, réveillé, ricochet, risqué, roué, sachet, soirée, tabouret, toupee, valet, visé

A**
data \ˈdā-tə\ *or*
\ˈdä-tə\
see
ABRA, ACA, ADA, AGA,
AH, ALA, ALPHA,
AMA*, AMA**, ANA,
ANDA, ANNA, ANZA,
ARA, ATA, AVA, AWAY,
AY, AYA, EA**, EBRA,
EDDA, ELLA, EMA, ENA,
ENNA, ERA, ESTA, IA,
ICA, IGMA, IKA, ILLA,
IMA, INA, IRA, ISTA,
ITA, OA, ODA, OGA,
OLA, OMA, ONA, ONDA,
ONNA, ORA, OSA, OTA,
ULA, UMBRA, USA, YA,
YDRA, UH

abracadabra, addenda, Aetna, Ahura Mazda, Alaska, alfalfa, algebra, Alhambra, alpaca, alpha, amoeba, ampulla, anaconda, anathema, Andromeda, apocrypha, aqua, Aquila, aria, arietta, Armenia, Atlanta, Attila, aura, Ba, Bermuda, bertha, beta, biretta, bonanza, Brahma, Buddha, Burma, Calcutta, Canada, calla, candelabra, caramba, Casablanca, Casanova, cascara, catalpa, cineraria, Cleopatra, Clepsydra, cloaca, cobra, coma, comma, contra, copra, Cordova, corolla, Cuba, data, delta, deva, dharma, digamma, dilemma, dogma, eureka, Europa, ex cathedra,

A**

extra, farina, fauna, felucca,
fra, gala, gamma, gardenia,
geisha, Geneva, grandpa,
hacienda, Hagiographa, ha-
ha, Hiawatha, Himalaya,
Hybla, hydra, hydrangea,
impedimenta, Inca, infanta,
influenza, infra, Jamaica,
jinricksha, Judaea, Kaaba,
kalpa, Kamchatka, kappa,
Karma, kiblah, Krishna, Lady
Godiva, lamina, larva, Lhasa,
Libra, Lima, lira, lobelia, Lyra,
ma, Madeira, magenta, Magna
Carta, maharaja, mahatma,
malacca, malaria, Malta, mama,
Manila, mantra, marimba,
mascara, Maya, mazurka, mea
culpa, Mecca, mesa, miasma,
millennia, Minerva, Minnehaha,
Mona Lisa, Mount Shasta,
naphtha, Odessa, okra, Omaha,
omega, operetta, orchestra,
Ouida, Ouija, pa, paca, Padua,
pagoda, palestra, Palmyra,
pampa, Panama, papa, paprika,
parhelia, pasha, per capita,
peseta, piazza, Pietà, Pisa,
polka, portulaca, puma, pupa,
Pyrrha, regatta, retina, rotunda,
rutabaga, saga, Sahara, savanna,
schizophrenia, scintilla, Scylla,
Seneca, seta, Sheba, Shiva,
sierra, Smyrna, soda, sofa,
solfatara, spa, Sparta, Spinoza,
stamina, swastika, Sumatra,
sura, syringa, taffeta, Tampa,
tapioca, tarantula, ta-ta, terra
firma, tiara, Topeka, tuba,
tundra, Uganda, ultra, umbra,
Ursa, Valhalla, Vega, vendetta,
Venezuela, veranda, vice versa,
viva, vodka, yucca, Zarathushtra,
zebra

AAL
kraal \ˈkrȯl\ *or* \ˈkräl\
see
AL**, ALL*

kraal, Transvaal

AB*
blab \ˈblab\
see
ARAB

ab, Ahab, blab, cab, confab, crab,
dab, drab, fab, flab, gab, grab,
jab, Moab, nab, prefab, sand dab,
scab, slab, stab, tab, taxicab

AB**
swab \ˈswäb\
see
OB

squab, swab, Punjab

ABBLE*
babble \ˈba-bəl\
see
EL, LE

babble, dabble, gabble, grabble,
rabble, scrabble

ABBLE**
squabble \ˈskwä-bəl\
LE, EL, OBBLE

squabble

ABBY
crabby \ˈkra-bē\
see
E*, EE*, I**, IE*, Y**

abbey, cabby, crabby, drabby,
flabby, gabby, scabby, shabby,
tabby

ABE
babe \ˈbāb\

Abe, astrolabe, babe

ABEL
label \ˈlā-bəl\
see
ABLE**, EL, LE

Abel, Babel, label

ABLE*
adorable
\ə-ˈdȯr-ə-bəl\
see
EABLE, EL, ERABLE,
IABLE***, ITABLE, LE,
OUBLE, UABLE, UBBLE

adorable, affable, allowable,
amicable, answerable, arable,
assessable, available, breakable,
calculable, capable, censurable,
changeable, commendable,

ABLE*

commensurable, comparable,
conceivable, consolable,
constable, delectable,
demonstrable, deplorable,
desirable, despicable,
detachable, disputable,
durable, equable, escapable,
estimable, evaporable, execrable,
explicable, formidable,
friable, getatable, hall table,
immeasurable, immutable,
impassable, impeccable,
impenetrable, imperishable,
impermeable, implacable,
impracticable, impregnable,
improbable, inalienable,
inapplicable, incalculable,
incapable, incommensurable,
incomparable, inconsolable,
incontestable, indefatigable,
indefinable, indemonstrable,
indescribable, indispensable,
indisputable, ineffable,
ineffaceable, ineradicable,
inescapable, inexcusable,
inexorable, inflammable,
inscrutable, inseparable,
insurmountable, interminable,
invaluable, inviolable,
invulnerable, irrefragable,
irrefutable, irrevocable,
jumpable, knowable, laudable,
likable, lovable, malleable,
memorable, monosyllable,
mutable, navigable, notable,
palatable, palpable, parable,
pardonable, passable, peaceable,
peccable, perishable, permeable,
pleasurable, polysyllable,
portable, practicable, pregnable,
presentable, printable, probable,
punishable, questionable,
readable, reasonable, receptable,
redoubtable, refutable,

ABLE*

regrettable, removable, resolvable, revocable, scrutable, seasonable, serviceable, sizeable, spankable, suitable, surmountable, syllable, tarnishable, taxable, teachable, tenable, terminable, traceable, tractable, unassailable, unavoidable, unbearable, unbelievable, unchangeable, undiminishable, unfathomable, unmentionable, unprintable, unseasonable, unshakable, unspeakable, unstridable, unsuitable, unsurpassable, unwarrantable, usable, valuable, vegetable, vocable, vulnerable, warrantable

ABLE**
table \\ ˈtā-bəl\
see
ABEL, EL, LE

able, cable, disable, enable, fable, gable, retable, Round Table, sable, stable, table, timetable, unable, unstable

ABLY*
see
ABLE+*y*, E*, EE*, I**,
IE*, Y**

ably, adorably, amicably, favorably, inevitably, irrevocably, irritably, justifiably, preferably, presumably, unspeakably

ABLY**
favorably
\\ ˈfā-v(ə-)rə-blē\
or \\ ˈfā-vər-blē\
see
E*, EE*, I**, IE*,
UBBLY, Y**

adorably, amicably, favorably, inevitably, irrevocably, irritably, justifiably, preferably, presumably, unspeakably

ABOO
taboo \tə-ˈbü\ *or*
\ta-ˈbü\
see
EW*, IEW, IEU, O*,
OE**, OU*, OUGH****,
OUS**, OUT**, OUX,
U, UE*, UT***

baboo, bugaboo, peekaboo, taboo

A SOUNDS

AC
shellac \shə-ˈlak\
see
ACH*, ACK, AK, IAC

almanac, Armagnac, Balzac, bivouac, bric-à-brac, cognac, cul-de-sac, ipecac, lac, lilac, sandarac, Saranac, shellac, sumac

ACE*
see
AIS, ASE*

ace, Alsace, apace, birthplace, brace, commonplace, deface, disgrace, displace, doughface, dwelling place, efface, embrace, face, grace, hiding place, interlace, interspace, lace, mace, macramé lace, marketplace, misplace, open-face, pace, place, point lace, poker face, Queen Anne's lace, race, refuge place, replace, resting place, retrace, Samothrace, scapegrace, shame face, space, tailrace, trace, unlace, whey-face

ACE**
palace \ˈpa-ləs\
see
IS*, ISS

furnace, grimace, Horace, menace, necklace, palace, populace, preface, solace, surface, terrace

ACENT
adjacent \ə-ˈjā-sᵊnt\
see
ENT**

adjacent, complacent, nascent

ACH*
Bach \ˈbach\
see
OCK

Bach

ACH**
stomach \ˈstə-mək\
or \ˈstə-mik\
see
IC, ICK

stomach

ACH***
see
ATCH*

detach

ACH****
spinach \ˈspi-nich\
see
ITCH*

spinach

ACHE*
mustache
\ˈməs-ˌtash\ *or*
\mə-ˈstash\
see
ASH*

cache, mustache, panache

ACHE**
headache \ˈhed-ˌāk\
see
AKE, AQUE**, EAK**,
IK**

ache, headache, heartache,
stomachache

ACHT
see
OT*

yacht

ACIOUS
gracious \ˈgrā-shəs\
see
IOUS, OUS*

audacious, bodacious,
contumacious, curvacious,
edacious, efficacious, gracious,
loquacious, mendacious,
mordacious, perspicacious,
pertinacious, predacious,
pugnacious, rapacious, sagacious,
sequacious, spacious, veracious,
vivacious, voracious

ACITY
capacity
\kə-ˈpa-sə-tē\
see
E*, EE*, I**, IE*, ITY

capacity, mendacity, opacity,
perspicacity, pertinacity,
pugnacity, rapacity, sagacity,
tenacity, veracity, vivacity, voracity

ACK
back \ˈbak\
see
AC, ACH*, AK

aback, Adirondack, alack,
applejack, attack, back, bareback,
black, book rack, book stack,
bootblack, bootjack, canvasback,
clack, comeback, Cossack, crack,

A SOUNDS

ACK

crackerjack, drawback, flapjack, flashback, fullback, gimcrack, greenback, gripsack, gunnysack, hack, hackmatack, hardtack, hat rack, haversack, hayrack, high-low-jack, hijack, horseback, hunchback, Jack, knack, knapsack, knickknack, lack, lampblack, leatherback, lumberjack, pack, paddywhack, piggyback, pitch-black, quack, quarterback, rack, ransack, razorback, rickrack, sack, setback, shack, shoeblack, sidetrack, slack, slapjack, smack, smokestack, snack, squirrel track, stack, steeplejack, switchback, tack, tamarack, thumbtack, thwack, track, Union Jack, unpack, whack, wisecrack, wrack, zwieback

ACKEN
blacken \ˈbla-kən\
see
EN**, IN

blacken, bracken, slacken

ACKER
cracker \ˈkra-kər\
see
AR**, ER*, OR*

backer, blacker, cracker, hijacker, nutcracker, slacker

ACKET
jacket \ˈja-kət\
see
AIT**, AT***, ATE**,
EDIT, EIT**, ERATE**,
ERIT, ET**, ETTE**,
IATE**, IBIT, ICATE**,
ICIT, ICKET, IDGET,
IGOT, IMATE*, INATE**,
IOT**, IT, ITE***,
OLATE*, ORATE**, OSET,
OT***, UET***, UGGET,
UIT*, ULATE**, URATE*

bluejacket, bracket, jacket, packet, racket, straitjacket

ACKLE
tackle \ˈta-kəl\
see
EL, LE

cackle, crackle, grackle, hackle, ramshackle, shackle, spackle, tackle

ACKS
barracks \ˈber-əks\
see
ACK+*s*, AXE, ICK+*s*

barracks

ACLE
miracle \ˈmir-i-kəl\
see
EL, LE

barnacle, binnacle, debacle, manacle, miracle, obstacle, oracle, pinnacle, receptacle, spectacle, tabernacle, tentacle

ACRE*
acre \ˈā-kər\
see
AKER, AR**, ER*, OR*

acre, nacre, simulacre, wiseacre

ACRE**
massacre
\ˈma-si-kər\
see
AR**, ER*, OCCUR, OR*

massacre

ACT
act \ˈakt\
see
ACK+*ed*, ED

abstract, act, attract, bract, cataract, compact, contract, counteract, detract, distract, enact, exact, extract, fact, impact, inexact, intact, interact, matter-of-fact, pact, protract, react, refract, retract, riot act, Stamp Act, subtract, tact, tract, transact

ACTIC
tactic \ˈtak-tik\
see
IC, ICK

didactic, lactic, prophylactic, tactic

ACTOR
actor \ˈak-tər\
see
AR**, ER*, OR*

actor, chiropractor, compactor, detractor, extractor, factor, tractor

A SOUNDS

ACY*
legacy \ ˈle-gə-sē\
see
E*, EA*, EE*, I**,
ICACY, ICY**, IE*,
IRACY, Y**

accuracy, adequacy, advocacy,
aristocracy, celibacy, confederacy,
conspiracy, contumacy,
democracy, diplomacy,
effeminacy, fallacy, gynecocracy,
illiteracy, intimacy, legacy,
literacy, lunacy, obstinacy, papacy,
pharmacy, piracy, plutocracy,
privacy, supremacy, theocracy

ACY**
lacy \ ˈlā-sē\
see
ACE*+y

lacy, racy, spacy

AD*
bad \ ˈbad\
see
ADD, AID***, IAD, YAD

Accad, ad, add, bad, Baghdad,
ballad, brad, cad, Carlsbad,
chad, clad, dad, doodad, egad,
fad, farad, footpad, forbad,
gad, Galahad, glad, grad, had,
ironclad, lad, lily pad, mad,
mail-clad, monad, naiad,
Olympiad, pad, sad, salad, shad,
Sinbad, snow-clad, steel-clad,
tetrad, triad, Trinidad

AD**
wad \ ˈwäd\
see
ADE***, OD*, ODD,
UAD

jihad, Upanishad, wad

AD***
myriad \ ˈmir-ē-əd\
see
ID

jeremiad, myriad

ADA*
cicada \sə-ˈkā-də\
see
A**

armada**, cicada**, Granada,
Haggada, posada, Torquemada

ADA**
armada \är-´mä-də\
see
A**

armada*, cicada*

ADD
add \´ad\
see
AD*

add

ADDLE*
paddle \´pa-dᵊl\
see
ATTLE, EL

addle, paddle, saddle, skedaddle,
staddle, straddle, twaddle

ADDLE**
waddle \´wä-dᵊl\
see
ODDLE, OTTLE

swaddle, waddle

ADE*
blade \´blād\
see
AID*, AY+*ed*, ENADE,
UADE

abrade, accolade, ambuscade,
arcade, balustrade, barricade,
blade, blockade, brigade,
brocade, cannonade, cascade,
cavalcade, centigrade, charade,
cockade, colonnade, crusade,
deadly nightshade, decade,
degrade, escalade, escapade,
esplanade***, evade, everglade,
fade, free trade, fusillade, glade,
harlequinade, homemade, invade,
jade, lade, lampshade, lemonade,
marmalade, masquerade,
nightshade, orangeade, palisade,
parade, pasquinade, pervade,
pomade, ready-made, renegade,
retrograde, shade, shoulder
blade, spade, stockade, sunshade,
tirade, trade, wade, well-made

ADE**
comrade \´käm-͵rad\
see
AD*, ADD

comrade

ADE***
facade \fə-ˈsäd\
see
AD**, OD*, ODD,
UAD

esplanade*, facade, fusillade,
Scheherazade

ADER
trader \ˈtrā-dər\
see
AR**, ER*, OR*

crusader, grader, masquerader,
tax evader, trader

ADES*
Hades \ˈhā-(ˌ)dēz\
see
EA*+*s*, EASE*, EE*+*s*,
EEZE, ESE*

Cyclades, Hades, Miltiades,
Pleiades

ADES**
palisades
\ˌpa-lə-ˈsādz\
see
ADE*+*s*, AID*+*s*

crusades, palisades

ADGE
badge \ˈbaj\

badge, cadge

ADIC
sporadic
\spə-ˈra-dik\
see
ATIC, IC

monadic, nomadic, sporadic

ADO*
avocado
\ˌä-və-ˈkä-(ˌ)dō\
see
EAU, EW**, O*,
OE*, OTTO, OT***,
OUGH*, OW*, OWE

avocado, bastinado, bravado,
Colorado*, cruzado, desperado,
El Dorado, mikado, renegado,
stoccado

ADO**
tornado
\tȯr-ˈnā-(ˌ)dō\
see
ATO**, EW**, O*, OE*,
tornado

ADOR*   ambassador
ambassador
\am-ˈba-sə-dər\
see
AR**, ER*, OR*

ADOR**   conquistador, Ecuador, Labrador,
Labrador   matador, picador, San Salvador,
\ˈla-brə-ˌdȯr\   toreador
see
OOR, OR**, ORE

ADY   lady, landlady, malady, milady,
lady \ˈlā-dē\   shady
see
E*, EA*, EE*, I**, IE*, Y**

AE*   algae, antennae, aqua vitae, arbor
algae \ˈal-(ˌ)jē\   vitae, dramatis personae, larvae,
see   lignum vitae, minutiae, Mycenae,
E*, EA*, EE*, I**, IE*, Y**   Parcae

AE**   brae, dies irae, sundae
brae \ˈbrā\
see
A*, AY, EIGH*

AEL   Ishmael, Israel, Raphael
Israel \ˈiz-rē-əl\ *or*
\ˈiz(ˌ)rā-əl\
see
EL, LE

AFE*
safe \ˈsāf\
see
AIF

chafe, safe, strafe, unsafe, vouchsafe

AFE**
carafe \kə-ˈraf\
see
AFF, AUGH

carafe

AFF
staff \ˈstaf\
see
AFE**, AFFE, ALF, APH

chaff, distaff, draff, Falstaff, flagstaff, gaff, pikestaff, riffraff, sclaff, shandygaff, staff

AFFE
giraffe \jə-ˈraf\
see
AFE**, AFF

gaffe, giraffe

AFT*
craft \ˈkraft\
see
AFF+*ed*, APH+*ed*, AUGHT**

abaft, aft, aircraft, antiaircraft, craft, daft, draft, graft, haft, handicraft, kingcraft, priestcraft, shaft, statecraft, waft**, witchcraft

AFT**
waft \ˈwäft\
see
OFT, OUGH*****+*ed*

waft

AFTER
after \ˈaf-tər\
see
AR**, ER*, OR*

after, hereafter, rafter, thereafter

AG
bag \ˈbag\

bag, beanbag, black-flag, blue flag, brag, carpetbag, crag, ditty bag, drag, duffel bag, fag, flag, gag, hag, handbag, jutting crag, lag, mailbag, nag, rag, ragtag, saddlebag, sag, sandbag, scallawag, scrag, shag, slag, sleeping bag, snag, stag, starry flag, swag, tag, wag, water bag, wigwag, zigzag

AGE*
village \ ˈvi-lij\
see
AUGE, EAGE, EDGE,
EGE, ERAGE, IAGE,
IDGE, ORAGE, OTAGE,
UAGE

acreage, adage, advantage,
amperage, anchorage, appanage,
appendage, assemblage, average,
baggage, bandage, beverage,
bondage, boscage, brokerage,
cabbage, Carthage, cartilage,
cleavage, coinage, cold storage,
cordage, cottage, courage, cribbage,
damage, discourage, disparage,
dosage, drainage, encourage,
ensilage, equipage, espionage,
forage, frontage, fruitage, fuselage,
garbage, greengage, Greenwich
Village, herbage, heritage, homage,
hostage, image, language, leafage,
leakage, leverage, lineage, luggage,
manage, mileage, mismanage,
mortgage, mucilage, nonage,
orphanage, ossifrage, package,
parentage, parsonage, pasturage,
patronage, peerage, percentage,
personage, pilgrimage, pillage,
plumage, portage, postage,
pottage, presage, ravage, rummage,
sabotage, salvage, sausage, savage,
saxifrage, scrimmage, scrummage,
scutage, seepage, sewage, shortage,
shrinkage, silage, spoilage, steerage,
Stone Age, stoppage, storage,
suffrage, tallage, tankage, tillage,
tutelage, umbrage, usage, vantage,
vassalage, vicarage, village, vintage,
visage, voyage, wreckage

AGE**
age \ ˈāj\
see
AUGE

age, assuage, birdcage, cage,
enrage, flowering sage, Golden
Age, middle age, page, outrage,
rage, rampage, sage, stage, Stone
Age, teenage, upstage, wage

AGE***
massage \mə-ˈsäzh\
or \mə-ˈsäj\

badinage, bon voyage, camouflage,
entourage, espionage, garage,
massage, ménage, mirage,
persiflage, sabotage

AGER
manager \ ˈma-ni-jər\
see
AR**, ER*, OR*

dowager, manager, onager, tanager

AGER*
wager \ ˈwā-jər\
see
AR**, ER*, OR*

pager, stager, tanager, teenager, wager

AGM
diaphragm
\ ˈdī-ə-ˌfram\
see
AM*, AMB, AME**, AMN

diaphragm

AGNE
Champagne
\sham-ˈpān\
see
AIGN, AIN*, AINE,
ANE, EIGN*, EIN*

Champagne, Charlemagne, Bretagne

AGO*
ago \ə-ˈgō\
see
EAU, EW**, O*, OE*,
OT***, OUGH*, OW*,
OWE

ago, archipelago

AGO**
virago \və-ˈrä-(ˌ)gō\
see
EAU, EW*, O*, OE*,
OT***, OUGH*, OW*,
OWE

farrago***, solidago***, virago***

AGO***
lumbago
\ ˌləm-ˈbā-(ˌ)gō\
see
EAU, EW**, O*, OE*,
OT***, OUGH*, OW*,
OWE

farrago**, lumbago, plumbago, sago, virago**

AGON*
paragon
\ ' per-ə- ˌ gän\
see
AN**, ON**

Aragon, flagon, hexagon,
octagon, paragon, pentagon,
tarragon, tetragon

AGON**
dragon
\ ' dra-gən\
see
ON*

dragon, snapdragon, wagon,
water wagon

AGRAM
diagram
\ ' dī-ə- ˌ gram\
see
AGM, AM*, AMB,
AME**, AMN

anagram, diagram, pentagram

AGUE
plague \ ' plāg\

Hague, plague, vague

AGUE**
league \ ' lēg\
see
UE**

colleague, league

AGUS
asparagus
\ə- ' sper-ə-gəs\
see
US

asparagus, sarcophagus

AH
cheetah \ ' chē-tə\
see
A**, IAH

Abdullah, ah, amah, bah,
Beulah, blah, cheetah,
Deborah, fellah, Gomorrah,
howdah, hurrah, huzzah,
Jehovah, Jonah, jubbah, Judah,
Methuselah, Micah, mullah,
Noah, oompah, purdah,
rajah, Rosh Hashanah, shah,
Shekinah, Shenandoah,
shillelagh, sirrah, Torah, yeah

AI
Sinai \ˈsī-ˌnī\
see
I*

Adonai, caravanserai, Mordecai, Shanghai, Sinai

AIC
prosaic \prō-ˈzā-ik\
see
IC

Aramaic, archaic, Hebraic, laic, mosaic, prosaic, Romaic, voltaic

AID*
afraid \ə-ˈfrād\
see
ADE*, AY+*ed*, EIGH*+*ed*

afraid, aid, air raid, bondmaid, braid, handmaid, inlaid, laid, maid, mermaid, milkmaid, overpaid, paid, raid, repaid, sea-maid, staid, unpaid, upbraid, waylaid

AID**
said \ˈsed\
see
EAD*, ED

aforesaid, said, unsaid

AID***
plaid \ˈplad\
see
AD*

plaid

AIF
waif \ˈwāf\
see
AFE*

naif, waif

AIGN
campaign \kam-ˈpān\
see
AGNE, AIN*, AINE,
ANE, EIGN*, EIN*

arraign, campaign

AIGHT
straight \ˈstrāt\
see
AIT*, ATE*, EAT**,
EIGHT*

straight

AIK
haik \ ' hīk\
see
IKE

haik

AIL*
bail \ ' bāl\
see
ALE, EIL

ail, assail, avail, bail, bewail,
blackmail, bobtail, cattail,
cocktail, curtail, derail, detail,
dovetail, draggle-tail, e-mail,
entail, fail, fan mail, fantail,
flail, foxtail, frail, grail, hail,
handrail, hangnail, hobnail,
jail, mail, mainsail, mare's tail,
monorail, nail, oxtail, pail,
pigtail, pintail, prevail, quail,
rail, retail, ringtail, sail, slap
tail, snail, staysail, swallowtail,
taffrail, tail, thumbnail, trail,
travail, vail, wagtail, wail,
wassail**

AIL**
wassail \ ' wä-səl\
see
AL*

wassail*

AILER
trailer \ ' trā-lər\
see /
AIL+*er*, ALE+*er*, AR**,
ER*, OR*

blackmailer, mailer, trailer

AIM
claim \ ' klām\
see
AME*

acclaim, aim, claim, declaim,
disclaim, Ephraim, exclaim,
maim, proclaim, quitclaim,
reclaim

AIN*
rain \ ' rān\·
see
AGNE, AIGN, AINE,
ANE, EIGN*, EIN*

abstain, main, appertain,
attain, blain, brain, Cain,
chain, chilblain, complain,
constrain, contain, coxswain,
cross-grain, etain, disdain,
domain, drain,

AIN*

enchain, entertain, explain, fain, foreordain, gain, grain, ingrain, legerdemain, main, maintain, Mark Twain, obtain, ordain, pain, plain, plantain, preordain, quatrain, rain, rattlebrain, refrain, regain, remain, restrain, retain, Spain, Spanish Main, stain, strain, sustain, suzerain, swain, terrain, train, twain, vain, vervain

AIN**
mountain
\ ˙maůn-tᵊn\
see
EN**, IN

again, bargain, boatswain, captain, certain, chamberlain, chaplain, chieftain, fountain, mountain, soda fountain, villain

AINE
migraine \ ˙mī- ˌgrān\
see
AIN*, ANE

Aquitaine, chatelaine, cocaine, Lorraine, migraine, moraine, ptomaine

AINT
faint \ ˙fānt\
see
EINT

ain't, acquaint, complaint, constraint, faint, paint, patron saint, plaint, quaint, restraint, saint, self-restraint, taint, war paint

AINTLY
faintly \ ˙fānt-lē\
see
EA*, E*, EE*, I**, IE*,
Y**

faintly, quaintly, saintly

AIR
chair \ ˙cher\
see
AIRE, ARE*, EAR**,
EIR*

affair, air, armchair, backstair, bath chair, camel hair, chair, Corsair, debonair, éclair, fair, flair, hair, horsehair, impair, lair, maidenhair, Mayfair, midair, mohair, open-air, pair, repair, rocking chair, stair, unfair, Vanity Fair

AIRE
billionaire
\bĭ(l)-yə-´ner\
see
AIR, ARE*

billionaire, Brumaire, debonaire, doctrinaire, legionnaire, millionaire, multimillionaire, questionnaire, savoir faire, secretaire, solitaire, Voltaire

AIRN
bairn \´bern\

bairn, cairn, Pitcairn

AIRY
fairy \´fer-ē\
see
ARY*, E*, EA, EE*,
ERRY, ERY**, I**, IE*,
Y**

airy, dairy, fairy, hairy

AIS
dais \´dā-əs\
see
IS*

dais, Sais

AISE
raise \´rāz\
see
A*+s, AISSE, AIZE, ASE**,
AY+s, AZE, EIGH*+s

braise, chaise, malaise, Marseillaise, mayonnaise, polonaise, post chaise, praise, raise

AISSE
bouillabaisse
\ˌbü-yə-´bās\
see
AISE

bouillabaisse

AIST
waist \´wāst\
see
ACE*+ed, ASE*+ed, ASTE

waist

AIT*
bait \´bāt\
see
AIGHT, AIT*, ATE*,
EAT**, EIGHT*

bait, fish bait, gait, plait, portrait**, strait, wait, whitebait

AIT**
portrait \ ˙ pȯr-trət\
see
ACKET, AT***,
ATE**, EDIT, EIT**,
ERATE**, ERIT, ET**,
ETTE**, IATE**,
IBIT, ICATE**, ICIT,
ICKET, IDGET, IGOT,
IMATE*, INATE**,
IOT**, IT, ITE***,
OLATE*, ORATE**,
OSET, OT***, UET***,
UGGET, UIT*,
ULATE**, URATE*

portrait*

AITER
waiter \ ˙ wā-tər\
see
AR**, ATER, ER*, OR*

baiter, congress gaiter, gaiter, waiter

AITH
faith \ ˙ fāth\

faith, wraith

AIVE
waive \ ˙ wāv\
see
AVE*

glaive, waive

AIZE
maize \ ˙ māz\
see
AISE, AZE

baize, maize

AK
yak \ ˙ yak\
see
AC, ACH*, ACK

Iraq, Karnak, kodak, yak, yashmak

AKE
bake \ ˙ bāk\
see
ACHE**, AQUE**,
EAK**, IK**

air brake, bake, betake, brake, cake, canebrake, clambake, coaster brake, cornflake, drake, earthquake, fake, flake, forsake, garter snake, give-and-take,

AKE

griddle cake, handshake, intake, keepsake, kittiwake, lake, make, mandrake, mistake, namesake, overtake, pancake, partake, quake, rake, rattlesnake, retake, sake, sea snake, shake, sheldrake, shortcake, snake, snowflake, spake, stake, sweepstake, take, undertake, wideawake

AKEN
mistaken
\mə-ˈstāk -kən\
see
EN**

awaken, betaken, godforsaken, mistaken, shaken, taken

AKER
baker \ˈbā-kər\
see
AR**, ER*, OR*

baker, breaker, caretaker, dressmaker, haymaker, lawbreaker, maker, matchmaker, peacemaker, Quaker, sailmaker, Shaker, shoemaker, tentmaker, undertaker

AL*
crystal \ˈkris-tᵊl\
see
AAL, ANAL, EAL, EGAL,
ENAL, ENTAL, ERAL,
ERIAL, ERNAL, ESTAL,
ETAL, EVAL, IAL**,
IBAL*, IBAL**, ICAL,
IDAL, IMAL, INAL,
ION*+al, IPAL, ITAL,
IVAL, OCAL, ONAL,
OPAL, ORAL, ORMAL,
ORTAL, OVAL, OYAL,
UAL, UGAL, URAL,
URNAL, USAL, UTAL

abnormal, abysmal, admiral, anecdotal, antidotal, antipodal, apocryphal, arbital, arsenal, astral, austral, autumnal, avowal, Bengal, betrayal, betrothal, carousal, carnal, cathedral, caudal, causal, central, cerebral, cloistral, coastal, colossal, coronal, corral, crystal, demoniacal, deposal, dihedral, disavowal, dismal, dismissal, dorsal, ducal, enthral, Episcopal, epochal, espousal, feudal, Funchal, gyral, herbal, integral, interval, isothermal, jackal, Jubal, juvenal, lachrymal, lethal, madrigal, magistral, mammal, marshal, medal, missal, mistral, modal, nasal, naval, offal, orchestral, papal, paschal, pedal, phenomenal, portrayal, postal,

AL*

primal, prodigal, proposal, quintal, rascal, rebuttal, rehearsal, renewal, reprisal, reversal, sacerdotal, sandal, scandal, seneschal, sepulchral, signal, spectral, spiral, spousal, survival, synagogal, teetotal, thermal, total, tribunal, triumphal, universal, upheaval, vandal, vassal, venal, verbal, withdrawal

AL**
narwhal \ ´när-ˌwäl\
see
ALL*, OLL**

cabal, narwhal, Provençal, Taj Mahal, withal, wherewithal

AL***
pal \ ´pal\
see
ALL**, ANAL***

gal, pal

ALA*
Guatemala
\ ˌgwä-tə-´mä-lə\
see
A**

Cabala, gala*, Guatemala, La Scala, marsala, Shambala

ALA**
gala \ ´gā-lə\
see
A**

gala**

ALC
talc \ ´talk\

talc

ALD*
bald \ ´bȯld\
see
ALL*+*ed*, AUL+*ed*

bald, piebald, ribald, scald, skald

ALD**
emerald \ˈem-rəld\
see
ULL+*ed*

emerald, herald

ALDRY
heraldry \ˈher-əl-drē\
see
E*, EA*, EE*, I**, IE*,
Y**

heraldry, ribaldry

ALE
ale \ˈāl\
see
AIL*, AILLE, EIL

Airedale, ale, bale, chippendale,
dale, exhale, farthingale, female,
gale, gunwale, hale, impale,
inhale, kale, male, martingale,
musicale, nightingale, pale,
percale, regale, sale, scale, shale,
stale, swale, tale, telltale, vale,
whale, wholesale, Yale

ALENT
equivalent
\i-ˈkwi-və -lənt\
see
ENT**

equivalent, prevalent

ALF
calf \ˈkaf\
see
APH

behalf, calf, half, half-and-half

ALI
Somali \sə-ˈmä-lē\
see
I**

Ali, Bali, Bengali, Kali, Somali

ALIA
Australia
\ȯ-ˈstrāl-yə\
see
IA

Australia, bacchanalia, genetalia,
paraphernalia, Parentalia,
penetralia, regalia, saturnalia

ALID*
invalid
\\(ˌ)in-ˈva-ləd\\
see
ID, UID**

invalid**, valid

ALID**
invalid \\ˈin-və-ləd\\
see
ID, UID*

invalid*

ALIS
chrysalis \\ˈkri-sə-ləs\\
see
ICE**, IS*, ISE****

aurora borealis, chrysalis, cum grano salis, digitalis, oxalis

ALISM
vandalism
\\ˈvan-də-ˌli-zəm\\
see
ISM

bilingualism, fatalism, formalism, idealism, imperialism, individualism, nationalism, rationalism, revivalism, royalism, socialism, vandalism

ALITY
reality \\rē-ˈa-lə-tē\\
see
E*, EA*, EE*, I**, IE*, ITY, Y**

abnormality, actuality, banality, beastiality, carnality, conviviality, duality, eternality, ethereality, fatality, finality, formality, frugality, generality, hospitality, intellectuality, liberality, locality, mentality, modality, mortality, municipality, neutrality, normality, originality, partiality, personality, plurality, potentiality, principality, prodigality, rascality, reality, speciality, substantiality, technicality, tonality, totality, triviality, vitality

ALIZE
localize \\ˈlō-kə-ˌlīz\\
see
IES*, ISE*, IZE

amortize, equalize, idealize, immortalize, individualize, legalize, localize, materialize, moralize, mortalize, neutralize, penalize, rationalize, realize, scandalize, signalize, specialize, tantalize, visualize, vocalize

ALK
talk \ˈtȯk\
see
AWK

balk, beanstalk, cakewalk, calk, chalk, cornstalk, jaywalk, ropewalk, sheep walk, sidewalk, sleepwalk, small talk, stalk, talk, walk

ALL*
all \ˈȯl\
see
AL**, AUL, AWL, OL**, OLL**

all, appall, ball, baseball, basketball, befall, birdcall, blackball, bookstall, buttonball, call, carryall, catcall, Chinese Wall, Cornwall, coverall, dance hall, downfall, enthrall, eyeball, fall, footfall, forestall, gall, hall, highball, holdall, install, mall, mudwall, music hall, nightfall, overall, pall, pitfall, puffball, rainfall, recall, roll call, seawall, small, spitball, squall, stall, stonewall, tall, tea ball, thrall, wall, waterfall, windfall

ALL**
shall \ˈshal\
see
AL***

shall

ALLOW*
shallow \ˈsha-(ˌ)lō\
see
EAU, EW**, O*, OE*, OT***, OUGH*, OW*, OWE

callow, fallow, hallow, mallow, marshmallow, sallow, shallow, tallow

ALLOW**
wallow \ˈwä-(ˌ)lō\
see
EAU, EW**, O*, OE*, OT***, OUGH*, OW*, OWE

wallow

ALLY*
totally \ˈtō-tᵊl-ē\
see
E*, EE*, Y**

cynically, diametrically, eternally, graphically, ideally, mathematically, morally, occasionally, paradoxically, personally, pragmatically,

ALLY*

prosaically, rascally, reverentially, rurally, stoically, technically, totally, typically, tyrannically, vitally

ALLY**
dally \ ˈda-lē\
see
E*, EE*, Y**

dally, dillydally, rally, sally, shilly-shally, tally

ALLY***
ally \ə- ˈlī\
see
I*, IE**, IGH, Y*

ally

ALM
balm \ ˈbä(l)m\
see
UALM

balm, becalm, calm, embalm, palm, psalm, qualm

ALOUS
scandalous
\ ˈskan-də-ləs\
see
OUS*

anomalous, bicephalous, megacephalous, scandalous

ALP
alp \ ˈalp\

alp, scalp

ALRY
rivalry \ ˈrī-vəl-rē\
see
E*, EE*, Y**

cavalry, chivalry, rivalry

ALS
annals \ ˈa-nᵊlz\
see
AL*+*s*, OL***+*s*, ULL+*s*

annals

ALT
salt \ ˈsȯlt\
see
AULT

alt, asphalt, basalt, cobalt, exalt, halt, malt, rock salt, salt, smalt, springhalt

A SOUNDS

ALTO
alto \ ˈal-(ˌ)tō\
see
O*

alto, contralto, Rialto

ALTY
see
E*, EA*, EE*, I**, IE*,
Y**

casualty, fealty, loyalty, mayoralty,
penalty, realty, royalty, salty,
viceroyalty

ALTZ
waltz \ ˈwȯl(t)s\
see
ALT+s

schmaltz, waltz

ALUS
see
US

Bucephalus, Daedalus, Tantalus

ALVE*
valve \ ˈvalv\

bivalve, valve

ALVE**
calve \ ˈkav\
see
AVE**

calve, halve, salve

AM*
am \ ˈam\
see
AGM, AGRAM, AME**,
AMB, AMME, AMN,
ASM, OGRAM

am, cablegram, cam, clam,
cram, dam, dram, epigram,
gam, gram, grand slam,
ham, jam, jimjam, lam,
marconigram, milldam, pam,
pram, program, radiogram,
ram, scam, scram, sham, Siam,
slam, swam, telegram, Uncle
Sam, wham

AM**
balsam \ ˈbȯl-səm\
see
OM*, UM, UMB

amalgam, balsam, bantam,
bedlam, buckram, flotsam,
gingham, in memoriam, jetsam,
macadam, madam, marjoram,
sweet William

AM***
Islam \is-ˈläm\
or \iz-ˈläm\
see
OM***

imam, Islam, salaam

AMA*
drama \ˈdrä-mə\
see
A**

Bahama, cyclorama**, Dalai Lama, drama, Fujiyama, Kama, lama, llama, mama, melodrama, pajama**, panorama**, Rama, Yokohama

AMA**
Alabama
\ˌa-lə-ˈba-mə\
see
A**

Alabama, cyclorama*, pajama*, panorama*

AMB
lamb \ˈlam\
see
AGM, AM*, AME**,
AMN

dithyramb, iamb, jamb, lamb

AMBLE
amble \ˈam-bəl\
see
EL, OL

amble, bramble, gamble, preamble, scramble, shamble

AME*
blame \ˈblām\
see
AIM

aflame, blame, came, dame, defame, fame, flame, frame, game, hame, inflame, kame, lame, name, nickname, overcame, pen name, same, selfsame, shame, surname, tame

AME**
madame
\mə-ˈdam\
see
AGM, AM*, AMB,
AMN

madame

AMEL
camel \ ˈka-məl\
see
EL, ULL

camel, caramel, enamel

AMENT
lament \lə-ˈment\
see
ENT**

armament, filament, firmament, lament, ligament, lineament, medicament, ornament, parliament, predicament, sacrament, temperament, testament, tournament

AMIC
dynamic \dī-ˈna-mik\
see
IC, ICK

Adamic, balsamic, ceramic, dynamic, hydrodynamic, panoramic

AMIN
gamin \ ˈga-mən\
see
IN

gamin

AMN
damn \ ˈdam\
see
AGM, AM*, AMB, AME**

damn

AMOR
clamor \ ˈkla-mər\
see
AMOUR, OR

clamor, enamor

AMP*
clamp \ ˈklamp\

aide-de-camp, champ, clamp, cramp, damp, decamp, encamp, firedamp, lamp, postage-stamp, ramp, safety lamp, scamp, stamp, tamp, tramp, vamp

AMP**
swamp \ ˈswämp\
see
OMP

swamp

AMPA
Tampa \ ˈtam-pə\
see
A**

pampa, Tampa

AMPER
damper \ ˈdam-pər\
see
AR**, ER*, OR*

damper, hamper, pamper, scamper, tamper

AMPLE
ample \ ˈam-pəl\
see
EL

ample, example, sample, trample

AMPUS
campus \ ˈkam-pəs\
see
US

campus, grampus, hippocampus

AMUS*
calamus \ ˈka-lə-məs\
see
US

calamus, hippopotamus, ignoramus**, mandamus, Nostradamus

AMUS**
ignoramus
\ ˌig-nə-ˈrā-məs\
see
US

ignoramus*

AMY
bigamy \ ˈbi-gə-mē\
see
E*, EA*, EE*, I**, IE*, Y**

bigamy, infamy, monogamy, polygamy

AN*
ban \ ˈban\
see
AN**, ARIAN, EDIAN, ERAN, ESAN, IAN, ICAN, ICIAN, ISAN, ITAN, OMAN, UAN

Afghan, Ahriman, Alaskan, Aldebaran, astrakhan, backwoodsman, Balkan, ban, banyan, barrel organ, began, bogeyman, Brahman, bran, brogan, bushman, can, cancan, capstan, caravan, catamaran,

AN*

caveman, clan, corbandivan, dustpan, fan, fantan, frying pan, G-man, hardpan, harmattan, he-man, Hindustan, hitman, kaftan, Ku Klux Klan, madman, mailman, man, marzipan, medicine man, middleman, minuteman, Norman, pan, pecan, Peter Pan, plan, ragman, ran, rataplan, rattan, redan, reman, sampan, sandman, saucepan, scan, sedan, snowman, Sudan, span, spick-and-span, stewpan, suntan, superman, switchman, than, tin can, toucan

AN**
human \ ˈhyü-mən\
see
EN**, IN

alderman, birdman, cattleman, clansman, clergyman, courlan, Cretan, dolman, draftsman, Elizabethan, Etruscan, everyman, fireman, fisherman, foreman, Franciscan, freshman, gargantuan, gentleman, hackman, Harridan, helmsman, henchman, horseman, human, inhuman, interurban, Jordan, layman, leviathan, Libyan, longshoreman, Magellan, marksman, merchantman, midshipman, molluscan, Norseman, organ, orphan, oysterman, pagan, policeman, postman, Pullman, quartan, raglan, rifleman, Roman, rowan, sacristan, Satan, Scotsman, seaman, shaman, showman, sylvan, slogan, Spartan, spokesman, steersman, suburban, suffragan, sultan, superhuman, sylvan, talisman, tartan, Tibetan, Titan, toboggan, watchman, Welshman, woman, yeoman

AN***
swan \ˈswän\
see
ON**, UAN

Iran, Kashan, khan, Kurdistan, Ramadan, swan, wan

ANA*
bandana \ban-ˈda-nə\
see
A**

ana, banana, bandana, cabana, Diana, dulciana, Ecbatana, fata morgana, Guiana, gymkhana, Havana**, Louisiana, sultana

ANA**
iguana \i-ˈgwä-nə\
see
A**

Havana*, iguana, lantana, liana, mañana, Nirvana

ANA
arcana \är-ˈkā-nə\
see
A**

arcana, Cana

ANAL*
anal \ˈā-nᵊl\
see
AL*

anal

ANAL**
banal \bə-ˈnal\
see
AL**, ALL*, OLL**

bacchanal, banal

ANAL***
canal \kə-ˈnal\
see
AL***

canal

ANCE*
allowance
\ə-ˈlaủ-ən(t)s\
see
ANSE, ENSE, ENT*+*s*,
IANCE, IENCE, UANCE

abeyance, abidance, abundance, acquaintance, admittance, allowance, ambulance, annoyance, appearance, arrogance, assistance, assurance, attendance, avoidance, balance,

ANCE*

buoyance, clairvoyance, clearance, concomitance, concordance, connivance, contrivance, conveyance, countenance, discordance, dissonance, distance, disturbance, durance, elegance, encumbrance, endurance, extravagance, fragrance, furtherance, governance, grievance, guidance, hindrance, ignorance, importance, inelegance, inheritance, instance, insurance, jubilance, maintenance, misfeasance, monstrance, nonchalance, nuisance, obeisance, observance, ordinance, ordnance, outdistance, overbalance, parlance, penance, performance, perseverance, petulance, piquance, pittance, predominance, protuberance, pursuance, quittance, reappearance, reconnaisance, redundance, relevance, reluctance, remembrance, remittance, remonstrance, renaissance, repugnance, resemblance, resonance, riddance, semblance, severance, sibilance, significance, substance, superabundance, surveillance, temperance, tolerance, unbalance, utterance, valance, vengeance, vigilance

ANCE**
advance \əd-ˈvan(t)s\
see
ANSE, ANT*+*s*

advance, askance, bechance, chance, circumstance, dance, enhance, entrance, finance, France, freelance, glance, lance, mischance, perchance, prance, romance, stance, trance

A SOUNDS

ANCH*
ranch \ ˈranch\
see
ANCHE

blanch, branch, olive branch, ranch

ANCH**
staunch \ ˈstȯnch\
see
AUNCH*

stanch

ANCHE
avalanche
\ ˈa-və-ˌlanch\
see
ANCH*

avalanche, carte blanche

ANCY*
diplomacy
\də-ˈplō-mə-sē\
see
E*, EA*, EE*, I**, IE*,
Y**

blatancy, buoyancy, chiromancy, dactylomancy, discrepancy, expectancy, flagrancy, flippancy, hesitancy, inconstancy, infancy, necromancy, occupancy, oneiromancy, pyromancy, radiancy, redundancy, relevancy, sycophancy, tenacy, truancy, vacancy, vagrancy, vibrancy

ANCY**
fancy \ ˈfan(t)-sē\
see
E*, EA*, EE*, I**, IE*,
Y**

fancy

AND*
and \ ˈan(d)\
see
AN*+*ed*

aforehand, and, band, beforehand, behindhand, bland, borderland, brand, brigand, cabstand, chateau briand, command, contraband, countermand, demand, disband, elfland, expand, fairyland, Ferdinand, firebrand, freehand, gland, grand, grandstand, grassland,

AND*

hand, headland, Holy Land, husband, inkstand, land, Lapland, misunderstand, moorland, offhand, quicksand, remand, reprimand, salt land, Samarqand, sand, saraband, secondhand, shorthand, sleight of hand, stand, strand, tableland, Tallyrand, underhand, understand, unhand, upland, washstand, wasteland, withstand, witness stand

AND**
husband \ ´hǝz-bǝnd\
see
UND

England, garland, Greenland, highland, husband, Iceland, inland, island, Long Island, lowland, mainland, New England, Newfoundland, New Zealand, Shetland, Switzerland, thousand, viand, woodland

AND***
wand \ ´wänd\
see
OND

gourmand, wand

ANDA
panda \ ´pan-dǝ\
see
A**

Ananda, panda, propaganda, veranda

ANDER*
slander \ ´slan-dǝr\
see
AR**, ER*, OR*

Alexander, bystander, commander, corriander, gander, grander, Highlander, islander, meander, oleander, pander, philander, pomander, salamander, slander

ANDER**
wander \ ´wän-dǝr\
see
ONDER*, OR*

squander, wander

A SOUNDS

ANDLE
candle \ˈkan-dᵊl\
see
EL

candle, chandle, handle,
manhandle, panhandle

ANDY
candy \ˈkan-dē\
see
E*, EA*, EE*, I**, IE*,
Y**

apple brandy, bandy, brandy,
candy, cherry brandy, handy,
Normandy, randy, rock candy,
sandy

ANE
cane \ˈkān\
see
AGNE, AIGN, AIN*,
AINE, EIGN*, EIN*

aeroplane, arcane, bane, biplane,
cane, cellophane, chicane,
counterpane, crane, Dane,
dogbane, elecampane, fleabane,
henbane, humane, hurricane,
hydroplane, inane, insane, lane,
mane, membrane, mundane,
pane, plane, profane, purslane,
sane, sugarcane, thane, triplane,
urbane, vane, volplane, wane,
weathervane, windowpane

ANG
hang \ˈhaŋ\
see
ANGUE, INGUE

bang, boomerang, chain gang,
clang, fang, gang, hang, mustang,
overhang, pang, rang, sang,
shebang, slang, sprang, tang,
twang, whang, whizbang

ANGE*
change \ˈchānj\

arrange, change, derange, estrange,
exchange, grange, interchange,
mange, range, strange

ANGE**
flange \ˈflanj\

flange, mélange

ANGER
danger \ˈdān-jər\
see
AR**, ER*, OR*

danger, endanger, manger, money
changer, ranger

ANGLE
angle \ ˈaŋ-gəl\
see
EL

angle, bangle, bespangle, dangle, disentangle, entangle, mangle, newfangle, quadrangle, spangle, strangle, tangle, triangle, wangle, wrangle

ANGO
tango \ ˈtaŋ-(ˌ)gō\
see
O*, OE*, OUGH*, OW*

fandango, mango, tango

ANGUE
harangue \hə-ˈraŋ\
see
ANG

cangue, gangue, harangue

ANIA
mania \ ˈmā-nē-ə\
or \ ˈmā-nyə\
see
IA

decalcomania, dipsomania, kleptomania, mania, miscellania, Tasmania, Transylvania

ANIC
panic \ ˈpa-nik\
see
IC, ICK

Galvanic, inorganic, mechanic, Messianic, morganic, oceanic, organic, panic, satanic, titanic, transoceanic, volcanic

ANITY
sanity \ ˈsa-nə-tē\
see
E**, EA*, EE*, I**, IE*,
ITY, Y**

Christianity, humanity, inanity, insanity, sanity, urbanity, vanity

ANK
bank \ ˈbaŋk\
see
ANC

bank, blank, clank, crank, dank, drank, embank, flank, frank, gangplank, hank, lank, mountebank, plank, point-blank, prank, rank, sank, shank, shrank, spank, stank, swank, tank, thank, yank

A SOUNDS

ANNA
savanna \sə-'va-nə\
see
A**, ANA

Anna, canna, hosanna, manna,
pollyanna, savanna, Susquehanna

ANNS
banns \'banz\
see
AN*+s

banns

ANNY
nanny \'na-nē\
see
E*, EA*, EE*, I**, IE*,
Y**

canny, cranny, fanny, granny,
nanny, tyranny, uncanny

ANS
sans \'sanz\
see
AN*+s, ANN+s

sans

ANSE
expanse \ik-'span(t)s\
see
ANCE**

expanse, manse

ANT*
ant \'ant\
see
AUNT**, EANT, ERANT,
ICANT, ILANT, ITANT,
UANT

air plant, ant, aslant, cant,
can't, chant, cormorant, decant,
descant, eggplant, enchant,
fondant, gallivant, grant,
hierophant, implant, pant,
pedant, plant, power plant, rant,
shant, slant, supplant, sycophant,
transplant

ANT**
elephant \'e-lə-fənt\
see
ENT**, INT, UNT

aberrant, abundant, adamant,
arrant, arrogant, ascendant,
aspirant, benignant, blatant,
buoyant, celebrant, claimant,
clairvoyant, cognizant, confidant,
consonant, constant, contestant,

ANT**

covenant, currant, descendant, discordant, dormant, elegant, elephant, emigrant, equidistant, errant, expectant, extravagant, flagellant, flagrant, flamboyant, flippant, fragrant, gallant, hydrant, ignorant, immigrant, important, incessant, inconstant, inelegant, infant, informant, instant, irrelevant, lieutenant, malignant, merchant, ministrant, miscreant, natant, observant, occupant, octant, participant, passant, peasant, pendant, pennant, petulant, pheasant, pleasant, poignant, postulant, predominant, pregnant, protestant, pursuivant, quadrant, recreant, redundant, regnant, relevant, reluctant, remnant, repugnant, resonant, resultant, ruminant, search warrant, sextant, stagnant, supplicant, tenant, termagant, tolerant, trenchant, triumphant, tyrant, unimportant, unpleasant, vacant, vagrant, verdant, vibrant, visitant, warrant

ANT***
want \ˈwȯnt\
see
AUNT*, ONT***

au courant, courant, debutant, en passant, nonchalant, piquant, puissant, restaurant, soi-disant, want

ANTH
amaranth
\ˈa-mə-ˌran(t)th\

amaranth

ANTIC
antic \ˈan-tik\
see
IC, ICK

antic, Atlantic, frantic, gigantic, pedantic, romantic, transatlantic, unromantic

ANTO
canto \ˈkan-(ˌ)tō\
see
EAU, EW**, O*, OE*,
OT***, OUGH*, OW*,
OWE

canto, coranto, santo

ANTRY*
pleasantry
\ˈple-zᵊn-trē\
see
E*, EA*, EE*, I**, IE*,
Y**

errantry, gallantry, infantry,
pageantry, peasantry, pedantry,
pleasantry

ANTRY**
pantry \ˈpan-trē\
see
E*, EA*, EE*, I**, IE*,
Y**

pantry

ANTY
panty \ˈpan-tē\
see
E*, EA*, EE*, I**, IE*,
Y**

panty, scanty, shanty, slanty

ANX
Manx \ˈmaŋ(k)s\
see
ANK+*s*

Manx, phalanx

ANY*
company
\ˈkəm-pə-nē\
see
E*, EA*, EE*, I**, IE*,
Y**

botany, Brittany, company,
dittany, epiphany, litany,
mahogany, Romany, Tammany,
theophany, Tuscany

ANY**
many \ˈme-nē\
see
E*, EA*, EE*, ENNY,
I**, IE*, Y**

any, many

A SOUNDS

ANY*
zany \ ˈzā-nē\
see
AIN+*y*, E*, EA*, EE*,
I**, IE*, Y**

miscellany, zany

ANZA
stanza \ ˈstan-zə\
see
A**

bonanza, extravaganza, stanza

AP*
cap \ ˈkap\
see
APPE

afterclap, burlap, cap, catnap,
chap, clap, claptrap, crap,
earlap, entrap, enwrap, flap,
flytrap, foolscap, gap, handicap,
hap, kidnap, knap, kneecap,
lap, madcap, mayhap, mishap,
mobcap, mousetrap, nap,
nightcap, overlap, pap, rap,
rattletrap, sap, satrap, scrap,
skullcap, slap, snap, stopgap,
strap, tap, thunderclap, trap,
unwrap, whap, wrap, yap, zap

AP**
swap \ ˈswäp\
see
OP*

swap

APE
ape \ ˈāp\
see
EPE

ape, agape, cape, drape,
escape, fire escape, gape, grape,
landscape, misshape, nape,
rape, red tape, scrape, shape,
shipshape, tape

APER
caper \ ˈkā-pər\
see
AR**, ER*, OR*

draper, newspaper, paper, rice
paper, sandpaper, skyscraper,
wallpaper

APES
drapes \ ˈdrāps\
see
APE+*s*

drapes, jackanapes

CLOSE, BUT NO CIGAR
NEAR RHYMES VS. TRUE RHYMES

GLORIOUS AND *NEFARIOUS*: you can call them *near rhymes*, *false rhymes*, *slant rhymes*, or *pararhymes*. These terms describe anything that's not a **true rhyme**, or words whose end syllables sound identical, as in *plate/fate*, *mountain/fountain*, and *precarious/nefarious*. Many near rhymes are not deliberate choices, but the result of writer fatigue or wishful thinking.

True rhymes do not have to be spelled exactly alike. For example, *pain*, *pane*, *rain*, and *reign* all rhyme with each other. Complicating matters, many words that are spelled the same do not rhyme. For example, *again* does not rhyme with *rain*, and *reign* and *sovereign* do not rhyme with each other. One might guess that *again* would rhyme with words ending in *–in* as in *tin*, but that's not quite right, either. It's a much closer rhyme than *rain/again*, but the end sound of *again* is actually a true rhyme with *men*.

So what's an aspiring poet or songwriter to do? Sometimes you can combine words to rhyme with syllables of the problematic word. For example, *riot* rhymes with the phrases *try it*, *buy it*, *deny it*, and so forth. Songwriters and free-verse poets looking for internal rhymes or alliteration can stretch, as in *wasp* and *clasp*, but for traditional rhyming verse, imperfect end rhymes are generally frowned upon.

Synonyms are a great fix for bad rhymes. Does your song or poem have to include a *wasp*? *Bee* would be infinitely easier to rhyme. So would *stinger*: *bringer*, *clinger*, *humdinger*, *flinger*, *ringer*, *singer*, *zinger*. *Hornet* isn't much help but you could try *pest* and use a verb such as *sting* to convey that it's the kind of insect that causes intense pain.

Still stumped? Try changing the word order. Instead of ending a line with *kiln*, why not use *kiln* earlier in the phrase and end with something that's easier to rhyme, such as *bake* or even *burn*. You could pair those with *ache*, *cake*, *fake*, *break*, *rake*, *stake*, *take*, or *learn*, *turn*, *spurn*, *churn*. Consider using metaphors . . . objects in a kiln are still being formed, aren't they? Vases-in-waiting? Clay hopes and dreams? Brainstorm fifteen or twenty other ways (literal and metaphorical) to describe the image or feeling you're describing . . . chances are you can find a fresher and less clunky way to say it. (Caveat: resist the temptation to invert your word order so the syntax is no longer natural. This just draws attention to the uncooperative line.)

As you iron out the rough spots in your verse, be careful not to create new wrinkles. Rearranging a line or verse may lead to another dreaded faux pas: the *forced rhyme*. At best, forced rhymes simply call attention to sticky wickets. At worst, they dictate plot and can reduce a meaningful phrase into a mere placeholder.

Is it ever okay to use near rhymes? Yes. Adding an *–s* to one word in a rhyming pair usually isn't jarring. Songwriters have more leeway because music softens the sound of not-quite rhymes. In fact, many songs today don't rely on end rhymes, instead using internal rhyme, alliteration, and other flourishes to give the song structure. Poets (particularly those who write for adults) may choose to use an occasional near rhyme when the troublesome word is the only way to precisely say what they're trying to convey. Writers for beginning readers should avoid near rhymes whenever possible because young children rely on rhyming sounds to help them learn to read.

All of these rhyme-wrangling techniques can also help improve more cooperative end rhymes, by the way. Don't settle for easy fits—strive to find a turn of phrase that is evocative, recognizable, *and* unique.

A SOUNDS

APH
graph \ ˈgraf\
see
AFE**, AFF, ALF,
AUGH, UAFF

epigraph, epitaph, graph,
holograph, lithograph, paragraph,
phonograph, photograph, seraph,
stenograph, telegraph

APHY
biography
\bī- ˈä-grə-fē\
see
E*, EA*, EE*, I**, IE*,
Y**

autobiography, bibliography,
biography, cacography, geography,
lexicography, oceanography,
orography, orthography,
phonography, photography,
pyrography, telephotography,
topography

APPE
lagniappe \ ˈlan- ˌyap\
see
AP*

force de frappe, lagniappe, nappe

APPER
wrapper \ ˈra-pər\
see
AR**, ER*, OR*

clapper, dapper, flapper,
scrapper, snapper, tapper,
trapper, wrapper, yapper, zapper

APPLE
apple \ ˈa-pəl\
see
EL, LE

apple, crab apple, dapple,
grapple, pineapple, scrapple

APPY
happy \ ˈha-pē\
see
E*, EA*, EE*, I**, IE*,
Y**

crappy, happy, nappy, sappy,
scrappy, snappy, yappy

APS
perhaps \pər- ˈhaps\
see
AP*+s, APSE

craps, drumtaps, perhaps, snaps,
taps

APSE
lapse \ ˈlaps\
see
AP*+s

apse, collapse, elapse, lapse,
relapse, synapse

APT
apt \ ˈapt\
see
AP*+ed

adapt, apt, inapt, rapt

AQUE*
plaque \ ˈplak\
see
AC, ACK

plaque

AQUE**
opaque \ō- ˈpāk\
see
ACHE**, AKE, EAK**,
IK**

opaque

AR*
bar \ ˈbär\
see
ARE**, ARRE, ILAR,
OLLAR, ULAR, ULGAR

afar, Alcazar, astylar, avatar,
bar, bazaar, Bolivar, car, char,
cigar, cinnabar, coal tar, cookie
jar, crossbar, crowbar, czar,
debar, exemplar, far, feldspar,
gar, guitar, handlebar, horsecar,
hussarisobar, jacktar, jaguar, jar,
lascar, lazar, lodestar, Magyar,
Malabar, mar, morningstar,
motor car, par, registrar, samovar,
sandbar, scar, scimitar, shooting
star, sidecar, sitar, solar, spar,
star, tar, Templar, trolley car,
Zanzibar, Zohar

AR**
burglar \ ˈbər-glər\
see
ER*, OR*

altar, antimacassar, beggar,
bipolar, burglar, bursar, Caesar,
calendar, caterpillar, cellar,
cheddar, cougar, excalibar,
Gibraltar, grammar, hangar,
interstellar, lascar, lazar, linear,
lunar, Madagascar, medlar,
molar, mortar, nectar, pillar,
polar, poplar, realgar, salt cellar,
scholar, solar, stellar, sugar,
tartar, Trafalgar, vicar, vinegar

AR***
war \\\`wȯr\
see
OOR, OR, ORE, OUR**

Civil War, man-of-war, prewar, war

ARAB
Arab \\\`a-rəb\
see
UB

Arab, scarab

ARB
barb \\\`bärb\

barb, garb, rhubarb

ARBLE*
marble \\\`mär-bəl\
see
EL, LE

garble, marble

ARBLE**
warble \\\`wȯr-bəl\
see
EL, LE

warble

ARC
arc \\\`ärk\
see
ARK*

arc, Joan of Arc, marc, narc

ARCH*
arch \\\`ärch\

arch, countermarch, larch, march, outmarch, overarch, parch, starch

ARCH**
monarch \\\`mä-närk\
see
ARK*

anarch, hierarch, monarch, oligarch, patriarch, Petrarch, Plutarch, tetrarch

ARCHY
monarchy
\\\`mä-nər-kē\
see
E*, EA*, EE*, I**, IE*,
Y**

anarchy, heptarchy, hierarchy, monarchy, oligarchy, tetrarchy

ARD*
backward \ˈbak-wərd\
see
ERD, IRD, URD

afterward, awkward, backward, bastard, blizzard, canard, costard, coward, custard, dullard, eastward, forward, foulard, forward, gizzard, gold standard, haggard, halyard, haphazard, Harvard, hazard, homeward, inward, izzard, laggard, leeward, leopard, lizard, mallard, mustard, niggard, northward, onward, orchard, outward, placard, pochard, reynard, scabbard, seaward, shoreward, skyward, sluggard, southward, standard, steward, straightforward, tankard, turkey buzzard, upward, vineyard, wayward, westward, windward, wizard

ARD**
yard \ˈyärd\

backyard, bard, bombard, boulevard, brickyard, buzzard, card, chard, churchyard, calling card, camelopard, discard, disregard, dockyard, hard, lard, mansard, nard, pard, petard, postcard, regard, retard, sard, Scotland Yard, shard, shipyard, steelyard, stockyard, trump card, yard

ARD***
see
ORD*, ORE+*ed*, OURD

award, greensward, reward, sward, toward, ward

ARDLY*
cowardly
\ˈkaů(-ə)rd-lē\
see
E*, EA*, EE*, I**, IE*,
Y**

cowardly, inwardly, niggardly, outwardly

ARDLY**
hardly \ˈhärd-lē\
see
E*, EA*, EE*, I**, IE*,
Y**

hardly

ARE*
bare \ˈber\
see
AIR, EIR*, ERE**, IARE

aware, bare, beware, blare, care, compare, dare, declare, delftware, earthenware, ensnare, fanfare, fare, flare, flatware, glare, hardware, hare, insnare, mare, nightmare, pare, pebbleware, plowshare, prepare, rare, scare, share, snare, spare, square, stoneware, tableware, tare, threadbare, thoroughfare, unaware, ware, warfare, welfare

ARE**
are \ˈär\
see
AR*

are, caviare

ARER
bearer \ˈber-ər\
see
AIR+*er*, AR**, ER*, OR*

bearer, cupbearer, shearer, talebearer, wayfarer, wearer

ARF*
barf \ˈbärf\

barf, scarf

ARF**
dwarf \ˈdwȯrf\

dwarf, wharf

ARGE
large \ˈlärj\

barge, charge, countercharge, discharge, enlarge, large, marge, overcharge, recharge, surcharge

ARGO
cargo \ˈkär-(ˌ)gō\
see
O*, OE*, OUGH*, OW*

cargo, embargo, largo, supercargo

ARIAN
vegetarian
\ˌve-jə-ˈter-ē-ən\
see
AN**

abecedarian, agrarian, antiquarian, barbarian, contrarian, humanitarian, librarian, nonagenarian, proletarian, sectarian, sexagenarian, utilitarian, vegetarian

ARING*
daring \ ˈder- iŋ\
see
ARE*+ *ing*, EAR**+*ing*

ball bearing, caring, clearing, daring, faring, glaring, hearing, paring, seafaring

ARIO
scenario
\sə- ˈner-ē- ˌō\ *or*
\sə- ˈnär -ē- ˌō\
see
IO

impresario, Lothario, scenario

ARITY
charity \ ˈcher-ə-tē\
see
E*, EA*, EE*, I**, IE*,
Y**

charity, clarity, disparity, hilarity, irregularity, jocularity, parity, particularity, peculiarity, polarity, popularity, rarity, regularity, similarity, singularity, solidarity, vulgarity

ARK*
park \ ˈpärk\
see
ARCH**

ark, bark, birthmark, bookmark, dark, Denmark, disembark, earmark, embark, hark, high-water mark, landmark, lark, mark, mudlark, Ozark, park, pitch-dark, pockmark, postmark, quotation mark, remark, sark, shagbark, shark, skylark, snark, spark, stark, thumbmark, titlark, watermark

ARK**
bulwark
\ ˈbu̇l-(ˌ)wərk\
see
ERK, ORK**

bulwark

ARL
snarl \ ˈsnär(-ə)l\

gnarl, marl, snarl

ARLY
early \ ˈər-lē\
see
E*, EA*, EE*, I**, IE*,
Y**

early, pearly, popularly, scholarly, similarly, singularly

ARM*
arm \ˈärm\
see
ARME

alarm, arm, charm, disarm, false
alarm, farm, forearm, harm,
unharm

ARM**
warm \ˈwȯrm\
see
ORM*

lukewarm, swarm, warm

ARME
gendarme
\ˈzhän-ˌdärm\
see
ARM*

gendarme

ARMS
arms \ˈärmz\
see
ARM*+s

arms, coat of arms, firearms,
man-at-arms

ARMTH
warmth \ˈwȯrm(p)th\

warmth

ARN*
barn \ˈbärn\

barn, darn, spun yarn, tarn, yarn

ARN**
warn \ˈwȯrn\
see
ORN

forewarn, warn

ARP*
carp \ˈkärp\

carp, harp, Jew's harp, scarp,
sharp, tarp

ARP**
warp \ˈwȯrp\
see
ORP

warp

ARRE
bizarre \bə-ˈzär\
see
AR*, ARE**

bizarre

A SOUNDS

ARROW
barrow \ ˈber-(ˌ)ō\
see
EAU, EW**, O*, OE*,
OT***, OUGH*, OW*,
OWE

arrow, barrow, harrow, marrow,
narrow, sparrow, wheelbarrow,
yarrow

ARRY*
carry \ ˈka-rē\
see
AIRY, ARY*, E*, EA*,
EE*, ERY**, I**, IE*, Y**

carry, charry, glengarry, harry,
marry, parry, remarry, tarry

ARRY**
quarry \ ˈkwȯr-ē\
see
E*, EA*, EE*, I**, IE*, Y**

quarry

ARRY***
starry \ ˈstär-ē\
see
E*, EA*, EE*, I**, IE*,
Y**

starry

ARS
Mars \ ˈmärz\
see
AR*+s

Mars

ARSE
sparse \ ˈspärs\

arse, marse, parse, sparse

ARSH
harsh \ ˈhärsh\

harsh, marsh, salt marsh

ART*
art \ ˈärt\
see
EART

apart, art, cart, chart,
counterpart, dart, depart, dog
cart, go-cart, handcart, hart,
impart, mart, Mozart, oxcart,
part, pushcart, rampart, smart,
start, tart, upstart, weather chart

A SOUNDS

ART**
wart \ˈwȯrt\
see
ORT*

athwart, thwart, wart

ART***
braggart \ˈbra-gərt\
see
ERT, URT

braggart, stalwart

ARTER
starter \ˈstär-tər\
see
AR**, ER*, OR*

barter, carter, charter, garter,
self-starter, starter

ARVE*
Carve \ˈkärv\

carve, starve

ARY*
library \ˈlī-ˌbrer-ē\
see
AIRY, E*, EA*, EE*,
ERRY, ERY**, I**, IARY*,
IARY**, IE*, INARY,
ONARY, UARY, Y**

adversary, apothecary, arbitrary,
binary, canary, cassowary,
chary, cinerary, commentary,
commissary, constabulary,
contemporary, contrary,
corollary, customary, dietary,
dignitary, disciplinary, dispensary,
dromedary, eleemosynary,
emissary, fragmentary,
functionary, honorary,
intercalary, involuntary,
itinerary, lapidary, legendary,
library, literary, mercenary,
military, momentary, monetary,
pituitary, planetary, primary,
quaternary, rosemary, rotary,
salary, sanitary, secondary,
secretary, sedentary, solitary,
supernumerary, temporary,
tercentenary, tributary, tutelary,
unitary, unwary, vary, vocabulary,
voluntary, wary

A SOUNDS

ARY**
notary \ ˈnō-tə-rē\
see
E*, EA*, EE*, ERY*,
I**, IE*, Y**

anniversary, boundary, calvary,
caravansary, cavalry, dispensary,
documentary, elementary,
glossary, granary, hoary, notary,
ovary, palimentary, plenary,
quandary, rosary, rudimentary,
summary, vagary, votary

AS*
gas \ ˈgas\
see
ASS*

alas, gas, hippocras, laughing gas,
poison gas, sassafras

AS**
atlas \ ˈat-ləs\
see
ICE**, IS, ISS, USS

alias, arras, atlas, bias,
Candlemas, canvas, Caracas,
Christmas, embarrass,
fracas, Hatteras, Honduras,
Kansas, madras, Martinmas,
Michaelmas, Midas, Mithras,
Pallas, Pocahontas, Puranas,
Pythagoras, St. Nicholas, upas,
Vedas, X-mas

AS***
has \ ˈhaz\
see
AZ, AZZ

as, has, whereas

AS***
was \ ˈwäz\
see
AUSE**

was

ASE*
base \ ˈbās\
see
ACE*

airbase, base, bookcase, case,
chase, crankcase, debase, erase,
lowercase, paperchase, pillowcase,
purchase, showcase, staircase,
steeplechase, suitcase

ASE**
phase \ ˈfāz\
see
AISE, AZE

chrysoprase, metaphrase,
paraphrase, phase, phrase, tase

ASH*
ash \ ˈash\
see
ACHE*

abash, ash, balderdash, bash, brash, calabash, calash, cash, clash, crash, dash, flash, gash, gnash, hash, lash, mash, potash, plash, rash, sash, slapdash, slash, smash, soda ash, spatterdash, splash, succotash, thrash, trash, Wabash

ASH**
wash \ ˈwȯsh\
see
UASH

backwash, wash, whitewash

ASH***
goulash \ ˈgü- ˌläsh\
see
OSH

goulash, swash

ASHER
dasher \ ˈda-shər\
see
AR**, ER*, OR*

dasher, gate-crasher, haberdasher, potato masher, rasher

ASIA
Asia \ ˈā-zhə\
see
IA

aphasia, Asia, Australasia, Eurasia, fantasia, paronomasia

ASION
abrasion
\ə- ˈbrā-zhən\
see
IAN**, ION*

abrasion, evasion, invasion, occasion, persuasion, pervasion

ASIS*
basis
\ ˈbā-səs\
see
IS*

basis, homeostasis, oasis, stasis

ASIS**
emphasis
\ˈem(p)-fə-səs\
see
IS*, ISS

emphasis, hypostasis, protasis

ASK
see
ASQUE

ask, bask, cask, flask, gas mask,
Iron Mask, mask, task, unmask

ASK**
damask
\ˈda-məsk\
see
ISK

damask

ASKET
basket
\ˈbas-kit\
see
ET

basket, casket, gasket, wastebasket

ASM
chasm \ˈka-zəm\
see
AM**, EM**, UM

cataplasm, chasm, ectoplasm,
enthusiasm, iconoclasm, orgasm,
phantasm, pleonasm, protoplasm,
sarcasm, spasm

ASON
mason \ˈmā-sᵊn\
see
IN, ON*

diapason, Freemason, mason

ASP*
clasp \ˈklasp\

asp, clasp, gasp, grasp, handclasp,
hasp, rasp, unclasp

ASP**
wasp \ˈwäsp\ *or*
\ˈwȯsp\

wasp

ASQUE
Basque \ˈbask\
see
ASK

Basque, casque, masque

ASS*
ass \ˈas\
see
AS*, EAS, IAS

ass, bass***, brass, class, come to pass, crass, crevass, cuirass, eelgrass, eyeglass, fieldglass, glass, grass, harass, hourglass, isinglass, jackass, lass, looking glass, mass, middle class, morass, opera glass, outclass, overpass, pass, plateglass, repass, sandglass, sea bass, spun glass, spyglass, stained glass, sunglass, surpass, trass, trespass, underpass, upperclass, wineglass

ASS**
compass \ˈkəm-pəs\
see
ICE**, IS*, ISE****, ISS

carcass, compass, cutlass, embarrass, encompass, windlass

ASS***
bass \ˈbās\
see
ASE*, ACE*

bass*

ASSE
demitasse
\ˈde-mi-ˌtas\
see
AS*, ASS*

demitasse, en masse

ASSY
brassy \ˈbra-sē\
see
AS*+*y*, ASS*+*y*, E*, EA*,
EE*, I**, IE*, Y**

brassy, classy, embassy, glassy, grassy, massy, sassy

AST*
past \ˈpast\
see
AS*+*ed*, ASS*+*ed*, ASTE**

aghast, avast, blast, bombast, breakfast, broadcast, cast, contrast, downcast, enthusiast, fast, flabbergast, forecast, foremast, half-mast, hast, iconoclast, jiggermast, last, mast, metaphrast, outcast, outlast, overcast, paraphrast, past,

AST*

peltast, plaster cast, repast,
sandblast, seablast, steadfast,
topmast, vast

AST**
gymnast \ ˈjim-nəst\
see
EST, IST

ballast, gymnast

ASTE*
baste \ ˈbāst\
see
ACE*+*d*, AIST, ASE*+*d*

baste, chaste, cotton waste,
distaste, foretaste, haste,
lambaste**, paste, posthaste, taste,
unchaste, waste

ASTE**
caste \ ˈkast\
see
ASS*+*ed*, AST

caste, half-caste, lambaste*

ASTER
aster \ ˈas-tər\
see
AR**, ER*, OR*

alabaster, aster, burgomaster,
caster, court plaster, disaster,
faster, headmaster, master,
piaster, pilaster, plaster, quarter
master, schoolmaster, taskmaster,
Zoroaster

ASTIC
plastic \ ˈplas-tik\
see
IC, ICK

bombastic, drastic, ecclesiastic,
elastic, fantastic, mastic,
monastic, plastic, sarcastic,
scholastic, spastic

ASTLY
lastly \ ˈgast-lē\
see
E*, EA*, EE*, I**, IE*,
Y**

ghastly, lastly, vastly

ASTY*
tasty \ ˈtā-stē\
see
E*, EA*, EE*, I**, IE*,
Y**

hasty, pasty**, tasty

ASTY**
nasty \ ˈnas-tē\
see
E*, EA*, EE*, I**, IE*,
Y**

dynasty, nasty, pasty*

ASURE
measure \ ˈme-zhər\
see
URE

measure, pleasure, tape measure,
treasure

ASY
fantasy \ ˈfan-tə-sē\
see
E*, EA*, EE*, I**, IE*, Y**

apostasy, ecstasy, fantasy,
idiosyncrasy, phantasy

AT*
at \ ˈat\
see
IAT

acrobat, aerostat, aristocrat,
assignat, at, autocrat, automat,
bat, blat, bobcat, brat, brickbat,
cat, chat, chitchat, combat,
concordat, cravat, crush hat,
democrat, diplomat, fat,
format, ghat, gnat, habitat,
hat, heliostat, hellcat, jurat,
Maat, Magnificat, mudflat,
muscat, muskrat, pat, pit-a-pat,
plutocrat, polecat, rat, rat-a-tat,
Rubaiyat, sat, slat, spat, tat, that,
that's that, theocrat, thereat,
tit for tat, tomcat, top hat, vat,
wharfrat, whereat, wildcat,
ziggurat

AT**
what \ ˈhwät\
see
UT*

arhat, caveat, somewhat, what

AT***
nougat \ ´nü-gət\
see
ACKET, AIT**, ATE**,
EDIT, EIT**, ERATE**,
ERIT, ET**, ETTE**,
IATE**, IBIT, ICATE**,
ICIT, ICKET, IDGET,
IGOT, IMATE*,
INATE**, IOT**, IT,
ITE***, OLATE*,
ORATE**, OSET, OT***,
UET***, UGGET, UIT*,
ULATE**, URATE*

carat, ducat, nougat

AT****
swat \ ` swät \
see
OT*

squat, swat

ATA*
data \ ´dā-tə\
see
A**

automata, cantata, data, errata,
persona grata, pro rata, strata,
ultimata

ATA**
sonata \sə- ´nä-tə\
see
A**

cantata, inamorata, Mahabharata,
sonata

ATAL
fatal \ ´fā-tᵊl\
see
AL*

fatal, natal, perinatal, prenatal

ATAN
charlatan
\ ´shär-lə-tən\
see
AN**

charlatan, tarlatan, Yucatan

A SOUNDS

ATCH*
batch \ˈbach\
see
ACH**

batch, boxing match, catch,
crosspatch, dispatch, hatch, latch,
match, nuthatch, overmatch,
patch, potlatch, scratch, snatch,
thatch, unlatch

ATCH**
watch \ˈwȯch\
see
otch

dogwatch, nightwatch, stopwatch,
watch, wristwatch

ATE*
date \ˈdāt\
see
AIGHT, AIT*, AVATE,
EAT**, EATE, EBATE,
ECATE, EGATE,
EIGHT*, ELATE,
ENATE, ERATE, ETE,
IATE*, ICATE, IDATE,
IGATE, ILATE, IMATE,
INATE, IPATE, ITATE,
IVATE, OATE, OBATE,
OCATE, OGATE, OLATE,
ONATE, ORATE, OVATE,
UATE, ULATE, URATE

abate, accommodate, adumbrate,
annotate, antedate, ate, aureate,
belate, bifurcate, billingsgate,
bookplate, breastplate, caliphate,
carbohydrate, celebrate,
checkmate, cognate, compensate,
concentrate, confiscate,
conflagrate, conflate, conjugate,
coordinate, copperplate,
correlate, corrugate, coruscate,
crate, create, cremate, date,
debate, deflagrate, deflate,
delegate**, demonstrate,
deprecate, desecrate, designate,
dictate, dinnerplate, distillate,
divagate, donate, doorplate,
edentate, elate, electroplate,
elevate, elongate, elucidate,
emigrate, equilibrate, estate,
exculpate, exhilarate, expurgate,
extirpate, fashion plate, fate,
filtrate, first-rate, floodgate,
folate, frustrate, gate, Golden
Gate, graduate, grate, gyrate,
hate, helpmate, hibernate,
hydrate, hypothecate, illustrate,
imprecate, impregnate, incubate,
inculcate, inflate, ingrate, inmate,
innate, insenate, instate, insulate,
interpenetrate, interrogate,
interstate, inundate, irate, late,
lucubrate, lustrate, magistrate,

ATE*

magnate, mandate, mate,
messmate, methylate, migrate,
miscreate, narrate, nauseate,
negate, nictate, nitrate, obfuscate,
orchestrate, ornate, oscillate, ovate,
overrate, overstate, pate, penetrate,
permeate, permutate, perpetrate,
phosphate, placate, plate, playmate,
potentate, procreate, promulgate,
propagate, prostrate, pulsate,
rate, rebate, recapitulate, recreate,
reinstate, relate, remonstrate,
rollerskate, roseate**, rotate,
sate, schoolmate, scintillate,
second mate, second-rate, sedate,
separate**, serrate, skate, slate,
stagnate, stalemate, state, syncopate,
tergiversate, tessellate, tinplate,
titillate, tollgate, translate, truncate,
up-to-date, vacate, vacillate,
variegate, vegetate, vertebrate,
vibrate, Vulgate

ATE**
palate \ ˈpa-lət\
see
ACKET, AIT**, AT***,
EDIT, EIT**, ERATE**,
ERIT, ET**, ETTE**,
IATE**, IBIT, ICATE**,
ICIT, ICKET, IDGET,
IGOT, IMATE*,
INATE**, IOT**, IT,
ITE***, OLATE*,
ORATE**, OSET, OT***,
UET***, UGGET, UIT*,
ULATE**, URATE*

adequate, agate, baccalaureate,
celibate, delegate*, discaranate,
frigate, graduate*, importunate,
inadequate, incarnate, inchoate,
laureate, obdurate, palate,
passionate, pirate, pomegranate,
prelate, private, postgraduate,
roseate*, senate, separate*,
surrogate, triumvirate,
undergraduate

ATELY*
accurately
\ ˈa-kyə-rət-lē\
see
E*, EE*, ELY, I**, IE*,
Y**

accurately, alternately, desolately,
intimately, passionately, philately,
precipitately, separately

ATELY**
lately \\ ˈlāt-lē\
see
E*, EA*, EE*, ELY, I**,
IE*, Y**

lately, innately, irately, ornately, sedately, stately

ATES*
see
ATE*+*s*

United States

ATES**
Socrates
\\ ˈsä-krə- ˌtēz\
see
ES*

Hippocrates, Socrates

ATH*
math \\ ˈmath\
see
OPATH

aftermath, bath, bridle path, footbath, footpath, hath, lath, math, mudbath, path, sandbath, showerbath, sitz bath, towpath, Turkish bath, warpath, wrath

ATH**
Sabbath \\ ˈsa-bəth\
see
ETH, ITH

Sabbath

ATHE
lathe \\ ˈlāth\

bathe, enswathe, lathe, scathe, spathe, swathe

ATHY
apathy \\ ˈa-pə-thē\
see
E*, EA*, EE*, I**, IE*,
Y**

allopathy, antipathy, apathy, homeopathy, idiopathy, neuropathy, sympathy, telepathy

ATIC
automatic
\\ ˌȯ-tə- ˈma-tik\
see
IC, ICK

acrobatic, anastigmatic, aristocratic, aromatic, Asiatic, autocratic, automatic, axiomatic, chromatic, climatic, diplomatic, dogmatic, dramatic, ecstatic, Eleatic, emblematic, emphatic,

ATIC

epigrammatic, erratic, fanatic, fluviatic, hieratic, hypostatic, idiomatic, lymphatic, mathematic, melodramatic, miasmatic, morganatic, operatic, phlegmatic, piratic, plutocratic, pneumatic, polychromatic, pragmatic, prismatic, problematic, rheumatic, sabbatic, static, systematic, thematic, theocratic, trichromatic

ATIN
satin \ ˈsa-tᵊn\
see
IN

Latin, matin, satin, statin

ATING
rating \ ˈrā-tiŋ\
see
AIT*+*ing*, ATE*+*ing*, ING

fascinating, grating, hibernating, lubricating, pulsating, rating

ATION
nation \ ˈnā-shən\
see
IATION, ION*

abdication, acclamation, accusation, administration, admiration, adulation, adumbration, affectation, affirmation, agitation, alteration, amplification, animation, appellation, arborization, attenuation, autointoxication, avocation, calculation, cantillation, carnation, causation, cessation, circulation, citation, civilization, collation, combination, communication, compensation, concatenation, concentration, condemnation, condensation, configuration, confirmation, conformation, conglomeration, congregation, consolation, constellation, consternation, consultation, consummation, contamination, contemplation, cooperation,

ATION

coordination, coronation,
corporation, culmination,
dedication, degustation,
delegation, deportation,
destination, dilapidation,
dilation, discrimination,
disintegration, dispensation,
dissertation, dissipation,
distillation, donation, duration,
elevation, elimination,
elucidation, emanation,
embrocation, emigration,
emulation, encrustation,
enumeration, equation,
eradication, estimation,
evocation, exaggeration,
exaltation, exhiliration,
expectation, expiration,
exploitation, expostulation,
extenuation, exudation,
exultation, fixation, flirtation,
fluctuation, fornication,
fortification, fulmination,
fumigation, generalization,
gestation, glorification,
gradation, graduation,
gravitation, gurgitation,
gustation, hallucination,
hesitation, identification, illation,
illumination, illustration,
imitation, impersonation,
incantation, incarnation,
incineration, incrustation,
individualization, individuation,
inflammation, inflation,
information, innovation,
insolation, inspiration,
installation, insubordination,
insulation, interpenetration,
interpolation, interpretation,
interrogation, intoxication,
inundation, investigation,
irritation, isolation, iteration,
jubilation, laceration, legation,

ATION

levitation, libation, liberation, libration, limitation, location, lubrication, lucubration, lustration, manifestation, manipulation, materialization, mediation, meditation, mensuration, migration, miscalculation, miscreation, mitigation, moderation, modulation, mutation, mutilation, natation, nation, negation, notation, nullification, obfuscation, oblation, obligation, observation, occupation, oration, organization, orientation, oscillation, osculation, ossification, ostentation, ovation, pagination, participation, particularization, peculation, peregrination, perspiration, plantation, population, potation, precipitation, predestination, presentation, preservation, privation, probation, proclamation, prolongation, propagation, provocation, publication, pulsation, punctuation, purification, quotation, radiation, ramification, ration, recantation, recapitulation, reclamation, recreation, recrimination, recuperation, reformation, reforestation, refrigeration, regeneration, regimentation, regulation, reincarnation, reiteration, relation, reparation, repastination, representation, reputation, reservation, respiration, resuscitation, revelation, reverberation, revocation, rotation, ruination, salutation, salvation, sanitation, simulation, speculation, stabilization,

ATION

stagnation, station, stimulation, subordination, supererogation, supplication, tabulation, temptation, tergiversation, tintinnabulation, transfiguration, translation, transmigration, transmogrification, transmutation, transportation, trepidation, tribulation, undulation, unification, vacation, vaccination, valuation, vaticination, vegetation, veneration, ventilation, verification, vexation, vibration, violation, visitation, visualization, vituperation, vocalization, vocation

ATIVE
decorative
\\ˈde-k(ə-)rə-tiv\\
see
IVE**

affirmative, alternative, causative, communicative, comparative, corroborative, curative, decorative, derivative, evocative, excitative, figurative, formative, germinative, illative, illustrative, imaginative, imperative, initiative, insinuative, laxative, legislative, lucrative, mediative, meditative, modificative, narrative, native, negative, nominative, operative, optative, palliative, predicative, prerogative, preservative, provocative, purgative, putative, relative, remunerative, representative, restorative, sanative, sedative, superlative, talkative, tentative, terminative, vocative

ATO*
staccato
\\stə-ˈkä-(ˌ)tō\\
see
EAU, EW**, O*, OE**,
OT***, OUGH*, OW*,
OWE

agitato, animato, inamorato, obligato, pizzicato, potato**, rabato, staccato, tomato**, vibrato

ATO**
Plato \ ˈplā-(ˌ)tō\
see
EAU, EW**, O*, OE**,
OT***, OUGH*, OW*,
OWE

Cato, Plato, potato*, tomato*

ATOR*
educator
\ ˈe-jə-ˌkā-tər\
see
AR**, OAR, OR

accelerator, administrator, agitator,
alligator, arbitrator, aviator,
curator, depredator, dictator,
educator, elevator, emigrator,
equator, escalator, fornicator,
generator, gladiator, impersonator,
incinerator, incorporator,
incubator, indicator, instigator,
insulator, investigator, liberator,
lubricator, mediator, moderator,
narrator, navigator, nominator,
perambulator, percolator,
perpetrator, prestidigitator,
prevaricator, procrastinator,
procurator, prognosticator,
promulgator, radiator, refrigerator,
spectator, speculator, testator,
translator, ventilator, vibrator

ATOR**
senator \ ˈse-nə-tər\
see
AR**, ER*, OR*

imperator, orator, senator

ATORY
lavatory
\ ˈla-və-ˌtȯr-ē\
see
E*, EA*, EE*, I**, IE*,
ORY**, Y**

amatory, anticipatory, conservatory,
consignatory, dedicatory,
depreciatory, derogatory, dilatory,
evocatory, feudatory, fumatory,
gyratory, indicatory, inflammatory,
laboratory, laudatory, lavatory,
mandatory, migratory, objurgatory,
obligatory, observatory, oratory,
predatory, prefatory, preparatory,
propitiatory, purgatory,
reformatory, respiratory, sudatory,
vibratory

ATRY
psychiatry
\sə-ˈkī-ə-trē\
see
E*, EA*, EE*, ETRY,
I**, IE*, Y**

idolatry, ophiolatry, psychiatry

ATT
watt \ˈwät\
see
OT*

kilowatt, watt

ATTER
batter \ˈba-tər\
see
ADDER, AR**, ER*, OR*

batter, chatter, clatter, fatter,
flatter, hatter, matter, natter,
patter, platter, pratter, scatter,
shatter, smatter, spatter, splatter,
subject matter

ATTLE*
cattle \ˈka-tᵊl\
see
ADDLE, EL

battle, cattle, prattle, rattle,
Seattle, tattle, tittle-tattle

ATTLE**
wattle \ˈwä-tᵊl\
see
EL, ODDLE, OTTLE

wattle

ATUM*
stratum \ˈstrā-təm\
see
AM**, UM

erratum, stratum, substratum,
superstratum

ATUM**
ultimatum
\ˌəl-tə-ˈmā-təm\
see
AM**, UM

ageratum, ultimatum

ATURE*
temperature
\ˈtem-pə(r)-ˌchu̇r\
see
EUR, URE

armature, caricature, curvature,
entablature, feature, immature,
judicature, ligature, literature,
mature, miniature, premature,
signature, temperature

ATURE**
nature \ˈnā-chər\
see
AR**, ER*, OR*

denature, legislature, nature, nomenclature

ATUS
hiatus \hī-ˈā-təs\
see
US

afflatus, apparatus, flatus, hiatus

AU*
landau \ˈlan-ˌdau\
see
OUGH**, OW**

Frau, landau, pau, tau

AUB
daub \ˈdȯb\
see
AB**, OB*

bedaub, daub

AUCE
sauce \ˈsȯs\
see
OS*, OSS

sauce

AUCH
debauch \di-ˈbȯch\
see
OTCH

debauch

AUD
fraud \ˈfrȯd\
see
AW+*ed*

applaud, defraud, fraud, gaud, laud, maraud

AUGE
gauge \ˈgāj\
see
AGE**

gauge

AUGH
laugh \ˈlaf\
see
AFE**, AFF, AFFE, ALF

laugh

AUGHT*
caught \ ˈkôt\
see
AUT, OUGHT*

aught, caught, distraught,
fearnaught, fraught, naught,
onslaught, self-taught, taught,
untaught

AUGHT**
draught \ ˈdräft\
see
AFT, AUGH+*ed*

draught

AUGHTY
naughty \ ˈnô-tē\
see
E*, EA*, EE*, I**, IE*,
Y**

haughty, naughty

AUL
haul \ ˈhôl\
see
ALL*, AUL, AWL

caterwaul, caul, Gaul, haul, maul,
overhaul

AULT
fault \ ˈfôlt\
see
ALT

assault, catapault, default, fault,
somersault, vault

AUM
meerschaum
\ ˈmir-shəm\
see
AM**, UM

meerschaum

AUN
faun \ ˈfôn\
see
AWN

faun

AUNCH
launch \ ˈlônch\
see
ANCH**

haunch, launch, paunch, staunch

AUNT*
daunt \ˈdȯnt\
see
ONT***

aunt**, daunt, flaunt, gaunt,
haunt, jaunt, taunt, vaunt

AUNT**
aunt \ˈant\
see
ANT*

aunt*

AUR
dinosaur
\ˈdī-nə-ˌsȯr\
see
OR, ORE

centaur, dinosaur, minotaur,
plesiosaur

AURUS
taurus
\ˈtȯr-əs\
see
ORUS, URUS, US

ichthyosaurus, plesiosaurus,
Taurus, thesaurus

AUSE*
cause \ˈkȯz\
see
AUS, AW+s

applause, because**, cause,
clause, pause

AUSE**
because \bi-ˈkəz\
see
AS***, UZZ

because*

AUST
exhaust \ig-ˈzȯst\
see
OST*

exhaust, holocaust

AUT
taut \ˈtȯt\
see
AUGHT*, OUGHT*

aeronaut, Argonaut, astronaut,
juggernaut, taut

AUVE
mauve \ ˈmȯv\ *or*
\ ˈmōv\
see
OVE*

mauve

AUZE
gauze \ ˈgȯz\
see
AUSE*

gauze

AVA
lava \ ˈlä-və\
see
A**

cassava, guava, Java, lava

AVATE
aggravate
\ ˈa-grə-ˌvāt\
see
AIGHT, AIT*, ATE*,
EAT**, EIGHT*

aggravate, enervate, excavate

AVE*
cave \ ˈkāv\
see
AIVE

architrave, behave, brain wave,
brave, cave, close shave, concave,
conclave, crave, deprave, engrave,
enslave, forgave, grave, hair
wave, heat wave, knave, margrave,
misbehave, nave, rave, save,
shave, shortwave, slave, stave,
wave

AVE**
have \ ˈhav\
see
AV

have

AVE***
octave \ ˈäk-tiv\
see
IVE*

octave

AVEL*
gravel \\ ˈgra-vəl\
see
EL, LE

gavel, gravel, ravel, travel, unravel

AVEL**
navel \\ ˈnā-vəl\
see
AL*, EL

navel

AVEN
raven \\ ˈrā-vən\
see
EN**

clean-shaven, craven, graven, haven, raven, shaven

AVER*
shaver \\ ˈshā-vər\
see
AR**, ER*, OR*

engraver, graver, quaver, shaver, waver

AVER**
cadaver \kə-ˈda-vər\
see
AR**, ER*, OR*

cadaver, palaver

AVY
gravy \\ ˈgrā-vē\
see
E**, EA*, EE*, I**, IE*,
Y**

gravy, navy, wavy

AW
claw \\ ˈklȯ\
see
AWE

blue law, bucksaw, caw, Choctaw, claw, coleslaw, draw, flaw, forepaw, foresaw, gewgaw, guffaw, handsaw, haw, hee-haw, in-law, jackdaw, jackstraw, jaw, jigsaw, kickshaw, law, lockjaw, macaw, mackinaw, maw, outlaw, paw, papaw, pshaw, raw, rickshaw, Saginaw, scroll saw, seesaw, straw, taw, thaw, Warsaw, withdraw

AWAY
away \ə-ˈwā\
see
A*, AY

away, caraway, castaway, fadeaway, faraway, flyaway, rockaway, runaway, stay away, stowaway, straightaway

AWDRY
tawdry \ˈtȯ-drē\
see
E*, EA*, EE*, I**, IE**,
Y**

bawdry, tawdry

AWE
awe \ˈȯ\
see
AW

awe, overawe

AWK
hawk \ˈhȯk\
see
ALK, AUK

awk, fish hawk, gawk, hen hawk, Mohawk, news hawk, sparrow hawk, squawk, tomahawk

AWL
bawl \ˈbȯl\
see
AL**, ALL*

awl, bawl, brawl, cawl, crawl, drawl, scrawl, shawl, sprawl, trawl, yawl

AWN
dawn \ˈdȯn\
see
ONE**

brawn, dawn, drawn, fawn, lawn, overdrawn, pawn, prawn, rosy-fingered dawn, sawn, spawn, withdrawn, yawn

AX
wax \ˈwaks\
see
AC+s, ACHS, ACK+s

Ajax, anthrax, anticlimax, battle-ax, beeswax, borax, climax, flax, Halifax, income tax, lax, overtax, Pax, pickax, poll tax, relax, sax, sealing wax, smilax, surtax, syntax, tax, thorax, wax, zax

AY
day \ˈdā\
see
A*, AWAY, EE**,
EIGH*, EY**, UAY,
UET**

affray, airway, allay, All Fool's Day, All Soul's Day, alpha ray, alway, anyway, arbor day, archway, array, assay, astray, ay, bay, Bay of Biscay, belay, beta ray, betray, birthday, bluejay, Bombay, Botany Bay,

AY

bray, breakfast tray, byway, causeway, clay, cutaway, daresay, day, decay, defray, delay, disarray, dismay, display, doomsday, doorway, dray, everyday, essay, fay, flay, foray, fray, Friday, gainsay, gamma ray, gangway, gay, gray, halfway, hatchway, hay, headway, heyday, highway, holiday, horseplay, hurray, inlay, jay, lay, leeway, mainstay, Malay, Mandalay, may, midday, midway, Milky Way, mislay, Monday, nay, noonday, Norway, nosegay, nowaday, Ojibway, outlay, out-of-the-way, outstay, passageway, pathway, pay, play, popinjay, portray, pray, prepay, railway, ray, red-letter day, relay, repay, roundelay, runaway, runway, sashay, Saturday, say, shay, slay, sluiceway, soothsay, speedway, spillway, splay, spray, stay, stingray, stray, subway, Sunday, sway, Thursday, today, Tokay, Tuesday, underpay, underway, waterway, waylay, Wednesday, workaday, X-ray, yesterday

AYER
layer \ ˈlā-ər\
see
AR**, AY+*er*, ER*, OR*

assayer, brayer, layer, payer, player, prayer, slayer, soothsayer, sprayer, taxpayer

AYS
sideways \ ˈsīd-wāz\
see
AY+*s*, EIGH*+*s*

nowadays, salad days, sideways

AZ
topaz \ ˈtō-ˌpaz\
see
AS***, AZZ

Alcatraz, Boaz, topaz

AZE
blaze \ ˈblāz\
see
AISE, AY+*s*, EIGH*+*s*

ablaze, amaze, blaze, craze, daze,
emblaze, faze, gaze, glaze, haze,
maze, raze, stargaze

AZZ
jazz \ ˈjaz\
see
AS***, AZ

jazz

AZY
lazy \ ˈlā–zē\
see
E*, EA*, E**, I**, IE*,
Y**

crazy, glazy, hazy, lazy

– E –
SOUNDS

E*
acme \ˈak-mē\
see
EA*, EE*, I**, IE*, Y**

acme, acne, adobe, Ananke, anemone, ante, Apache, Aphrodite, Ariadne, Astarte, be, campanile, canzone, Chile, cicerone, Circe, Comanche, coyote, Daphne, dele, Don Quixote, epitome, Euterpe, extempore, festina lente, finale, fricasse, Gethsemane, he, Hebe, Il Trovatore, Lao-Tse, Lethe, maybe, me, MD, Melpomene, Miserere, Nepenthe, netsuke, Nike, Niobe, nota bene, Persephone, phoebe, Proserpine, Psyche, recipe, sake, Selene, sesame, she, sotto voce, stele, the, tsetse, ukulele, viva voce, we, would-be, Yangtse, ye

EA*
sea \ˈsē\
see
E*, EE*, I**, IE*, Y**

asea, beef tea, flea, guinea, lea, pea, plea, Red Sea, sea, sweet pea, tea

EA**
area \ˈer-ē-ə\
see
A**

Adrastea, area, azalea, Bona Dea, Chaldea, Crimea, Galatea, kea, Korea, Medea, nausea, panacea, Rhea, spirea, trachea

EA***
yea \ˈyā\
see
A*, AY, EIGH*

shea, yea

EACE
peace \ˈpēs\
see
EASE**, EECE, ESE**, ICE***, IECE

peace

EACH
beach \ ˈbēch\
see
EECH

beach, bleach, each, impeach, overreach, peach, preach, reach, teach

EACON
beacon \ ˈbē-kən\
see
ON*

beacon, deacon

EAD*
spread \ ˈspred\
see
AID**, ED

arrowhead, bedspread, bedstead, behead, blockhead, Book of the Dead, bread, brown bread, bulkhead, bullhead, cabbagehead, copperhead, dead, deadhead, dread, dunderhead, figurehead, forehead, gingerbread, hammerhead, head, hogshead, homestead, instead, lead**, loggerhead, masthead, overhead, overspread, pinhead, read**, roadstead, Roundhead, saphead, shewbread, shortbread, sleepyhead, sorehead, spearhead, spread, squarehead, stead, sweetbread, thread, towhead, tread, turtlehead, unread

EAD**
plead \ ˈplēd\
see
EDE, EED, YD

bead, knead, lead*, mead, plead, read*, reread

EAF*
leaf \ ˈlēf\
see
EEF, IEF*

bay leaf, cloverleaf, fig leaf, flyleaf, gold leaf, leaf, palm leaf, rose leaf, sheaf

EAF**
deaf \ ˈdef\
see
EF

deaf

EAGLE
eagle \ ˈē-gəl\
see
EGAL, EL

beagle, eagle, gold eagle, spread-eagle

EAGUE**
league \ ˈlēg\
see
UE**

colleague, league

EAK*
speak \ ˈspēk\
see
EEK, EKE, IEK, IK*,
IQUE

beak, bespeak, bleak, creak, freak, grosbeak, leak, outspeak, peak, sneak, speak, spring a leak, squeak, streak, teak, tweak, weak, wreak

EAK**
break \ ˈbrāk\
see
ACHE**, AKE, AQUE**,
IK**

beefsteak, break, daybreak, heartbreak, outbreak, steak

EAL
deal \ ˈdēl\
see
EEL, ILE***

anneal, appeal, armorial seal, cochineal, commonweal, conceal, congeal, deal, heal, leal, meal, misdeal, New Deal, oatmeal, peal, piecemeal, repeal, reveal, seal, self-heal, Solomon's seal, squeal, steal, teal, veal, weal, zeal

EALM
realm \ ˈrelm\
see
ELM

realm

EALT
dealt \ ˈdelt\
see
ELT

dealt

EALTH
health \ ˈhelth\

commonwealth, health, stealth, wealth

EALTHY
healthy \ˈhel-thē\
see
E**, EA*, EE*, I**, IE*,
Y**

healthy, stealthy, wealthy

EAM
dream \ˈdrēm\
see
EAM, EEM, IME**

beam, bream, cold cream, cream, crossbeam, daydream, dream, gleam, Gulf Stream, hornbeam, ice cream, midstream, moonbeam, ream, scream, seam, steam, stream, sunbeam, team

EAN*
clean \ˈklēn\
see
EEN, ENE, IEN**,
INE**

bean, bemean, clean, dean, demean, dry-clean, glean, jean, lean, mean, string bean, unclean, wean

EAN**
Korean \kə-ˈrē-ən\
see
AN**, IN, IEN*

Caribbean, cerulean, Epicurean, Herculean, hyperborean, Korean, Mediterranean, nectarean, paean, Promethean, protean, pygmean, subterranean, superterranean, terpsichorean, terranean

EAN***
ocean \ˈō-shən\
see
AN**, EN**, UN*

cetacean, crustacean, mid-ocean, ocean

EAP
leap \ˈlēp\
see
EEP

ash heap, cheap, heap, leap, neap, reap, sand heap

EAR*
ear \ˈir\
see
EER, ERE*, IER***

appear, blear, clear, crystal clear, dear, disappear, dogear, drear, ear, endear, fear, gear, hear, King Lear, lean year, leap year, near, overhear, reappear, rear, sear, shear, smear, spear, steering gear, tear**, year, yesteryear

EAR**
pear \ ˈper\
see
AIR, ARE*

bear, bugbear, forebear, Great Bear, koala bear, northern bear, pear, polar bear, prickly pear, swear, tear*, teddy bear, underwear, wear

EARCH
search \ ˈsərch\
see
ERCH, IRCH, URCH

research, search

EARD*
heard \ ˈhərd\
see
ERD, IRD, ORD**,
URD

heard, overheard, unheard

EARD**
beard \ ˈbird\
see
EAR*+*ed*, EER*+*ed*

beard

EARE
Shakespeare
\ ˈshāk- ˌspir\
see
EAR*, EER, ERE*,
IER***

Shakespeare

EARING
hearing \ ˈhir-iŋ\
see
EAR*+*ing*, EER+*ing*

clearing, endearing, god-fearing, hearing

EARL
pearl \ ˈpər(-ə)l\
see
IRL, URL

earl, mother-of-pearl, pearl, seed pearl

EARN
learn \ ˈlərn\
see
ERN, URN

earn, learn, unlearn, yearn

EARSE
hearse \ ˈhərs\
see
ERCE, ERSE, URSE

hearse, rehearse

EART
heart \ ˈhärt\
see
ART*

bleeding heart, broken heart, faintheart, heart, sweetheart

EARTH*
earth \ ˈərth\
see
ERTH

dearth, earth, fuller's earth, unearth

EARTH**
hearth \ ˈhärth\

hearth

EAS*
pancreas
\ ˈpan-krē-əs\
see
AS**, US

Boreas, pancreas

EAS**
see
EA*+*s*, EE*+*s*, IE*+*s*

fleas, pleas

EASE*
please \ ˈplēz\
see
E*+*s*, EA*+*s*, EE*+*s*,
EESE*, EEZE, EIZE,
EZE, IEZE

appease, disease, displease, ease, heart disease, please, tease

EASE**
increase
\in- ˈkrēs\
see
EACE, EECE, EESE**,
ICE***, IECE

axle grease, cease, crease, decease, decrease, elbow grease, increase, lease, release, surcease

EASH
leash \ˈlēsh\
see
EESH

leash

EASON
reason \ˈrē-zᵊn\
see
ASON, ON*

high treason, rainy season,
reason, season, treason

EAST*
east \ˈēst\
see
EECE+*ed*, IECE+*ed*,
IEST**, ISTE, YST**

beast, east, Far East, feast, least,
Near East, northeast, southeast,
yeast

EAST**
breast \ˈbrest\
see
EST, ESS+*ed*, IEST*,
UESS+*ed*, UEST

abreast, breast, redbreast

EAT*
beat \ˈbēt\
see
EET, EIT*, ITE***

backseat, bearded wheat, beat, bleat,
box seat, browbeat, buckwheat,
carseat, cheat, cleat, countryseat,
crabmeat, deadbeat, defeat,
drumbeat, eat, entreat, feat,
forcemeat, heartbeat, heat, maltreat,
meat, mincemeat, mistreat, neat,
overeat, peat, repeat, reseat, seat,
sweetmeat, treat, unseat, wheat

EAT**
great \ˈgrāt\
see
AIGHT, AIT*, ATE*,
EIGHT*

great

EAT***
threat \ˈthret\
see
ET

sweat, threat

EATER*
beater \ˈbē-tər\
see
AR**, EAT*+*er*, ER*,
OR*

beater, eggbeater, eater, maneater,
two-seater

EATER**
theater
\ˈthē-ə-tər\
see
AR**, EATRE, ER*, OR*

amphitheater, theater

EATER***
sweater \ˈswe-tər\
see
AR**, ER*, ETTER, OR*

sweater

EATRE
theatre
\ˈthē-ə-tər\
see
AR**, EATER**, ER*,
OR*

amphitheatre, theatre

EATURE
creature \ˈkrē-chər\
see
EACH+*er*

creature, feature

EATH*
wreath \ˈrēth\
see
EATHE, EETH

beneath, bequeath, heath,
'neath, sheath, smoke wreath,
underneath, wreath

EATH**
death \ˈdeth\
see
ETH

breath, death

EATHE
breathe \ˈbrēth\
see
EATH*

breathe, sheathe, unsheathe,
wreathe

EATHER
leather \ ˈle-thər\
see
AR**, ER*, OR*

feather, heather, leather,
pinfeather, sole leather, weather

EAU
bureau \ ˈbyu̇r-(ˌ)ō\
see
BO*, O*, OE*, OT***,
OUGH*, OW*, OWE

bandeau, beau, bureau, chateau,
manteau, plateau, portmanteau,
rondeau, Rousseau, tableau,
tonneau, trousseau, weather
bureau

EAVE
weave \ ˈwēv\
see
EEVE, EVE, IEVE

bereave, cleave, eave, heave,
interweave, leave, sheave, sick
leave, weave

EAVER
beaver \ ˈbē-vər\
see
AR**, ER*, OR*

beaver, weaver

EB
web \ ˈweb\
see
EBB

cobweb, cubeb, deb, neb, pleb,
spiderweb, web

EBB
ebb \ ˈeb\
see
EB

ebb

EBE
plebe \ ˈplēb\

glebe, grebe, plebe

EBT
debt \ ˈdet\
see
ET

debt

EC
sec \ ˈsek\
see
ECK

Aztec, Quebec, sec, spec, Toltec,
xebec

ECENT
decent \ ˈdē-s³nt\
see
ENT**

decent, indecent, recent

ECK
deck \ ˈdek\
see
EK, EQUE

beck, bedeck, breakneck, by
heck, check, crookneck, deck,
fleck, flyspeck, gooseneck,
henpeck, leatherneck, longneck,
mizzen deck, neck, peck,
pinchbeck, quarter deck, rebeck,
recheck, reck, roughneck,
rubberneck, shipwreck,
speck, stiff neck, swan neck,
upperdeck, wreck

ECKLE
freckle \ ˈfre-kəl\
see
EL, LE

deckle, freckle, heckle, speckle

ECT*
collect \ ˈkä-lekt\
see
ECK+*ed*

abject, affect, architect, bisect,
circumspect, collect, confect,
connect, correct, defect, deflect,
deject, detect, dialect, direct,
disinfect, disrespect, dissect,
effect, eject, elect, erect, expect,
genuflect, incorrect, indirect,
infect, inflect, inject, insect,
inspect, intellect, intersect,
introspect, neglect, object,
perfect, prefect, prelect, project,
prospect, protect, recollect,
reflect, reject, respect, resurrect,
retrospect, sect, select, self-
respect, stage effect, stick insect,
subject, suspect

ECT**
imperfect
\im-ˈpər-fikt\
see
ICT, ICK+*ed*

imperfect, perfect*, pluperfect

ECTOR
collector \kə-ˈlek-tər\
see
AR**, ER*, OR*

collector, deflector, detector, director, elector, erector, inspector, lector, projector, prospector, protector, rector, reflector, sector, stamp collector, tax collector, vector

ECY
secrecy \ˈsē-krə-sē\
see
E*, EA*, EE*, I**, IE*, Y**

prophecy, secrecy

ED*
bed \ˈbed\
see
AID**, EAD*

aged, bed, biped, bled, bloodshed, bobsled, bred, double bed, featherbed, fed, fled, garden bed, homebred, hotbed, ill-bred, imbed, inbred, infrared, led, low-bred, milk-fed, misled, newlywed, overfed, oyster bed, quadruped, red, sacred, shed, shred, single bed, sled, snowshed, sped, spoon-fed, ted, thoroughbred, trundle bed, underbred, underfed, unwed, watershed, well-fed, woodshed, zed

ED**
talented \ˈta-lən-təd\
see
ACT+*ed*, ANT*+*ed*,
ASP+*ed*, AST+*ed*,
ASTE+*d*, ATE*+*ed*,
AUD+*ed*, AUNT*+*ed*,
EAD*+*ed*, EAD**+*ed*,
EAT*+*ed*, EDE+*d*,
END*+*ed*, ET+*ed*,
ICT+*ed*, ID, IDE+*d*,
IELD+*ed*, IFT+*ed*,
IGHT+*ed*, ILT+*ed*, IT+*ed*,
OAST+*ed*, OINT+*ed*,
ORD*+*ed*, OST*+*ed*,
UID, ULT+*ed*, UTE+*ed*

accented, accosted, accredited, addlepated, affrighted, agitated, anointed, antiquated, barricaded, beloved**, benighted, bigoted, bird-witted, blended, blessed, booted, bowlegged, branded, brooded, bruited, buffeted, carted, cat-footed, closefisted, coasted, cold-blooded, comforted, conceited, confounded, corroded, cursed**, dark red, defeated, deflected, dim-witted, disquieted, dumbfounded, elated, elected, ended, evil-minded, fair-minded, false-hearted, featherbed, fed, fretted, halfhearted, high-minded, hoisted, hotheaded,

ED**

hundred, indebted, invented, jagged, jewel-studded, kilted, kindred, knotted, lamented, learned, left-handed, light-footed, long-winded, Manfred, Mohammed, naked, narrow-minded, nodded, one-sided, pixilated, precipitated, prompted, railroaded, recommended, red-handed, reported, resounded, restricted, resuscitated, Samoyed, shredded, single-handed, slab-sided, sober-minded, spirited, spotted, stark naked, stilted, stouthearted, surefooted, talented, translated, unabated, unaccented, uncomforted, unpolluted, unspotted, unsuited, untested, untranslated, unwarranted, unwonted, variegated, vested, wafted, weighted, wholehearted, wicked, wooded, worsted, wretched

ED***
breathed \ ´bretht

accursed, airconditioned, Argus-eyed, barelegged, beloved**, bereaved, bleached, brazen-faced, breathed, caracoled, cloyed, cowled, crabbed, crowned, cured, cursed*, curtained, dark-eyed, dead-eyed, delved, deranged, drenched, drowsed, electrotyped, endorsed, enveloped, etched, far-fetched, fettered, flagged, fringed, frog-eyed, full-fledged, gnarled, gypped, hallowed, hardboiled, henpecked, honeyed, horned, keyed, landlocked, low-necked, mottled, mullioned, pampered, parcelled, peopled, petered, pillowed, refurbished, reserved, riprapped, rock-ribbed, scowled, sequestered, shamefaced, skewered, slack-jawed, snarled,

ED***

so-called, star-spangled, stitched, straitlaced, straight-faced, stuccoed, swaybacked, tattered, tempered, three-cornered, two-faced, unlaced, unlettered, unpeopled, unreined, unremembered, unscathed, untrammeled, well-groomed, winced, winged, withered

EDE
cede \ ˈsēd\
see
EAD**, EED, YD

accede, antecede, cede, centipede, concede, expede, impede, intercede, precede, recede, rede, retrocede, secede, stampede, supersede, Swede, velocipede, Venerable Bede

EDGE*
ledge \ ˈlej\
see
EAGE, EGE

dredge, edge, fledge, kedge, keen edge, ledge, mountain edge, on edge, pledge, sedge, selvedge, sledge, water's edge, wedge

EDGE**
knowledge \ ˈnä-lij\
see
AGE*, EGE, IDGE

acknowledge, foreknowledge, knowledge

EDIAN
median \ ˈmē-dē-ən\
see
AN**, IAN*

comedian, median

EDIT*
edit \ ˈe-dət\
see
AIT**, AT***, EIT**,
ET**, ETTE**, UET***,
UIT*

accredit, credit, edit, discredit

EDO
tuxedo
\ ˌtək-ˈsē-(ˌ)dō\
see
EAU, EW**, O*, OE*,
OT***, OUGH*, OW*,
OWE

credo, teredo, Toledo, torpedo, tuxedo

EDY
comedy
\ˈkä-mə-dē\
see
E*, EA*, E*, I**, IE*, Y**

comedy, higgledy-piggledy, remedy, tragedy

EE*
tree \ˈtrē\
see
E*, EA*, I**, IE*,
IGREE, Y**

absentee, agree, alee, apogee, banshee, bee, bootee, Bo tree, bumblebee, calipee, carefree, Chaldee, Cherokee, chick-a-dee, chimpanzee, coatee, coffee, committee, conferee, Cree, debauchee, degree, devotee, disagree, dungaree, employee, endorsee, fancy-free, fee, fiddle-dee-dee, flee, foresee, free, fricassee, Galilee, garnishee, gee, glee, goatee, grandee, guarantee, hard alee, hat tree, honeybee, jamboree, jubilee, Judas tree, knee, lee, legatee, lessee, levee, marquee, nominee, ogee, oversee, Parsee, patentee, Pawnee, payee, Pharisee, pledgee, pongee, presentee, prithee, puttee, quilting bee, referee, refugee, repartee, rupee, Sadducee, scot-free, scree, see. settee, Shawnee, snickersnee, soiree, spelling bee, spondee, spree, squeegee, suttee, tee, tee-hee, tepee, thee, third degree, three, toffee, tree, trustee, vendee, warrantee, wee, whoopee, Yankee

EE**
matinee \ˌma-tə-ˈnā\
see
A*, AY

coryphee, divorcée, fiancée, matinee

EECE
Greece \ˈgrēs\
see
EACE, EASE**, EESE**,
ESE**, ICE***, IECE,
ISE***

fleece, Golden Fleece, Greece

EECH
speech \ ˙spēch\
see
EACH

beech, beseech, breech, leech, screech, speech

EED
feed \ ˙fēd\
see
EAD**, EDE, YD

agreed, aniseed, Apostle's Creed, bindweed, birdseed, bleed, breed, chickweed, cotton seed, creed, crossbreed, decreed, deed, exceed, feed, flaxseed, freed, full speed, gleed, Godspeed, greed, hayseed, heed, indeed, Indian weed, ironweed, jewelweed, knock-kneed, knotweed, linseed, meed, misdeed, need, overfeed, pigweed, pokeweed, poppyseed, proceed, reed, screed, seaweed, seed, sneezeweed, speed, steed, stinkweed, succeed, title deed, tobacco weed, treed, tweed, weak-kneed, weed, whispering reed

EEDLE
needle \ ˙nē-dᵊl\
see
EL, LE

darning needle, pine needle, needle, wheedle

EEDY
greedy \ ˙grē-dē\
see
E*, EA*, EE*, I**, IE*,
Y**

greedy, needy, reedy, seedy, speedy, weedy

EEF
beef \ ˙bēf\
see
IEF*

beef, coral reef, reef

PARTNERS IN RHYME
POLISHING YOUR POETRY

So, your rhymes are golden. Your meter's flawless. What else can you do to polish up your poetry and lyrics? Plenty.

Alliteration uses words that begin with similar consonant sounds as in *Thumbelina was thrilled to take third place in the thumb-wrestling tournament.* A little bit of alliteration goes a long way, so use a light touch.

Assonance combines words with similar vowel sounds. For example, *Chase's pancakes were always as big as a plate.* Songwriters often use assonance in lieu of true rhymes to give songs shape.

With **consonance**, words share consonant sounds at any position: *The kitten's prickly, curling whiskers tickled Katerina's cheeks.*

Internal rhyme slips rhyming words into the middle of a line or phrase within a poem or song. *Tucked in bed, three sleepyheads . . .* Or, *Fog blanketed the trees in shrouds of clouds.* This technique is popular with songwriters, who may choose to rhyme the beginnings of lines with repetitive end phrases: *Lie to me, cry to me, but do not say good-bye to me.*

To add sensory details, use **onomatopoeia**: words that are spelled like the sound they make—*hiss, buzz, whap, bang!*

Puns, or words with humorous double meanings, are a clever way to add depth and interest: *The poet's new effort went from bad to verse.*

Variety is the spice of poetry, too. Changing the structure of a last stanza to include a repeated line lets the reader trail off or march away, depending on how it's used. Ending with an incomplete rhyme gives a kind of auditory punctuation mark. The following example from one of my books for children (*Baby Love*, Dutton 2003) uses both techniques: *Your cozy perch moves up and down / up and down / up and down . . . / eyelids heavy, not a sound / as you drift off to sleep.*

Visual cues give poetry physical structure that can enhance meaning.

- **Line breaks** force the reader to pause at particular points for added drama, while *compressingtext* (removing white space) encourages the reader to speed up.

- **Punctuation** (or intentional lack of it paces the reader.

- *Italics*, **bold print**, and font size add emotional elements to plain text.

- **Paragraph formatting** such as justification or line breaks gives poetry a graphic structure and uses white space to underscore a poem's theme or image. This is done on a large scale with concrete poetry.

EEK
cheek \ ˈchēk\
see
EAK*, EKE, IEK, IK*,
IQUE

cheek, cleek, creek, Greek, hide-and-seek, leek, meek, peek, reek, seek, sleek, week

EEL
steel \ ˈstēl\
see
EAL, ILE***

balance wheel, cartwheel, chainwheel, cogwheel, creel, despot's heel, eel, emery wheel, feel, Ferris wheel, flywheel, genteel, heel, high heel, Jezreel, keel, kneel, mill wheel, newsreel, paddlewheel, peel, potter's wheel, prayer wheel, reel, spinning wheel, steel, Virginia reel, waterwheel, wheel

EEM
seem \ ˈsēm\
see
EAM, EEM, EME, IME**

deem, esteem, redeem, seem, self-esteem, teem

EEN
teen \ ˈtēn\
see
EAN*, EIN**, ENE,
IEN**, INE**

Aberdeen, a-tween, baleen, between, bowling green, canteen, careen, colleen, e'en, eighteen, fellaheen, fifteen, fourteen, go-between, green, Halloween, keen, lateen, nankeen, nineteen, overween, peen, preen, putting green, queen, sateen, screen, seen, seventeen, sheen, sixteen, smoke screen, spleen, teen, thirteen, tureen, 'tween, umpteen, unseen, velveteen, village green, ween, wintergreen

EENS
greens \ ˈgrēnz\
see
EEN+*s*, INE**+*s*

greens, smithereens, teens

EEP
sweep \ ˈswēp\
see
EAP

asleep, Bo Peep, cheep, chimney sweep, clean sweep, creep, deep, keep, knee-deep, oversleep, peep, sheep, skin-deep, sleep, steep, sweep, upkeep, weep, well-sweep

EEPER
keeper \ ˈkē-pər\
see
AR**, EAP+*er*, ER*, OR*

carpet sweeper, creeper, deeper, gamekeeper, housekeeper, keeper, lighthouse keeper, peeper, sleeper, steeper, sweeper

EER
beer \ ˈbir\
see
EIR**, ERE*, IER***

auctioneer, beer, buccaneer, cameleer, carabineer, career, chanticleer, charioteer, cheer, compeer, decreer, deer, domineer, engineer, freer, gazetteer, ginger beer, jeer, leer, mountaineer, muleteer, musk deer, musketeer, mutineer, near beer, overseer, peer, pioneer, privateer, profiteer, queer, racketeer, reindeer, root beer, seer, sheer, sightseer, sneer, spruce beer, steer, veer, veneer, volunteer

EESE*
see
EASE*, EE*+*s*, EEZE,
EIZE, EZE, IEZE

cheese, headcheese

EESE**
see
EACE, EASE**, EECE,
ESE**, ICE***, IECE,
ISE***

geese

EESH
sheesh \ ˈshēsh\
see
EASH

baksheesh, hasheesh, sheesh

EET
feet \ ˈfēt\
see
EAT*, EIPT, EIT*, ETE,
ITE***

afreet, balance sheet, beet,
bittersweet, Blackfeet, crow's
feet, discreet, feet, fleet, greet,
indiscreet, meadowsweet, meet,
parakeet, proof sheet, sheet,
skeet, sleet, stern sheet, stocking
feet, street, sweet, tweet, Wall
Street, winding sheet

EETH
teeth \ ˈtēth\
see
EATH*

teeth

EETHE
seethe \ ˈsēth\
see
EATHE

seethe, teethe

EEVE
peeve \ ˈpēv\
see
EIVE

beeve, peeve, reeve, sleeve

EEZE
sneeze \ ˈsnēz\
see
E*+s, EASE*, EE*+s,
EIZE, IE*+s, IEZE

breeze, freeze, sneeze, squeeze,
tweeze, wheeze

EF
chef \ ˈshef\
see
EAF**

chef, clef

EFT
deft \ ˈdeft\
see

bereft, cleft, deft, eft, heft, left,
reft, theft, weft

EFY
defy \di- ˈfī\
see
I*, IE**, IGH, Y*

defy, liquefy, putrefy, stupefy

EG
peg \ ˈpeg\
see
EGG

beg, dreg, keg, leg, mumblety-peg, nutmeg, peg

EGAL
legal \ ˈlē-gəl\
see
AL*, EAGLE

illegal, legal, regal, viceregal

EGATE
segregate
\ ˈse-gri-ˌgāt\
see
AIGHT, AIT**, ATE*,
EAT**, EIGHT*

congregate, delegate, legate, relegate, segregate

EGE
college \ ˈkä-lij\
see
EDGE, IDGE

allege, college, cortege, privilege, sacrilege

EGG
egg \ ˈeg\
see
EG

egg, nest egg, yegg

EGION
region \ ˈrē-jən\
see
ION*

legion, region

EGM
phlegm \ ˈflem\
see
EM*

apothegm, phlegm

EGS
dregs \ ˈdregz\
see
EG+*s*

daddy longlegs, dregs, sea legs

EI
lei \ ˈlā\
see
A*, AY, EIGH*, EY**

lei

EIGE
beige \ ˈbāzh\
see
EGE

beige

EIGH
weigh \ ˈwā\
see
A*, AY, EY*, UET**

inveigh, neigh, outweigh, sleigh, weigh

EIGHT*
freight \ ˈfrāt\
see
AIGHT, AIT**, ATE*,
EAT**

eight, featherweight, freight, heavyweight, paperweight, pennyweight, weight

EIGHT**
height \ ˈhīt\
see
IGHT, ITE*

height, sleight

EIGN*
deign \ ˈdān\
see
AGNE, AIGN, AIN*,
AINE, ANE, EIN*

deign, feign, reign

EIGN**
foreign \ ˈfȯr-ən\
see
IN

foreign, sovereign

EIL
veil \ ˈvāl\
see
AIL*, ALE

nonpareil, unveil, veil

EIN*
vein \ˈvān\
see
AGNE, AIGN, AIN*,
AINE, ANE, EIGN*

Hussein, skein, vein

EIN**
stein \ˈstīn\
see
INE*

Frankenstein, Holstein,
Rubenstein, stein

EIN***
protein \ˈprō-ˌtēn\
see
EAN*, EEN, ENE,
IEN**, INE**

protein

EINE
Seine \ˈsān\
see
AIN*, ANE, EIGN*

Seine, vicereine

EING
being \ˈbē(-i)ŋ\
see
E*+*ing*, EE*+*ing*, ING

being, fleeing, freeing, seeing

EINT
feint \ˈfānt\
see
AINT

feint

EIPT
receipt \ri-ˈsēt\
see
EAT*, EET, EIT*, ITE***

receipt

EIR*
their \ˈth̲ər\
see
AIR, ARE*, ERE**

heir, their

EIR**
weir \\ ˈwir\
see
EAR*, ERE*

weir

EIRD
weird \\ ˈwird\
see
EAR*+*ed*, EARD**,
EER+*ed*

weird

EISS
gneiss \\ ˈnīs\
see
ICE*

edelweiss, gneiss

EIT*
deceit \di-ˈsēt\
see
EAT*, EET, EIPT, ETE,
ITE***

conceit, deceit

EIT**
forfeit \\ ˈfȯr-fət\
see
AIT**, AT***, ATE**,
EDIT, ERATE**, ERIT,
ET**, ETTE**, IATE**,
IBIT, ICATE**, ICIT,
ICKET, IDGET, IGOT,
IMATE*, INATE**,
IOT**, IT, ITE***,
OLATE*, ORATE**,
OSET, OT***, UET***,
UGGET, UIT*, ULATE**,
URATE*

counterfeit, forfeit, surfeit

EITY
deity \\ ˈdē-ə-tē\
see
E*, EA*, EE*, I**, IE*,
ITY, Y**

deity, homogeneity, ipseity, seity, spontaneity

EIVE
receive \ri-ˈsēv\
see
IEVE*

apperceive, conceive, deceive,
perceive, preconceive, receive

EIZE
seize \ˈsēz\
see
EAS, EE*+s, EEZE, ES*,
IEZE

seize

EK
trek \ˈtrek\
see
ECK

trek

EKE
eke \ˈēk\
see
EAK*, EEK, IEK, IK*,
IQUE

eke

EL*
angel \ˈān-jəl\
see
ABEL, AEL, AMEL,
AVEL*, AVEL**, ELL,
ENNEL, EREL, ERYL,
EVEL, IEL, IVEL, OVEL,
OWEL, UEL, UNNEL,
USEL, YL

angel, apparel, archangel,
barrel, brothel, calomel, camel,
cancel, canton flannel, chancel,
channel, charnel, chattel, chisel,
counsel, cudgel, damsel, easel,
evangel, fardel, flannel, flour
barrel, gambrel, gimel, hazel,
hostel, jewel, kernel, kummel,
laurel, libel, lintel, marvel,
minstrel, model, mongrel,
morsel, Mount Carmel, mussel,
nickel, panel, parcel, petrel,
pommel, pretzel, quarrel,
rebel, remodel, satchel, scalpel,
scoundrel, sentinel, shekel,
shrapnel, sorrel, spandrel,
spaniel, spiel, tael, tassel,
timbrel, tinsel, trammel, vessel,
wastrel, weasel, Whitechapel,
witch hazel, wood sorrel, yodel,
yokel

EL**
compel \kəm-ˈpel\
see
ELL

asphodel, citadel, clientele,
compel, corbel, dispel, El, excel,
expel, hydromel, impel, infidel,
Israel, Jezebel, lapel, muscatel,
Noel, parallel, pastel, personnel,
rebel*

LE
amble \ˈam-bəl\
see
ABBLE, ABLE*, ABLE**,
ACKLE, ACLE, ADDLE,
AMBLE, AMPLE,
ANDLE, ANGLE,
APPLE, ARBLE, ATTLE,
EABLE, EAGLE, ECKLE,
EEDLE, ELLE, EMBLE,
ESTLE, ETTLE, IABLE*,
IABLE**, IABLE***,
IBBLE, IBLE*, IBLE**,
ICKLE, ICLE, IDDLE,
IDLE, IFLE, IGGLE,
IMBLE, IMPLE, INDLE,
INGLE, INKLE, IPLE,
IPPLE, IRCLE, ISTLE,
ITTLE, IZZLE, OBBLE,
OBLE, OGGLE, OPLE,
OSTLE, UBLE, UCKLE,
UDDLE, UGGLE,
UMBLE, URDLE,
URTLE, USTLE, UZZLE,
YCLE

addle, amble, ample, ankle,
Aristotle, astraddle, axle, baffle,
bamboozle, battle, beagle, beetle,
boodle, bridle, bubble, bugle,
bundle, bungle, burble, burgle,
carbuncle, castle, cat's cradle,
cattle, chortle, church steeple,
cockle, coddle, Constantinople,
couple, cradle, crossword puzzle,
crumple, cuttle, dawdle, dazzle,
decouple, dingle, disciple,
dismantle, double, embezzle,
entitle, fettle, foible, fondle,
foozle, forecastle, frazzle, gargle,
gentle, gurgle, haggle, idle,
inveigle, jungle, kindle, kirtle,
ladle, mantle, maple, meddle,
mollycoddle, monocle, mottle,
muffle, muscle, myrtle, noodle,
nozzle, octuple, ogle, oodle,
pebble, peddle, peduncle,
people, piffle, pinochle, poodle,
purple, quadruple, quintuple,
raffle, rankle, razzle-dazzle,
reshuffle, Roman candle, rubble,
schnozzle, scuffle, septuple,
shuffle, shuttle, snaffle, snuffle,
socle, spangle, sparkle, stag
beetle, staple, startle, stubble,
subtle, supple, temple, tickle,
tinkle, tipple, title, toddle,
tousle, treacle, treadle, treble,
trouble, truffle, trundle, tussle,
tweedle, uncle, unruffle, waffle,
waggle

ELCH
belch \ ˈbelch\

belch, squelch

ELD
held \ ˈheld\
see
EL+*ed*, ELL+*ed*

beheld, geld, held, meld, upheld,
weld, withheld

ELDT
veldt \ ˈvelt\
see
ELT

veldt

ELESS
careless \ ˈker-ləs\
see
ESCE, ESS

careless, clueless, defenseless,
gestureless, guileless, homeless,
lifeless, measureless, nevertheless,
noiseless, priceless, purposeless,
senseless, shameless, shoeless,
spaceless, tasteless, timeless,
useless, vagueless, valueless,
verdureless, wireless

ELET
bracelet \ ˈbrās-lət\
see
ET

bandelet, bracelet, corselet,
omelet, wavelet

ELF
self \ ˈself\

delf, elf, herself, himself, itself,
myself, oneself, pantry shelf, pelf,
self, shelf, thing-in-itself, thyself,
yourself

ELIN
javelin \ ˈjav-lən\
see
IN, INE***, INN

javelin, zeppelin

ELK
elk \ ˈelk\
see
ILK

elk, whelk

ELL
bell \ ˈbel\
see
EL, ELLE

alarm bell, artesian well, befell, bell, bluebell, bombshell, buy and sell, cell, church bell, cockleshell, convent bell, cowbell, dell, diving bell, doorbell, dumbbell, dwell, eggshell, ell, fare-thee-well, farewell, fell, foretell, groundswell, harebell, heather bell, hell, jell, knell, misspell, nutshell, oversell, pell-mell, quell, resell, retell, school bell, seashell, sell, shell, sleigh bell, smell, spell, swell, tell, tortoiseshell, well, William Tell, yell

ELLA
umbrella
\ ˌəm-ˈbre-lə\
see
A**

a cappella, Capella, citronella, fenestrella, Isabella, nigella, pimpinella, predella, prunella, stella, tarantella, umbrella, villanella

ELLE
gazelle \gə-ˈzel\
see
ELL

bagatelle, belle, fontanelle, gazelle, immortelle, mademoiselle, Moselle, nacelle, spirituelle, villanelle

ELLER
teller \ ˈte-lər\
see
AR**, ELL+*er*, ER*, OR*

bookseller, feller, propeller, speller, storyteller, teller

ELLO
hello \hə-ˈlō\
see
EAU, EW**, O*, OE*, OT***, OUGH*, OW*, OWE

cello, hello, martello, Othello, punchinello, violoncello

ELLOW
yellow \ ˈye-(ˌ)lō\
see
EAU, EW**, O*, OE**, OT***, OUGH*, OW*, OWE

bedfellow, fellow, Longfellow, mellow, yellow

ELM
elm \ ´elm\
see
EALM

elm, helm, overwhelm, whelm

ELON
melon \ ´me-lən\
see
ON*

felon, melon, watermelon

ELP
help \ ´help\

help, kelp, whelp, yelp

ELRY
revelry \ ´re-vəl-rē\
see
E*, EA*, EE*, I**, IE*,
Y**

hostelry, jewelry, revelry

ELSE
else \ ´el(t)s\
see
ELL+*s*

else

ELT
felt \ ´felt\
see
EALT

belt, delt, dwelt, felt, heartfelt,
knelt, life belt, melt, pelt, smelt,
spelt, welt

ELTE
svelte \ ´svelt\
see
ELT

svelte

ELTER
shelter \ ´shel-tər\
see
AR**, ER*, OR*

helter-skelter, shelter, swelter,
welter

ELVE
twelve \ ´twelv\
see
ELF+*s*

delve, helve, shelve, twelve

ELVES
shelves \ ˈshelvz\
see
ELVE+*s*

elves, ourselves, selves, shelves, themselves, yourselves

ELY
lovely \ ˈləv-lē\
see
ATELY, E*, EE*, EL+*y*,
ELL+*y*, I**, IE*, Y**

antiquely, blithely, bravely, chastely, coarsely, comely, completely, concretely, contumely, conversely, crudely, divinely, entirely, exquisitely, freely, homely, inanely, infinitely, intuitively, lately, leisurely, lithely, lively, loosely, lovely, merely, naively, namely, obliquely, obtrusively, precisely, princely, profusely, purely, rarely, relatively, rely, safely, savagely, scarcely, shapely, sincerely, solely, sorely, strangely, sublimely, supremely, surely, tamely, tensely, timely, unlovely, untimely, vaguely, wifely

EM*
gem \ ˈjem\

anadem, cave canem, diadem, gem, hem, ibidem, idem, per diem, pro tem, stratagem, the rem

EM**
problem \ ˈprä-bləm\
see
AGM, AM**, AMB,
AME**, AMN, ASM,
EGM, EMN, IEM

ad valorem, anthem, emblem, harem, item, Jerusalem, Moslem, poem, postmortem, problem, proem, requiem, sachem, solar system, stem, system, tandem, theorem, totem

EMA
cinema \ ˈsi-nə-mə\
see
A*

anathema, cinema, eczema, enema, ulema

EMBER
ember \ ˈem-bər\
see
AR**, ER*, OR*

December, dismember, ember, member, November, remember, September

EMBLE
tremble \ ˈtrem-bəl\
see
EL, LE

assemble, dissemble, reassemble, resemble, tremble

EME
extreme \ik- ˈstrēm\
see
EAM, EEM, IME**

bireme, blaspheme, extreme, morpheme, phoneme, quinquereme, scheme, supreme, theme, trireme

EMENT
tenement
\ ˈte-nə-mənt\
see
ENT**

accoutrement, achievement, acquirement, amusement, assuagement, atonement, attunement, bereavement, casement, cement, cerement, chastisement, clement, displacement, divulgement, element, embezzlement, encouragement, enlargement, escapement, excitement, impalement, implement, improvement, inclement, infringement, management, measurement, movement, pavement, postponement, pronouncement, refinement, reimbursement, reinforcement, requirement, retirement, settlement, supplement, tenement, vehement

EMN*
condemn \kən- ˈdem\
see
EM*

condemn, contemn

EMN**
solemn \ ˈsä-ləm\
see
ONYM, YMN

solemn

EMP
hemp \ ˈhemp\

hemp, temp

EMPT
tempt \ ˈtem(p)t\

attempt, contempt, exempt,
preempt, tempt, unkempt

EMY
enemy \ ˈe-nə-mē\
see
E*, EA*, EE*, I**, IE*,
Y**

academy, alchemy, blasphemy,
enemy, Ptolemy

EN*
yen \ ˈyen\

amen, fen, ken, men, ten, then,
wen, when, wren, yen, Zen

EN**
quicken \ ˈkwi-kən\
see
AIN**, AKEN, AMEN,
AVEN, EAN**, EMEN,
ENNE, EVEN, IEN*,
IMEN, IN, IZEN, OGEN,
OKEN, OMEN, OVEN,
UMEN, YGEN

abdomen, ashen, barren, batten,
begotten, beholden, bitten,
boughten, brazen, brethren,
brighten, burden, chicken,
chosen, coven, cozen, crestfallen,
cyclamen, dampen, darken,
delicatessen, den, dew-laden,
dolmen, downtrodden, dozen,
Dryden, Eden, embolden,
enliven, fatten, flaxen,
forbidden, forgotten, foughten,
frighten, frozen, Galen, garden,
gentlemen, glen, glisten, gluten,
gotten, guinea hen, harden,
hasten, heathen, heaven, hen,
herb garden, hidden, hydrogen,
hymen, hyphen, ill-gotten,
kindergarten, kinsmen, kitchen,
kitten, laden, leaven, lengthen,
Lenten, lessen, lichen, lighten,
liken, linden, linen, listen,
madden, madmen, Magdalen,
maiden, menhaden, mitten,
mizzen, moisten, molten,
mullen, Munchausen, new-fallen,
oaken, oaten, often, olden, open,
Origen, overladen, oxygen,
paten, pen, pigpen, pollen,
poverty-stricken, quicken, quill
pen, redden, reopen, risen,
rotten, sadden, Saracen,

EN**

schoolmen, silken, siren,
smarten, soften, stamen, storm
driven, strengthen, stricken,
sudden, sullen, swollen, table
linen, terror-stricken, thicken,
tungsten, unforsaken, unloosen,
untrodden, vestrymen, vixen,
warden, warren, waxen,
weather-beaten, whiten,
wooden, worm-eaten, written,
Yemen

ENA*
hyena \hī-ˈē-nə\
see
A**

arena, Athena, hyena, novena,
subpoena, verbena

ENA**
phenomena
\fi-ˈnä-mə-nə\
see
A**

phenomena, prolegomena

ENADE
grenade \grə-ˈnād\
see
ADE*

grenade, hand grenade,
promenade, serenade

ENARY
mercenary
\ˈmər-sə-ˌner-ē\
see
AIRY, ARRY*, ARY*, E*,
EE*, ERRY, ERY**, I**,
IE*, Y**

centenary, mercenary, septenary

ENATE
hyphenate
\ˈhī-fə-ˌnāt\
see
AIGHT, AIT**, ATE*,
EAT**, EIGHT*

enate, hyphenate, oxygenate,
rejuvenate, senate

ENCE
fence \ ˈfen(t)s\
see
ANCE*, ANT*+*s*, ENSE,
ENT*+*s*, IENCE, UENCE

absence, abstinence, acquiescence, adolescence, appetence, back fence, belligerence, cadence, circumference, coincidence, commence, condolence, conference, confidence, continence, corpulence, correspondence, credence, decadence, defence, difference, diffidence, diligence, divergence, divulgence, effulgence, eminence, essence, evidence, excellence, excrescence, fence, Florence, florescence, fraudulence, hence, immanence, impertinence, impotence, impudence, inadvertence, incandescence, incidence, incompetence, inconsequence, independence, indigence, indolence, indulgence, inference, influence, innocence, insistence, intelligence, interference, intumescence, iridescence, irreverence, jurisprudence, magnificence, negligence, nonoccurrence, occurrence, offence, omnipotence, omnipresence, opulence, pence, penitence, persistence, Peter's pence, phosphorescence, preeminence, preference, presence, prevalence, prominence, providence, prudence, putrescence, quintessence, recurrence, redolence, reference, reminiscence, renascence, residence, resplendence, resurgence, reticence, reverence, self-defence, senescence, silence, sixpence, subsistence, sufference, thence, tower of silence, transference, turbulence, violence, virulence, whence

E SOUNDS

ENCH
bench \ ˙bench\

bench, blench, clench, drench,
entrench, French, monkey
wrench, quench, retrench,
stench, trench, unclench, wench,
workbench, wrench

ENCY
agency \ ˙ā-jən(t)-sē\
see
E*, SEA*, EE*, I*, IE*,
Y**

agency, clemency, cogency,
cognency, competency,
consistency, constituency,
contingency, currency, decency,
deficiency, delinquency,
despondency, efficiency,
emergency, exigency, fervency,
frequency, impotency,
inadvertency, incipiency,
inclemency, inconsistency,
incumbency, independency,
indigency, infrequency, leniency,
nascency, patency, permanency,
persistency, pertinency, potency,
pungency, regency, tendency,
transparency

END*
amend \ə-˙mend\
see
UEND

amend, append, ascend, attend,
befriend, bend, blend, commend,
comprehend, condescend,
contend, defend, depend,
descend, distend, dividend,
emend, end, expend, extend,
fend, forfend, friend, godsend,
impend, intend, interblend,
lend, mend, minuend, offend,
pend, perpend, portend,
pretend, recommend, rend,
reprehend, reverend, send, spend,
superintend, suspend, tail end,
tend, transcend, trend, unbend,
vend, vilipend, wend, Zend

END**
legend \ ˙le-jənd\
see
IND, UND

legend

ENDA
agenda
\ə-ˈjen-də\
see
A**

addenda, agenda, hacienda

ENDER
fender \ˈfen-dər\
see
AR**, ER*, OR*

bartender, defender, double-ender, engender, expender, fender, gender, legal tender, mender, offender, pretender, provender, sender, spender, surrender, suspender, tender

ENDO
crescendo
\krə-ˈshen-(ˌ)dō\
see
EAU, EW**, O*, OE*,
OT***, OUGH*, OW*,
OWE

crescendo, diminuendo, innuendo

ENDS
calends \ˈka-lən(d)z\
see
END*+s

calends, odds and ends

ENE
convene \kən-ˈvēn\
see
EAN*, EEN, EIN***,
IEN**, INE**

acetylene, contravene, convene, damascene, epicene, ethylene, gangrene, hygiene, intervene, kerosene, Nazarene, Nicene, obscene, pliocene, pyrene, scene, serene, supervene

ENER
opener \ˈō-pə-nər\
see
AR**, EN**+er, ER*,
OR*

eye-opener, gardener, listener, opener, scrivener, softener

ENET
tenet \ˈte-nət\
see
ET

genet, Plantagenet, tenet

ENG
ginseng \ ˈjin- ˌseŋ\
see
ING

ginseng

ENGE*
avenge \ə- ˈvenj\

avenge, revenge, Stonehenge

ENGE**
lozenge \ ˈlä-zᵊnj\
see
INGE

challenge, lozenge, scavenge

ENGTH
length \ ˈleŋ(k)th\

length, strength, wavelength

ENIC*
arsenic \ ˈär-sə- nik\
see
IC, ICK

arsenic, eugenic, hygienic,
Saracenic

ENIC**
scenic \ ˈsē-nik\
see
IC, ICK

scenic

ENITY
amenity
\ə- ˈme-nə-tē\
see
ITY

amenity, serenity

ENLY*
suddenly \ ˈsə-dᵊn-lē\
see
E*, EA*, EE*, EN**+*ly*,
I**, IE**, Y**

evenly, heavenly, openly, slovenly,
suddenly

ENLY**
keenly \ ˈkēn-lē\
see
E*, EA*, EAN+*ly*, EE*,
I**, IE*, Y**

keenly, queenly

ENNA
henna \ ˈhe-nə\
see
ENA

antenna, Gehenna, henna, senna,
Sienna, Vienna

ENNE
cayenne \(ˌ)kī-ˈen*\
see
EN*

cayenne, comedienne, doyenne,
Parisienne, tragedienne

ENNEL
kennel \ ˈke-nᵊl\
see
EL

fennel, kennel

ENNY
penny \ ˈpe-nē\
see
ANY**, E*, EA*, EE*,
I**, IE*, Y**

catchpenny, fenny, ha'penny,
penny, spinning jenny

ENS
lens \ ˈlenz\
see
EN*+s

Athens, Dickens, Homo sapiens,
lens, nolens volens

ENSE
dense \ ˈden(t)s\
see
ENCE, ENT*+s

condense, dense, dispense,
expense, frankincense, horse
sense, immense, incense, intense,
license, nonsense, offense,
pretense, recompense, sense,
suspense, tense

ENSER
condenser
\ kən-ˈden(t)-sər\
see
AR**, ER*, OR*

censer, condenser, denser, flenser

ENT*
bent \ ˈbent\

advent, accent, bent, cement,
cent, circumvent, comment,
consent, content, descent,
discontent, dissent, event,

ENT*

ferment, foment, gent, Ghent,
indent, intent, Lent, malcontent,
pent, percent, present**, red
cent, relent, rent, repent, resent,
scent, sent, spent, stent, tent,
torment, unbent, vent, went

ENT**
apartment
\ə-ˈpärt-mənt\
see
ACENT, AGENT, ALENT,
AMENT, ECENT,
EMENT, ERENT, ICENT,
IDENT, IENT, IMENT,
INENT, OLENT, ONENT,
UENT, ULENT, ULGENT,
UMENT

abandonment, abhorrent,
acknowledgment, adjournment,
adolescent, adornment,
agent, albescent, alignment,
amendment, annulment,
antecedent, apartment,
arborescent, ardent, argent,
ascent, astonishment, astringent,
beneficent, bewilderment,
bombardment, brazen serpent,
cerement, circumfluent,
cogent, competent, consent,
consignment, consistent,
convergent, co-respondent,
correspondent, covalent,
crescent, current, decadent,
deterrent, diligent, disalignment,
discernment, divergent,
embankment, emulgent,
encampment, endearment,
enjoyment, enrollment,
enthralment, environment,
equipment, escarpment,
establishment, evanescent,
excellent, existent, extent,
fervent, fragment, fulfilment,
horrentimpellent, impotent,
inadvertent, incandescent,
incoherent, incompetent,
inconsistent, incumbent,
independent, indictment,
indigent, innocent, insolvent,
insurgent, intelligent,
interlucent, intermittent,
intumescent, iridescent,

ENT**

judgment, lambent, latent, latescent, lucent, magnificent, maladjustment, munificent, nascent, nonexistent, nonpayment, oddment, ointment, omnipotent, omnipresent, opalescent, parchment, parent, patent, payment, pendent, penitent, permanent, persistent, phosphorescent, pigment, potent, precedent, present*, prevent, prudent, pungent, punishment, putrescent, quiescent, raiment, ravishment, recent, redolent, refreshment, refringent, refulgent, regent, relucent, reminiscent, repellent, resentment, resplendent, respondent, resurgent, reticent, retrenchment, rodent, segment, senescent, serpent, shipment, silent, solvent, spent, stringent, student, superincumbent, superintendent, talent, tangent, torrent, transcendent, translucent, transparent, treatment, tumescent, Turkish crescent, undercurrent, underwent, unravelment, urgent, vestment, vice-regent, went

ENTAL
mental \ ˈmen–tᵊl
see
AL*

accidental, continental, dental, detrimental, elemental, experimental, fundamental, incidental, instrumental, mental, monumental, occidental, Oriental, ornamental, parental, regimental, rental, sacramental, temperamental, transcontinental

ENTER
enter \ ˈen-tər\
see
AR**, ER*, OR*

carpenter, center, enter, reenter, renter, self-center

ENTH
tenth \ ˈten(t)th\

eleventh, nth, seventh, tenth

ENTIA
dementia
\di- ˈmen(t)-shə\
see
IA

amentia, dementia

ENTLY
gently \ ˈjent-lē\
see
E*, EA*, EE*,
ENT**+*ly*, I**, IE*,
Y**

eloquently, eminently, frequently, gently, imminently, innocently, intently, patiently, penitently, permanently, presently, prominently, prudently

ENTO
pimento
\pə- ˈmen-( )tō\
see
EAU, EW**, O*, OE*,
OT***, OUGH*, OW*,
OWE

lento, memento, pimento, pimiento

ENTRY
entry \ ˈen-trē\
see
E*, EA*, EE*, I**, IE*,
Y**

entry, gentry, sentry

ENTY
plenty \ ˈplen-tē\
see
E*, EA*, EE*, I**, IE*,
Y**

plenty, twenty

EO
cameo \\\`ka-mē-ˌō\
see
EAU, EW*, O*, OE*,
OT***, OUGH*, OW*,
OWE

Borneo, cameo, Galileo, Leo,
Montevideo, rodeo, Romeo, vireo

EOL
Sheol \shē-ˈōl\
see
OL*

Sheol

EON*
neon \\\`nē-ˌän\
see
AN***, ON**

eon, neon, peon

EON**
pigeon \\\`pi-jən\
see
IN

bludgeon, burgeon, clay pigeon,
curmudgeon, dudgeon, dungeon,
escutcheon, luncheon, pigeon,
stool pigeon, sturgeon, surgeon,
truncheon, wigeon

EON***
chameleon
\kə-ˈmēl-yən\
see
ION**, UN

chameleon, galleon, melodeon,
Napoleon, pantheon

EOUS*
erroneous
\i-ˈrō-nē-əs\
see
US

aqueous, beauteous,
cinereous, consanguineous,
contemporaneous, courteous,
erroneous, gaseous**,
heterogeneous, hideous,
homogeneous, igneous,
instantaneous, ligneous,
miscellaneous, osseous, piteous,
simultaneous, subaqueous,
subterraneous, succedaneous,
terraqueous, vitreous

EOUS**
courageous \kə-ˈrā-jəs\
see
ACIOUS, AMUS, EUS*,
IOUS, OUS*, UOUS, US

alliaceous, argillaceous,
courageous, fabaceous,
gallinaceous, gaseous*,
gorgeous, outrageous, righteous,
saponaceous, sebaceous

EP*
step \ˈstep\
see
EPPE

Amenhotep, doorstep, footstep,
goose step, instep, lockstep,
misstep, overstep, pep, prep,
quick step, rep, schlep, sidestep,
step, two-step

EP**
julep \ˈjü-ləp\
see
IP

julep, mint julep

EPE
crepe \ˈkrāp\
see
APE

crepe

EPPE
steppe \ˈstep\
see
EP

steppe

EPS
forceps \ˈfôr-səps\
see
EP+*s*

biceps, forceps, triceps

EPT
kept \ˈkept\
see
EP+*ed*

accept, adept, concept, crept,
except, inept, intercept, kept,
percept, precept, slept, stept,
swept, transept, unkept, well-
kept, wept, windswept

EQUE
cheque \ˈchek\
see
ECK

cheque

E SOUNDS

ER*
amber \ˈam-bər\
see

ACKER, ACRE, ADER,
AFTER, AGER, AILER,
AITER, AKER, AMER,
AMPER, ANDER,
ANGER, APER, APPER,
AR**, ARER, ARTER,
ARTYR, ASHER, ASTER,
ATER, ATRE, ATTER,
ATYR, AUR, AVER,
AYER, EATHER, EEPER,
ELLER, ELTER, EMBER,
EMER, ENDER, ENER,
ENSER, ENTER, EPHYR,
ERER, ERR, ESTER,
ETER*, ETER**, ETHER,
ETRE, ETTER, EUR,
EVER*, EVER**, EWER,
IAR*, IBRE, ICKER,
IDER, IDITY, IER*,
IGGER, ILDER, ILER,
ILLER, IMBER, IMMER,
INDER, INER, INGER,
INKER, INNER, INTER,
IPER, IPPER, IR*, ISER,
ISHER, ISTER, ITER*,
ITER**, ITER***,
ITTER, IVER, IZER,
OBBER, OBER, OCKER,
OCRE, OER, OFFER,
OGRE, OKER, OLDER,
OLVER, OMBER, OMER,
ONDER*, ONDER**,
ONER, OOMER,
OONER, OPHER,
OPPER, OR*, ORDER,
ORTER, OTHER,
OULDER, OUNDER,
OUR*, OVER, OW*+*er*,
OWDER, OWER, UBBER,
UCRE, UDDER, UER,

adder, adorer, alter, alma
mater, amber, anger, angler,
antler, archer, artificer, assayer,
astrologer, babbler, backwater,
badger, Baedeker, banker,
banner, banter, barber, bather,
beater, beleaguer, bellwether,
berserker, bill poster, bitter,
blasphemer, blather, boiler,
bolster, boner, booster,
bootlegger, bouncer, breakwater,
broiler, bunker, butler, buyer,
buzzer, caliber, caliper, camper,
cancer, canter, Casper, chamber,
chandler, chapter, charger,
Chaucer, checker, chiseler,
choler, chooser, chorister, cipher,
clabber, clapper, clinker, cloister,
cobbler, conceiver, condoler,
conger, consumer, costumer,
cowcatcher, coworker, crater,
creeper, cricketer, crosser,
cruiser, dabster, dagger, dapper,
daughter, decanter, deceiver,
decipher, differ, dissenter,
dodder, dowager, draper,
drawer, dreamer, dredger,
dresser, dulcimer, duller, duster,
eager, Easter, either, elder,
embroider, encounter, err,
ester, etcher, ether, exploiter,
falter, farmer, farther, faster,
father, feeler, fibber, fiber,
filter, fire-eater, flivver, fodder,
follower, forefather, forefinger,
forerunner, former, foster, four-
poster, frankfurter, freethinker,
fuller, further, gambler, gangster,
garner, gather, geyser, gibber,
glacier, golfer, gopher, gossamer,
grandfather, greater, greengrocer,
grosser, gutter, halter, hammer,
hanger, hanker, harder, hawker,

E SOUNDS

UIRE, UMBER, UMNER,
UNDER, UR, URER,
USTER, UTTER, UVRE,
PLUS WORDS FORMED
BY ADDING —er TO
ADJECTIVES AND
VERBS, FOR EXAMPLE,
bigger, PLUS NOUNS
FORMED BY ADDING
—er TO VERBS, FOR
EXAMPLE, *quitter*

hawser, headquarter, heather,
heckler, heifer, helicopter, her,
holster, hoosier, hostler, huckster,
hunger, idler, importer, improper,
jabber, Jacob's ladder, jammer,
jasper, jawbreaker, jaywalker,
juggler, juniper, kilter, kosher,
laborer, lacquer, ladder, lager,
lamplighter, lancer, larder, larger,
later, lather, laughter, launder,
lavender, lawyer, leader, ledger,
leper, lesser, lifer, lighter, lobster,
loiter, longer, loudspeaker, lounger,
Luther, madder, maneater,
maneuver, manner, manslaughter,
marker, masher, meager, merger,
milder, mineral water, minister,
minster, miter, monger, monster,
mossbunker, mouser, muffler,
mummer, murder, necromancer,
ne'er, neither, neuter,
newsmonger, nowhither, officer,
oldster, onlooker, ostler, outer,
oyster, pacer, panther, partner,
passenger, pater, paternoster,
pauper, peddler, pepper,
performer, pewter, pilfer, pitcher,
planter, platter, player, plumber,
plunder, plunger, poacher, pointer,
porker, potato masher, pouter,
preacher, presbyter, primer,
producer, prompter, proofreader,
propeller, proper, prosper, psalter,
pucker, punster, purser, pursuer,
quarter, quicksilver, quitter,
racer, rather, rathskeller, rattler,
receiver, reconnoiter, redeemer,
red pepper, reefer, reflector,
reformer, rejoiner, respecter,
rhymester, ringleader, roadster,
rooster, rosewater, roster, rougher,
saber, saucer, saunter, scalper,
scandalmonger, scavenger,

ER*

scepter, schemer, scooter,
scraper, scribbler, scriber,
scupper, seeker, seersucker,
seltzer, sepulcher, sharpshooter,
shock absorber, shoplifter,
shopper, shyer, shyster, silver,
simper, slaughter, sleepwalker,
slipper, smarter, smuggler,
snubber, snuffer, soccer,
sockdologer, soda water, soldier,
somber, sooner, sou'wester,
spanker, specter, spinster,
sprinkler, stage whisper, stagger,
stargazer, steam boiler, steamer,
steamroller, stenographer,
stepladder, stiffer, stomacher,
stopper, streamer, stretcher,
stroller, sucker, super,
sundowner, supper, sutler,
swagger, swashbuckler, sweater,
sweeter, swindler, talebearer,
tamer, Tam-o'-shanter, tanker,
tauter, teacher, teetotaler, temper,
tempter, tether, thaler, theater,
Tiber, timer, tipster, titer,
together, toper, tougher, trader,
transfer, transformer, traveler,
trickster, trooper, trotter,
tumbler, ulster, upholster, upper,
user, usher, vacuum cleaner,
Vancouver, verger, vesper,
vintner, voucher, Wagner, waiter,
waiver, warbler, warder, water,
waver, wayfarer, Webster, well-
wisher, whaler, whimper, whisker,
whisper, whiter, whither, wilder,
windjammer, wither, woodpecker,
wrapper, wrecker, youngster

ER**
prefer \pri-ˈfər
see
ERR, IR*, URR

confer, defer, deter, infer, inter,
prefer, refer

ERA*
camera \ ˈkam-rə\
see
A**

camera, chimera, cholera,
ephemera, genera, Hera,
lepidoptera, opera

ERA**
Riviera \ ˌri-vē- ˈer-ə\
see
A**

era, Hera, Riviera

ERABLE
tolerable
\ ˈtä-lə-rə-bəl\
see
ABLE*

conquerable, considerable,
discoverable, imponderable,
insuperable, intolerable,
invulnerable, miserable,
preferable, tolerable,
unconquerable, venerable,
vulnerable

ERAL
mineral \ ˈmi-nə- rəl\
see
AL*

bicameral, bilateral, collateral,
consul general, ephemeral,
equilateral, federal, feral, funeral,
general, lateral, liberal, literal,
mineral, numeral, quadrilateral,
several, trilateral, unilateral

ERAN
veteran \ ˈve-tə-rən\
see
AN**

Lateran, Lutheran, veteran

ERANT
tolerant \ ˈtä-lə-rənt\
see
ANT**, ENT**, INT

exuberant, intolerant, itinerant,
protuberant, tolerant

ERATE*
operate \ ˈä-pə- ˌrāt\
see
AIGHT, AIT**, ATE*,
EAT**, EIGHT*

adulterate, aerate, berate,
commiserate, enumerate,
exaggerate, exasperate, exhilarate,
exonerate, exuberate, federate,
generate, incarcerate, incinerate,
iterate, lacerate, liberate,
macerate, moderate**, numerate,

E SOUNDS

ERATE*

obliterate, operate, preponderate, recuperate, refrigerate, reiterate, remunerate, reverberate, tolerate, transliterate, vituperate, vociferate

ERATE**
confederate
\kən-ˈfe-d(ə-)rət\
see
AIT**, AT***, ATE**,
EDIT, EIT**, ERIT,
ET**, ETTE**, IATE**,
IBIT, ICATE**, ICIT,
ICKET, IDGET, IGOT,
IMATE*, INATE**,
IOT**, IT, ITE***,
OLATE*, ORATE**,
OSET, OT***, UET***,
UGGET, UIT*, ULATE**,
URATE*

confederate, conglomerate, considerate, degenerate, desperate, illiterate, immoderate, inconsiderate, intemperate, inveterate, literate, temperate

ERB
verb \ˈvərb\
see
URB

acerb, adverb, herb, kerb, potherb, proverb, reverb, Serb, superb, verb

ERCE
commerce
\ˈkä-(ˌ)mərs\
see
EARSE, ERSE, URSE

coerce, commerce, terce, sesterce

ERCH
perch \ˈpərch\
see
IRCH

perch

ERD
herd \ˈhərd\
see
EARD*, IRD, ORD**,
URD

cowherd, halberd, herd, potsherd, shepherd, swineherd

E SOUNDS

ERE*
mere \ˈmir\
see
EAR*, EER, IER***

adhere, ampere, belvedere,
atmosphere, austere, bathysphere,
cashmere, cassimere, cohere,
Guinevere, hemisphere, here,
inhere, insincere, interfere,
mere, Paul Revere, persevere,
revere, sere, severe, sincere,
sphere, stratosphere

ERE**
there \ˈt͟her\
see
AIR, ARE*, EAR**,
IARE, IERE

anywhere, confrere, elsewhere,
ere, everywhere, Gruyère,
nowhere, porte cochère,
somewhere, there, where

ERE***
were \ˈwər\
see
IR*, UR

were

EREL
mackerel
\ˈma-k(ə-)rəl\
see
AL*, EL

doggerel, mackerel, pickerel

ERENT*
coherent
\kō-ˈhir-ənt\
see
ENT**

adherent, coherent, incoherent,
inherent

ERENT*
different
\ˈdi-f(ə-)rənt\
see
ENT**, INT

belligerent, different, indifferent,
irreverent, reverent

ERER
wanderer
\ˈwän-dər-ər\
see
ER*, OR*

interferer, loiterer, philanderer,
roisterer, sorcerer, wanderer

ERF
serf \ˈsərf\
see
URF

serf

ERG
berg \ˈbərg\
see
URG

berg, erg, iceberg, Heidelberg, Nuremberg

ERGE
merge \ˈmərj\
see
IRGE, URGE

absterge, converge, deterge, diverge, emerge, merge, serge, submerge, verge

ERGY
energy \ˈe-nər-jē\
see
E*, EA*, EE*, I**, IE*, Y**

clergy, energy

ERIA*
bacteria
\bak-ˈtir-ē-ə\
see
IA

Algeria, bacteria, cafeteria, diphtheria, Egeria, Iberia, Siberia

ERIA**
hysteria
\his-ˈter-ē-ə\
see
IA

hysteria

ERIAL
material
\mə-ˈtir-ē-əl\
see
AL*, IAL**

aerial, immaterial, imperial, material, serial

ERIC
esoteric
\ˌe-sə-ˈter-ik\
see
IC, ICK

atmospheric, choleric, cleric, climacteric, congeneric, esoteric, etheric, exoteric, generic, Homeric, mesmeric, neoteric, turmeric, spheric

ERIE
menagerie
\mə-'na-zhə-rē\
see
EE, IE*

menagerie, reverie

ERIL
peril \'per-əl\
see
IL, ILE**

imperil, peril

ERIN
glycerin \'gli-sə- rən\
see
IN, INE***

glycerin

ERING
covering \'kə-və- riŋ\
see
ER+*ing*, ING

burnt offering, covering,
fingerling, gathering, offering

ERIS
ephemeris
\ e-fə-mə-rəs\
see
ICE**, IS*, ISE****, ISS

ephemeris, Eris, sui generis

ERISH*
perish \'per-ish\
see
ISH

cherish, perish

ERISH**
gibberish
\'ji-b(ə-)rish\
see
ISH

feverish, gibberish, impoverish

ERIT
merit \ ˈmer-ət\
see
AIT**, AT***, ATE**,
EDIT, EIT**, ERATE**,
ET**, ETTE**, IATE**,
IBIT, ICATE**, ICIT,
ICKET, IDGET, IGOT,
IMATE, INATE, IOT**,
IT, ITE***, OLATE*,
ORATE**, OSET, OT***,
UET***, UGGET, UIT*,
ULATE**, URATE*

demerit, inherit, merit

ERITY
posterity
\pä-ˈster-ə-tē\
see
ITY

asperity, austerity, celerity,
dexterity, insincerity, posterity,
prosperity, severity, sincerity,
temerity, verity

ERK
perk \ ˈpərk\
see
IRK, URK

clerk, berserk, hauberk, jerk, perk

ERLY
orderly \ ˈōr-dər-lē\
see
E*, EA*, EE*, ER*+*ly*,
I**, IE*, Y**

orderly, quarterly

ERM
term \ ˈtərm\
see
IRM, ORM**

berm, germ, isotherm,
pachyderm, sperm, term, therm

ERN*
fern \ ˈfərn\
see
EARN, ERN, OURN*,
URN

concern, discern, ern, fern,
intern, kern, lectern, stern, tern

ERN**
cavern \\ˈka-vərn\
see
EARN, ERN, OURN*,
URN

bittern, cavern, cistern, cithern,
eastern, govern, Hohenzollern,
jack-o'-lantern, lantern, leathern,
misgovern, modern, northern,
pattern, postern, quern, silvern,
slattern, southern, subaltern,
tavern, western

ERNAL
internal \in-ˈtər-nᵊl\
see
AL*

eternal, external, fraternal,
infernal, internal, maternal,
paternal, sempiternal, supernal,
vernal

ERO*
zero \\ˈzē-(ˌ)rō\ *or*
\\ˈzir-(ˌ)ō\
see
EAU, EW**, O*, OE*,
OT***, OUGH*, OW*,
OWE

hero, Nero, zero

ERO**
sombrero
\səm-ˈbrer-(ˌ)ō\
see
EAU, EW**, O*, OE*,
OT***, OUGH*, OW*,
OWE

bolero, caballero, pampero,
sombrero, Trocadero

ERO***
numero \\ˈnü-mə-rō\
see
EAU, EW**, O*, OE*,
OT***, OUGH*, OW*,
OWE

Cicero, numero

ERON
heron \\ˈher-ən\
see
ON*

heron, Oberon, Percheron

EROUS
thunderous
\ˈthən-d(ə-)rəs\
see
OUS*, US

adulterous, boisterous,
cadaverous, cantankerous,
dangerous, dexterous,
generous, lecherous, numerous,
obstreperous, odoriferous,
onerous, pestiferous, ponderous,
preposterous, prosperous,
slanderous, somniferous,
splendiferous, thunderous,
viperous

ERPT
excerpt \ek-ˈsərpt\
see
URP+*ed*

excerpt

ERR
err \ˈer\ *or* \ˈər\
see
AIR, ARE*, EAR**,
ER**, IR*, URR

err

ERRY
cherry \ˈcher-ē\
see
E*, EA*, EE*, ERY, I**,
IE*, Y**

berry, blackberry, blueberry,
cherry, cranberry, elderberry,
ferry, gooseberry, loganberry,
merry, mulberry, raspberry,
sherry, spiceberry, strawberry,
Tom and Jerry

ERS
vespers \ˈves-pərz\
see
ER*+*s*, OR*+*s*

bitters, divers, headquarters,
Ghebers, Vespers

ERSE
verse \ˈvərs\
see
EARSE, ERCE, URSE

adverse, asperse, converse,
disperse, diverse, Erse, immerse,
intersperse, inverse, obverse,
perverse, reverse, terse, transverse,
traverse, universe, verse

ERST
erst \ˈərst\
see
IRST

erst

ERT*
insert \in-ˈsərt\
see
IRT, UIRT, URT

advert, alert, assert, avert,
convert, covert, desert**, dessert,
disconcert, divert, exert, inert,
insert, invert, malapert, overt,
pert, pervert**, reassert, vert

ERT**
concert \ˈkän(t)-sərt\
see
IRT, UIRT, URT

concert, controvert, desert*,
expert, extrovert, filbert,
introvert, overt, pervert*,
sherbert

ERTH
berth \ˈbərth\
see
IRTH

berth

ERTY
liberty \ˈli-bər-tē\
see
E*, EA*, EE*, I**, IE*,
Y**

liberty, poverty, property

ERUS
Cerberus
\ˈsər-b(ə-)rəs\
see
US

Cerberus, Hesperus

ERVE
nerve \ˈnərv\
see
URVE

conserve, deserve, nerve, observe,
preserve, reserve, serve, swerve,
unnerve, unreserve, verve

ERY*
bakery \ˈbā-k(ə-)rē\
see
E*, EA*, EE*, ER*+y,
ORY*, URY, Y**

adultery, antislavery, archery,
artery, artillery, bakery, battery,
brewery, bribery, buffoonery,
cajolery, celery, cemetery,
chancery, chandlery, chicanery,
creamery, crockery, cutlery,
deanery, debauchery, discovery,
distillery, drapery, drudgery,
effrontery, embroidery, emery,
fakery, fernery, fiery, finery,
fippery, fishery, flattery, flummery,

ERY*

foolery, forgery, frippery, gallery,
greenery, grocery, gunnery,
haberdashery, hatchery, hosiery,
housewifery, imagery, ironmongery,
jewellery, jugglery, knavery,
lamasery, lottery, machinery,
mastery, millinery, misery,
mockery, monastery, mummery,
mystery, napery, nunnery, nursery,
ornery, perfumery, periphery,
phylactery, pottery, powdery,
prudery, psaltery, quackery, raillery,
recovery, refinery, revery, rockery,
roguery, rogues' gallery, rookery,
scenery, self-mastery, shivery,
showery, shrubbery, skulduggery,
slavery, silvery, slippery, soldiery,
sorcery, surgery, thievery, thuggery,
tomfoolery, tracery, treachery,
trickery, trumpery, upholstery,
venery, waggery, watery, witchery

ERY**
very \ ˈver-ē\
see
AIRY, ARRY*, ARY*, E*,
EA*, EE*, ERRY, I**,
IE*, Y**

query, very

ERYL
beryl \ ˈber-əl\
see
ERIL, IL

beryl

ES*
Hades \ ˈhā-(ˌ)dēz\
see
EA*+s, EASE*, EE*+s,
EESE*, EIZE, ESE*, EZE,
IEZE, PLUS PLURALS
ENDING IN —ies
FORMED BY ADDING
—s TO —y WORDS, FOR
EXAMPLE, *cookies*

Aborigines, Achilles, Albigenses,
Anchises, Andes, Antilles,
antipodes, Apelles, Archimedes,
Ares, Aristides, Aristophanes,
Buenos Aires, Ceres, Cervantes,
Corybantes, Damocles, degrees,
Demosthenes, Dives, Empedocles,
Epiphanes, Erinyes, Euphrates,
Ganges, Hades, Heracles,
Hercules, Hermes, herpes,

ES*

lares, Lemures, Mephistopheles, Mercedes, oases, Orestes, penates, Pericles, Pisces, Procrustes, similes, Ulysses, vortices, Xerxes

ES**
yes \ˈyes\
see
ESCE, ESS

yes

ESCE
coalesce \ˌkō-ə-ˈles\
see
ES**, ESS

acquiesce, coalesce, convalesce, effervesce, effloresce, evanesce, intumesce, opalesce

ESE*
these \ˈthēz\
see
EAS**, EIZE, IECE, IEZE, ISE***

Burmese, Cantonese, Chinese, Japanese, Maltese, manganese, Pekinese, Portuguese, Siamese, Singhalese, Sudanese, these, Viennese

ESE**
obese \ō-ˈbēs\
see
EACE, EASE**, EECE, EESE**, ICE***, IECE, ISE***

diocese, obese

ESET
beset \bē-ˈset\
see
ET

beset, preset, reset

ESH
mesh \ˈmesh\

afresh, enmesh, flesh, fresh, gooseflesh, horseflesh, mesh, refresh, thresh

ESIA
amnesia
\am-ˈnē-zhə\
see
IA

amnesia, anaesthesia, freesia, magnesia, Polynesia, Rhodesia, silesia

ESIS
hypothesis
\hī-ˈpä-thə-səs\
see
ICE**, IS*, ISE****, ISS

anamnesis, antithesis, exegesis,
Genesis, hypothesis, Lachesis,
nemesis, palingenesis,
parenthesis, parthenogenesis,
synthesis, telekinesis

ESK
desk \ˈdesk\
see
ESQUE

desk

ESQUE
grotesque
\grō-ˈtesk\
see
ESK

arabesque, burlesque, grotesque,
Moresque, Normanesque,
picturesque, Romanesque,
statuesque

ESS*
business \ˈbiz-nəs\
see
ELESS, ES**, ESCE,
ESSE, ILESS, INESS,
PLUS NOUNS FORMED
BY ADDING —*ness* OR
TO ADJECTIVES, FOR
EXAMPLE, *spaciousness*,
PLUS ADJECTIVES
FORMED BY ADDING
—*less* TO NOUNS, FOR
EXAMPLE, *fearless*

abbess, ageless, artless,
bloodless, bottomless, burgess,
business, buttress, childless,
congress, countless, cypress,
dauntless, deaconess, duchess,
egress, empress, enchantress,
eyewitness, forgiveness, goddess,
governess, harness, heiress,
hostess, huntress, laundress,
lioness, mattress, mistress,
ogress, peeress, *The Pilgrim's Progress*,
poetess, priestess, princess**,
prioress, progress, pythoness,
seamstress, shepherdess,
sorceress, stainless, stewardess,
tigress, traitress, waitress, witness

ESS**
bless \ˈbles\

access, address, bless, caress, chess,
clothespress, compress, confess,
cress, digress, dispossess, distress,
dress, duress, ess, express, guess,
impress, ingress, less, mess, ness,
obsess, oppress, overdress, possess,
prepossess, press, princess*,
process, profess, prowess,
readdress, recess, redress,

ESS**

regress, repress, retrogress,
success, suppress, transgress, tress,
undress, unless, watercress

ESSE
finesse \fə-ˈnes\
see
ESS**

finesse, largesse, noblesse

ESSION
session \ˈse-shən\
see
ION*

accession, cession, concession,
confession, depression, digression,
expression, impression,
intercession, obsession,
precession, procession, profession,
progression, recession, regression,
repression, retrocession,
retrogression, session, succession,
suppression, transgression

EST
see
EAST**, ESS+*ed*,
IEST*, UESS+*ed*, UEST,
PLUS COMPARATIVES
FORMED BY ADDING
—*est* TO ADJECTIVES,
FOR EXAMPLE, *cheapest*

acid test, alkahest, almagest,
arrest, behest, best, blest,
Budapest, chest, congest, contest,
crest, detest, digest, dishonest,
divest, earnest, Everest, forest,
harvest, honest, immodest,
infest, interest, invest, jest, lest,
manifest, mare's nest, Midwest,
modest, molest, nest, palimpsest,
pest, protest, reforest, request,
rest, rinderpest, second-best,
suggest, tempest, test, unrest,
vest, west, wettest, wrest, zest

ESTA
siesta \sē-ˈes-tə\
see
A**

fiesta, podesta, siesta, Vesta,
Zend-Avesta

ESTAL
vestal \ˈves-tᵊl\
see
AL*

festal, pedestal, vestal

ESTER*
fester \ ˈfes-tər\
see
AR**, ER*, OR*

ester, fester, forester, jester,
nor'wester, quester, rhymester,
semester, sequester, yester

ESTLE
nestle \ ˈne-səl\
see
EL, LE

nestle, pestle, trestle, wrestle

ESTO
pesto \ ˈpes-(ˌ)tō\
see
EAU, EW**, O*, OE*,
OT***, OUGH*, OW*
OWE

manifesto, pesto, presto

ESTY
modesty \ ˈmä-də-stē\
see
E*, EA*, EE*, I**, IE*, Y**

amnesty, dishonesty, honesty,
immodesty, lese majesty, majesty,
modesty, travesty, testy

ESY
courtesy \ ˈkər-tə-sē\
see
E*, EA*, EE*, I**, IE*,
Y**

courtesy, heresy, poesy, prophesy

ET*
yet \ ˈyet\
see
ANET, EAT***, EBT,
ELET, ENET, ESET,
ETTE, IET, INET, OSET,
UET*, ULET, UMPET

abet, alphabet, anchoret, asset,
beget, bet, brevet, cadet, calumet,
chaplet, clarinet, cornet, corset,
curvet, deep-set, dragnet, epithet,
fishnet, flageolet, floweret,
forget, fret, gas jet, get, inset,
jet, Kismet, landaulet, let, met,
minaret, net, offset, onset,
parapet, pet, quartet, quintet,
quodlibet, regret, reset, ret, set,
sextet, stet, stockinet, sublet,
sunset, tabouret, Tibet, thickset,
upset, videlicet, wet, whet, yet

ET**
bucket \ ˈbə-kət\
see
AIT**, AT***, ATE**,
EDIT, EIT**, ERATE**,
ERIT, ETTE**, IATE**,
IBIT, ICATE**, ICIT,
ICKET, IDGET, IGOT,
IMATE*, INATE**,
IOT**, IT, ITE***,
OLATE*, ORATE**,
OSET, OT***, UET***,
UGGET, UIT*, ULATE**,
URATE*

blanket, bonnet, booklet, brisket,
brooklet, bucket, budget, buffet,
bullet, circlet, claret, cloudlet,
comet, cosset, couplet, covet,
cresset, cygnet, dulcet, eaglet,
egret, emmet, facet, faucet, ferret,
flibbertigibbet, freshet, frisket,
gadget, garnet, garret, gauntlet,
gibbet, giblet, gimlet, goblet,
gorget, gusset, hamlet, hatchet,
helmet, hornet, inlet, interpret,
jennet, junket, lancet, latchet,
leaflet, leveret, linnet, magnet,
mallet, market, millet, moppet,
mullet, musket, outlet, owlet,
pallet, pamphlet, pellet, plummet,
poet, posset, privet, prophet,
pullet, puppet, ratchet, rennet,
ringlet, rivet, russet, scarlet, secret,
sherbet, signet, singlet, sonnet,
spinet, stock market, streamlet,
suet, sunbonnet, tablet, target,
tippet, toilet, Tophet, trinket,
troutlet, turret, ultraviolet, varlet,
velvet, violet, wallet, wristlet

ETAL*
metal \ ˈme-tᵊl\
see
AL*, EDAL, EDDLE,
ETTLE

gunmetal, metal, petal

ETAL**
centripetal
\sen- ˈtri-pə-tᵊl\
see
AL*

centripetal, decretal

ETCH
etch \ ˈech\

etch, fetch, homestretch, ketch,
outstretch, sketch, stretch, vetch,
wretch

ETE
concrete
\(͈)kän-ˈkrēt\
see
EAT*, EET, ITE***,
UITE*

athlete, compete, complete,
concrete, Crete, delete, deplete,
discrete, effete, esthete,
incomplete, mete, obsolete,
Paraclete, replete, secrete

ETER*
barometer
\bə-ˈrä-mə-tər\
see
ITER*, ER*, OR*

altimeter, anemometer,
barometer, cyclometer,
Demeter, diameter, heliometer,
hydrometer, kilometer, orometer,
pedometer, perimeter, pyrometer,
speedometer, thermometer,
trumpeter, variometer

ETER**
meter \ˈmē-tər\
see
EAD**+*er*, EAT*+*er*,
EET+*er*, ER*, ETRE,
ITER**, OR*

gas meter, meter, peter, saltpeter

ETHER
tether \ˈte-th͟ər\
see
AR**, EATHER, ER*,
OR*

bellwether, nether, tether,
together, wether, whether

ETIC
athletic \ath-ˈle-tik\
see
IC, ICK

aesthetic, apathetic, ascetic,
athletic, cosmetic, emetic,
energetic, frenetic, genetic,
geodetic, hermetic, homiletic,
magnetic, noetic, onomatopoetic,
parenthetic, pathetic, peripatetic,
phonetic, phrenetic, poetic,
polysynthetic, prophetic,
sympathetic, synthetic

ETO
veto \ˈvē-(͈)tō\
see
EAU, EW**, O*, OE*,
OT***, OUGH*, OW*,
OWE

Leto, magneto, veto

E SOUNDS

ETON
skeleton \ˈske-lə-tən\
see
ON*

phaeton, simpleton, skeleton

ETRE
metre \ˈmē-tər\
see
ETER**, ITER**

kilometre, metre, saltpetre

ETRY
poetry \ˈpō-ə-trē\
see
E*, EA*, EE*, I**, IE*, Y**

chronometry, coquetry, geometry, marquetry, musketry, parquetry, poetry, psychometry, symmetry, trigonometry

ETTE*
cigarette \ˌsi-gə-ˈret\
see
ET

aigrette, anisette, barette, blanquette, briquette, brochette, brunette, chemisette, cigarette, collarette, coquette, corvette, croquette, curette, dinette, epaulette, flannelette, fourchette, gazette, grisette, kitchenette, Lafayette, layette, leatherette, lorgnette, lunette, maisonnette, Marie Antoinette, mignonette, moquette, novelette, oubliette, parquette, pipette, planchette, poussette, rosette, roulette, satinette, serviette, silhouette, soubrette, statuette, suffragette, toilette, vedette, vignette, vinaigrette, wagonette

ETTE**
etiquette \ˈe-ti-kət\
see
AIT**, AT***, ATE**,
EDIT, EIT**, ERATE**,
ERIT, ET**, IATE**,
IBIT, ICATE**, ICIT,
ICKET, IDGET, IGOT,
IMATE*, INATE**, IOT**,
IT, ITE***, OLATE*,
ORATE**, OSET, OT***,
UET***, UGGET, UIT*,
ULATE**, URATE*

etiquette, palette

ETTER
better \ ˈbe-tər\
see
ET+*er*

begetter, bedwetter, better, dead letter, fetter, getter, go-getter, letter, red-letter, setter, typesetter, unfetter, wetter, whetter

ETTI
confetti \kən-ˈfe-tē\
see
E*, EA*, EE*, I**, IE*, Y**

confetti, Rossetti, spaghetti

ETTLE
kettle \ ˈke-tᵊl\
see
EL, LE

fettle, kettle, mettle, nettle, settle, teakettle

ETTO
ghetto \ ˈge-(ˌ)tō\
see
EAU, EW**, O*, OE*, OUGH*, OW*, OWE

allegretto, amoretto, falsetto, ghetto, libretto, palmetto, Rigoletto, stiletto, terzetto, Tintoretto

ETTY*
jetty \ ˈje-tē\
see
E*, EA*, EE*, I**, IE*, Y**

betty, jetty, petty

ETTY**
pretty \ ˈpri-tē\
see
E*, EA*, EE*, I**, IE*, ITTY, Y**

pretty

ETY*
fidgety \ ˈfi-jə-tē\
see
E*, EA*, EE*, I**, IE*, Y**

crotchety, fidgety, nicety, pernickety, rackety, rickety, subtlety, surety, velvety

ALL STRESSED OUT?
HOW TO USE METER

DOES HEARING THE phrase "iambic pentameter" strike fear in your gut? Poetry purists may cringe to hear it, but writers don't really need to know their *anapests* from their *dactyls* in order to compose decent verse. Those terms, and many others listed in this book's glossary, are simply very specific ways to describe poetic meter.

Meter is the pulse of a poem. The natural stresses of each word and combinations of words determine how the poem or song will be read or sung. Good meter has two components: matching stressed and unstressed beats, and natural stresses on each word. Unstressed syllables tend to disappear when poetry is read aloud. What needs to match from line to line is not the total number of syllables, but the number and pattern of stressed beats. When reviewing a couplet or stanza to see if it's symmetrical, count **accented** syllables. If the stressed syllables line up, the poetry will be said to *scan*; that is, it will be easy to read aloud correctly.

The dissected limerick below illustrates good, symmetrical meter. CAPS indicate stressed syllables, lowercase letters indicate unstressed ones.

there ONCE was a MAN from peRU,	u/S/uu/S/uu/S
who DREAMED he was EATing his SHOE,	u/S/uu/S/uu/S
he aWOKE in the NIGHT,	uu/S/uu/S
in a TERible FRIGHT,	uu/S/uu/S
and FOUND it was PERfectly TRUE.	a/S/uu/S/uu/S

See how nicely those stresses line up? When a poem feels clunky, write out your verse using this CAPS/lowercase trick to see if your meter has good symmetry.

Some writers assume that readers will adjust stresses to make meter "work," but that makes a poem awkward and forced. For example, peRU technically rhymes with HAIRdo, but those words don't work as a couplet because the stresses are different. If you're unsure where the natural stress falls in a given word, the phonetically spelled example at the beginning of each entry in this dictionary shows where the stresses lie for all words listed below it. Now go ahead—put your best metric foot forward!

ETUS
impetus \ˈim-pə-təs\
see
US

impetus, quietus

EUD
feud \ˈfyüd\
see
UDE

feud

EUM
museum
\myu̇-ˈzē-əm\
see
IUM, OM*

athenaeum, Colosseum, Herculaneum, linoleum, lyceum, mausoleum, museum, odeum, petroleum

EUR
grandeur \ˈgran-jər\
see
IR*, UR

amateur, coiffeur, connoisseur, entrepreneur, fleur, grandeur, liqueur, masseur, monsieur, raconteur, seigneur, voyageur

EUS
nucleus \ˈnü-klē-əs\
see
UCE, US

Alpheus, caduceus, coleus, Morpheus, nucleus, Orpheus, Peleus, Perseus, Prometheus, Proteus, Theseus

EUSE
chartreuse
\shär-ˈtrüs\
see
ERS, OOSE*, UICE,
URS, USE*

berceuse, Betelgeuse, chartreuse, danseuse, masseuse

EUTH
sleuth \ˈslüth\
see
UTH

sleuth

EVAL
primeval
\prī-ˈmē-vəl\
see
AL*, IL

coeval, medieval, primeval

EVE
eve \ ˈēv\
see
EAVE, EEVE, IEVE

eve

EVEL
level \ ˈle-vəl\
see
EL, IL

bevel, dishevel, level, revel, sea level

EVEN*
even \ ˈē-vən\
see
EN**

even

EVEN*
seven \ ˈse-vən\
see
EAVEN, EN**

eleven, seven

EVER*
sever \ ˈse-vər\
see
AR**, ER*, OR*

cantilever, dissever, ever, forever, lever**, never, sever, soever, whatever, whatsoever, whoever, whomsoever, whosoever

EVER**
fever \ ˈfē-vər\
see
AR**, ER*, OR*

fever, lever*, retriever

EVITY
brevity \ ˈbre-və-tē\
see
E*, EA*, EE*, I**, IE*,
ITY, Y**

brevity, levity, longevity

EVY
bevy \ ˈbe-vē\
see
E*, EA*, EE*, I**, IE*,
Y**

bevy, Chevy, levy

EW*
blew \ ˈblü\
see
IEU, IEW, O*, OE**,
OO, OU*, OUGH****,
OUS**, OUT**, OUX,
U, UE*, UT***

anew, askew, bedew, beef stew, beshrew, bestrew, blew, brand-new, brew, corkscrew, crew, curfew, curlew, dew, drew, eschew, feverfew, few, Hebrew, hew, honeydew, Jew, knew, mew, mildew, nephew, new, pew, phew, renew, screw, shrew, sinew, skeleton crew, skew, slew, smew, spew, stew, strew, threw, thumbscrew, unscrew, view, Wandering Jew, whew, withdrew, yew

EW**
sew \ ˈsō\
see
EAU, O*, OE*, OT***,
OUGH*, OW*, OWE

sew

EWD
lewd \ ˈlüd\
see
EUD, UDE

lewd, shrewd

EWEL
jewel \ ˈjü-əl\
see
EL, UEL

bejewel, crewel, jewel, newel

EWER
fewer \ ˈfyü-ər\
see
AR**, ER*, OR*

ewer, fewer, hewer, reviewer, sewer, skewer

EWN*
strewn \ ˈstrün\
see
OON, UGN, UNE

hewn, rough-hewn, strewn

EWN**
sewn \ ˈsōn\
see
OAN, OGNE, ONE*,
OWN*

sewn

E SOUNDS

EWS
news \ˈnüz\
see
EW*+*s*, IEW+*s*, OE*+*s*,
OOSE**, OSE***,
UE*+*s*, USE**

mews, news

EWT
newt \ˈnüt\
see
OOT*, UIT**, UTE

newt

EWY
chewy \ˈchü-ē\
see
E*, EA*, EE*, I**, IE*,
Y**

chewy, dewy, mildewy, screwy,
sinewy, skewy

EX
index \ˈin-ˌdeks\
see
ECK+*s*, ECT+*s*, EQUE+*s*

annex, apex, biconvex,
circumflex, codex, complex,
convex, duplex, flex, haruspex,
ibex, ilex, index, inflex,
multiplex, murex, perplex,
pollex, pontifex, reflex, rex, sex,
silex, simplex, vertex, vex, vortex

EXT
next \ˈnekst\
see
EX+*ed*

next, pretext, text

EY*
alley \ˈa-lē\
see
E*, EA*, EE*, I**, IE*,
Y**

abbey, Alderney, alley, attorney,
barley, blarney, bluey, bogey,
bowling alley, burley, chimney,
choosey, chop suey, chutney,
cockney, convey, covey, crikey,
donkey, dopey, fluey, flunkey,
galley, gluey, grey, Guernsey,
gully, hackney, jersey, jitney,
jockey, journey, key, Killarney,
lackey, linsey-woolsey, malmsey,
master key, medley, monkey,
motley, odyssey, okeydokey,

EY*

Orkney, osprey, palfrey, parley, parsley, passkey, phoney, phooey, posey, pulley, Shelley, shimmy, Sidney, skeleton key, surrey, tourney, trolley, turkey, turnkey, valley, volley, watch key, whimsey, whiskey

EY**
obey \ō-ˈbā\
see
A*, AY, EE**, UET**

bey, convey, disobey, hey, lamprey, Monterey, obey, osprey, prey, purvey, survey, they, trey, whey

EYE
eye \ˈī\
see
I*, IE**, IGH, Y*, YE

buckeye, bull's-eye, cockeye, evil eye, eye, walleye

EZ
fez \ˈfez\

Cortez, fez, oyez, Suez, Velasquez

EZE
trapeze \tra-ˈpēz\
see
EASE*, EIZE, EESE*,
EEZE, ESE*, IEZE

trapeze

EZZO
mezzo \ˈmet-(ˌ)sō\
see
EAU, EW**, O*, OE*,
OT***, OUGH*, OW*,
OWE

intermezzo, mezzo

—I—
SOUNDS

I*
alibi \ ˈa-lə-ˌbī\
see
AI, EFY, EYE, IE**, IFY,
IGH, ISFY, ULY**, Y*

alibi, alkali, alumni, Delphi, Eli,
fungi, Gemini, genii, I, Magi,
Malachi, modus operandi, pi,
rabbi, semi, vox populi

I**
taxi \ ˈtak-sē\
see
ALI, ATI, E*, EA*, EE*,
ETTI, IE*, IGREE, INI,
IORI, ITI, OLI, ONI

Agni, Amalfi, banditti, beriberi,
bhakti, cadi, Capri, chianti, Chili,
conoscenti, Cotopaxi, daiquiri,
Disraeli, do-re-mi, effendi,
ennui, Fascisti, Fiji, frangipani,
Gandhi, Ghazi, Gobi, Hadji,
Haiti, hara-kari, Hawaii, Hopi,
houri, khaki, kiwi, Lakshmi,
lapis lazuli, Leonardo da Vinci,
Loki, Machiavelli, Maori, Medici,
Miami, Midi, mufti, Nagasaki,
Nazi, obi, okapi, Pahlavi,
Parvati, patchouli, peccavi, peri,
piccalilli, potpourri, quasi, rishi,
salmagundi, sans souci, saki,
sakti, Saudi, scudi, ski, soldi,
spermaceti, sri, Sufi, Tauri, taxi,
Tiki, Tishri, Trimurti, tutti-frutti,
Uffizi, vermicelli, Visconti, yogi

IA
mania \ ˈmā-nē-ə\
see
A**, ALIA, ANIA, ARIA,
ASIA, EIA, ELIA, ENIA,
ENTIA, ERIA, ESIA,
OLIA, ONIA, OPIA,
ORIA

Abyssinia, acacia, Aglaia,
Alexandria, ambrosia, Andalusia,
aphrodisia, apologia, Arabia,
Arcadia, artemisia, Assyria,
Bessarabia, Bohemia, Bolivia,
braggadocia, Britannia, Calabria,
California, Cambodia, camellia,
Cappadocia, Cassiopeia, cassia,
claustrophobia, Columbia,
cyclopedia, Czechoslovakia,
dahlia, deutzia, Dionysia,
Discordia, dyspepsia,

IA

encyclopedia, euphorbia,
fuchsia, Hibernia, hydrophobia,
Hygeia, hypochondria, India,
inertia, insignia, insomnia,
intelligentsia, ischia,
kleptomania, loggia, mania,
Malaysia, Manchuria, media,
memorabilia, Mesopotamia,
militia, minutia, misericordia,
Moravia, neuralgia, nostalgia,
Nubia, Olympia, onomatopoeia,
paranoia, Persia, petunia,
phantasmagoria, pharmacopeia,
phobia, Phoenicia, pointsettia,
Portia, Prussia, raffia,
rudbeckia, Russia, salvia,
Scandinavia, Scythia, sedilia,
sepia, sequoia, stadia, stevia,
symposia, Syria, Thalia, tibia,
via, via media, Zenobia

IABLE*
amiable
\ˈā-mē-ə-bəl\
see
ABLE*, EL, LE

amiable, inexpiable, invariable,
pitiable, undeniable, variable

IABLE**
liable \ˈlī-ə-bəl\
see
ABLE*, EL, LE

justifiable, liable, pliable, reliable

IABLE***
sociable \ˈsō-shə-bəl\
see
ABLE*, EL, LE

insatiable, satiable, sociable

IAC
cardiac \ˈkär-dē-ˌak\
see
AC, ACK

ammoniac, aphrodisiac, cardiac,
celeriac, demoniac, elegiac,
hypochondriac, kleptomaniac,
maniac, pericardiac, symposiac,
Syriac, theriac, Zodiac

IAGE
marriage \ˈmer-ij\
see
AGE*, EDGE, IDGE

carriage, foliage, marriage, verbiage

IAH
pariah \pə-ˈrī-ə\
see
AH

messiah, Mount Moriah, pariah

IAL*
dial \ˈdī(-ə)l\
see
AL*, ISLE, ILE*, YLE

denial, dial, phial, retrial, sundial, self-denial, trial, vial

IAL**
burial \ˈber-ē-əl\
see
AL*

actuarial, alluvial, antimonial, Belial, bestial, biennial, burial, centennial, ceremonial, colonial, coloquial, congenial, connubial, convivial, decennial, diluvial, equatorial, Escurial, filial, finial, fluvial, imperial, industrial, jovial, labial, manorial, matrimonial, memorial, menial, mercurial, parochial, patrimonial, perennial, pluvial, postprandial, Prairial, prandial, primordial, proverbial, radial, secretarial, terrestrial, testimonial, trial, triennial, trivial, uncongenial, venial

IAL***
crucial \ˈkrü-shəl\
see
AL*

ambrosial, antisocial, celestial, circumferential, circumstantial, commercial, consequential, cordial, court-martial, credential, crucial, deferential, differential, equinoctial, essential, evidential, facial, financial, glacial, impartial, inconsequential, inessential, inferential, influential, initial, martial, nonessential, nuptial, official, palatial, partial,

IAL***

penitential, pestilential,
potential, preglacial, presidential,
providential, provincial,
prudential, racial, residential,
reverential, social, spatial, special,
substantial, torrential, uncial,
unsocial

IAN*
median \ ˈmē-dē-ən\
see
AN**, ARIAN, EDIAN,
ICAN, ICIAN, IDIAN,
ORIAN

amphibian, antediluvian,
antinomian, Arcadian, Assyrian,
Bacchanalian, Bodleian,
Bohemian, Brobdingnagian,
Castilian, Cimmerian,
Corinthian, custodian, Cyprian,
Dickensian, diluvian, Draconian,
durian, equestrian, Essenian,
Ethiopian, guardian, Hanoverian,
Hibernian, Indian, Ionian,
isthmian, Machiavellian, magian,
Manchurian, Merovingian,
median, Midian, Nubian,
Olympian, Ossian, Parthian,
pedestrian, Peruvian, Pierian,
plebian, Pomeranian, Pythian,
reptilian, riparian, ruffian,
salarian, Saturnalian, saurian,
Shakespearean, Siberian, simian,
Stygian, Sumerian, Swabian,
Tasmanian, Thespian, tragedian,
Umbrian, Uranian, Utopian,
valerian, Zoroastrian

IAN**
Asian \ ˈā-zhən\
see
AN**, EN**, IN, UN

Andalusian, artesian, Asian,
beautician, Carthusian,
Christian, Circassian,
Cistercian, Confucian,
Elysian, Ephesian, fringed
gentian, fustian, Lilliputian,
metaphysician, Norwegian,
Parisian, Peloponnesian, Persian,
Perugian, Rabelaisian, tertian,
theologian, Titian, Venetian

IANCE*
alliance \ə-ˈlī-ən(t)s\
see
ANCE*

affiance, alliance, appliance, compliance, defiance, reliance

IANCE**
variance \
ˈver-ē-ən(t)s\
see
ANCE*, ENCE

allegiance, brilliance, dalliance, insouciance, invariance, luxuriance, radiance, variance

IANT*
giant \ˈjī-ənt\
see
ANT**

compliant, defiant, giant, pliant, reliant

IANT**
valiant \ˈval-yənt\
see
ANT**, ENT**

brilliant, luxuriant, mediant, radiant, suppliant, valiant, variant

IAR*
liar \ˈlī(-ə)r\
see
AR**, ER*, IRE*, OR*

briar, friar, liar, sweetbriar, White Friar

IAR**
familiar \fə-ˈmil-yər\
see
AR**, ER*, OR*

familiar, peculiar, unfamiliar

IARD
billiard \ˈbi(l)-yərd\
see
ARD*, ERD, IRD, ORD**

billiard, galliard, poniard, Spaniard

IARY*
aviary \ˈā-vē-ˌer-ē\
see
AIRY, ARRY*, E*, EA*,
EE*, ERRY*, ERY**,
I**, IE*, UARY, Y**

apiary, auxiliary, aviary, breviary, incendiary, intermediary, judiciary, pecuniary, subsidiary, tertiary

IARY**
beneficiary
\ ˌbe-nə-ˈfi-shē-ˌe-rē\
see
E*, EA*, EE*, ERY*,
I**, IE*, Y**

beneficiary, penitentiary,
plenipotentiary

IARY***
diary \ ˈdī-(ə-)rē\
see
E*, EA*, EE*, I**, IE*,
Y**

diary

IAT
lariat \ ˈler-ē-ət\
see
AT***

commissariat, lariat, proletariat

IATE*
deviate \ ˈdē-vē-ˌāt\
see
AIGHT, AIT**, ATE*,
EAT**, ITATE, EIGHT*

abbreviate, affiliate**, alleviate,
appreciate, appropriate**,
associate**, collegiate, conciliate,
denunciate, depreciate,
deviate, dissociate, excruciate,
expatiate, expatriate, expediate,
expiate, expropriate, filiate,
foliate, humiliate, infuriate,
ingratiate, insatiate, luxuriate,
mediate, misappropriate,
negotiate, obviate, officiate,
palliate, propitiate, radiate,
repatriate, repudiate, retaliate,
satiate, striate, substantiate,
transubstantiate, vitiate

IATE**
immediate
\i-ˈmē-dē-ət\
see
AIT**, AT***, ATE**,
EDIT, EIT**, ERATE**,
ERIT, ET**, ETTE**,
IBIT, ICATE**, ICIT,
ICKET, IDGET, IGOT,
IMATE*, INATE**,
IOT**, IT, ITE***,
OLATE*, ORATE**,
OSET, OT***, UET***,
UGGET, UIT*, ULATE**,
URATE*

affiliate*, appropriate*, associate*,
immediate, inappropriate,
intercollegiate, intermediate,
novitiate, opiate, trifoliate

IATION
abbreviation
\ə-ˌbrē-vē-ˈā-shən\
see
ATION, ION*

abbreviation, appreciation,
aviation, denunciation,
expatriation, initiation,
negotiation, pronunciation,
renunciation

IB
bib \ˈbib\
see
UIB

ad lib, bib, Carib, corncrib, crib,
dib, drib, fib, glib, jib, nib, rib,
sahib, spare rib, squib

IBAL*
cannibal \ˈka-nə-bəl\
see
AL*, EL, LE, ULL*

cannibal, Hannibal

IBAL**
tribal \ˈtrī-bəl\
see
AL*, EL, IBEL, IBLE**,
LE

intertribal, tribal

IBBLE
nibble \ˈni-bəl\
see
EL, LE

dribble, fribble, nibble, quibble,
scribble

IBE
bribe \ ˈbrīb\

ascribe, bribe, circumscribe, describe, imbibe, inscribe, jibe, oversubscribe, prescribe, proscribe, scribe, subscribe, transcribe, tribe, vibe

IBEL
see
IBAL**, IBLE**, LE

libel

IBIT
prohibit \prō- ˈhi-bət\
see
AIT**, AT***, ATE**,
EIT**, EDIT, ERATE**,
ERIT, ET**, ETTE**,
IATE**, ICATE**, ICIT,
ICKET, IDGET, IGOT,
IMATE*, INATE**,
IOT**, IT, ITE***,
OLATE*, ORATE**,
OSET, OT***, UET***,
UGGET, UIT*, ULATE**,
URATE*

exhibit, inhibit, prohibit

IBLE*
visible \ ˈvi-zə-bəl\
see
ABLE*, EL, LE

accessible, audible, collapsible, combustible, comprehensible, compressible, contemptible, convertible, corrigible, corruptible, credible, crucible, dirigible, discernible, divisible, edible, eligible, exhaustible, fallible, feasible, flexible, forcible, frangible, fusible, gullible, horrible, illegible, impassible, imperceptible, impossible, inaccessible, inaudible, incombustible, incompatible, incomprehensible, incontrovertible, inconvertible, incorrigible, incorruptible, incredible, indefensible, indestructible, inedible,

IBLE*

inexhaustible, infallible, inflexible, insensible, intangible, intelligible, invincible, invisible, irascible, irresistible, irresponsible, legible, mandible, negligible, ostensible, partible, passible, perceptible, permissible, plausible, possible, reducible, refrangible, repressible, resistible, responsible, reversible, risible, sensible, susceptible, tangible, terrible, thurible, vendible, visible

IBLE**
Bible \\ ˈbī-bəl\\
see
IBAL**, IBEL

Bible

IBLY
possibly \\ ˈpä-sə-blē\\
see
E*, EA*, EE*, I**, IE*,
Y**

audibly, forcibly, glibly, indelibly, invisibly, possibly, terribly, visibly

IBUTE
tribute \\ ˈtri-(̣)byüt\\
see
EWT, OOT, UIT, UTE

attribute, contribute, distribute, tribute

IC
basic \\ ˈbā-sik\\
see
ACTIC, AIC, AMIC,
ANIC, ANTIC, ASTIC,
ATIC, ENIC, ERIC,
ETIC, ICK, IFIC, INIC,
ISTIC, ITIC, ODIC,
OGIC, OLIC, OMIC,
ONIC, OPIC, ORIC,
OTIC

acoustic, acrostic, agnostic, agrestic, alembic, allopathic, anelectric, angelic, Antarctic, anthropographic, antiseptic, antitoxic, Arabic, Arctic, arithmetic, ascetic, aseptic, aspic, attic, authentic, azoic, baldric, barbaric, basic, benefic, bishopric, black magic, cambric, cataclysmic, cathartic, caustic, Celtic, cherubic, chic, chivalric, civic, classic, concentric, Coptic, cosmic, cryptic, cubic, cynic,

IC

decasyllabic, Delphic, diagnostic, diametric, domestic, eccentric, eclectic, ecliptic, egocentric, elliptic, empiric, endemic, eolithic, epic, epidemic, epileptic, ethic, eupeptic, evangelic, fabric, forensic, formic, Gaelic, Gallic, garlic, geocentric, geodesic, geometric, gnomic, gnostic, Gothic, graphic, gum arabic, hectic, heliocentric, hermeneutic, heroic, hieroglyphic, hierographic, homeopathic, hydraulic, hydroelectric, iambic, Icelandic, idyllic, intrinsic, Ionic, Islamic, italic, karmic, lethargic, lyric, magic, majestic, malic, metallic, metamorphic, metric, mimic, monolithic, monosyllabic, mystic, mythic, natureopathic, neolithic, Nordic, obstetric, Olympic, optic, Orphic, orthopedic, orthorhombic, oxalic, paleolithic, panegyric, patronymic, phallic, physic, picnic, politic, polytechnic, polytheistic, pragmatic, prognostic, prussic, psychiatric, psychic, psychoanalytic, public, Punic, pyrotechnic, relic, republic, rhetoric, rhombic, rubric, runic, rustic, salicylic, sapphic, satiric, seismic, seraphic, Slavic, sic, skeptic, stenographic, stoic, strategic, sulphuric, styptic, syllabic, symmetric, syndic, technic, telepathic, thalassic, therapeutic, thermometric, theurgic, tonic, toreutic, toxic, traffic, tunic, tyrannic, unauthentic, Vedic

ICA*
Africa \ ˈa-fri-kə\
see
A**

Africa, America, angelica, arnica, Attica, basilica, Britannica, Corsica, harmonica, hepatica, japonica, majolica, materia medica, nux vomica, replica, sciatica, silica, veronica

ICA**
mica \ ˈmī-kə\
see
A**

mica, pica

ICACY
delicacy
\ ˈde-li-kə-sē\
see
ACY*, E*, EA*, EE*,
I**, IE*, Y**

delicacy, efficacy, indelicacy, intricacy

ICAL
medical \ ˈme-di-kəl\
see
AL*

aeronautical, allegorical, anthropological, artistical, biblical, biographical, biological, canonical, chemical, chronological, clerical, comical, conical, cosmical, cosmogonical, critical, cylindrical, cynical, diabolical, ecclesiastical, egotistical, emblematical, empirical, encyclical, ethnological, etiological, etymological, evangelical, farcical, finical, genetical, geographical, grammatical, heretical, hermeneutical, hierarchical, historical, horological, hypercritical, hypocritical, hypothetical, hysterical, identical, illogical, inimical, ironical, lackadaisical, logical, lyrical, magical, majestical, medical, meteorological, methodical, metrical, mimical, morphological, musical, mystical,

I SOUNDS

ICAL

mythological, nautical, nonsensical, numerical, ontological, optical, paradoxical, pathological, periodical, philosophical, physical, piratical, poetical, pontifical, practical, pragmatical, psychical, quizzical, radical, rhetorical, sabbatical, satirical, semitropical, skeptical, sophistical, spherical, stoical, surgical, symbolical, symmetrical, technical, technological, theatrical, theoretical, tragical, tropical, typical, tyrannical, unsophistical, vertical, vortical, whimsical

ICAN
pelican \ ˈpe-li-kən\
see
AN**, IAN**

African, American, Anglican, Mexican, Pan-American, pelican, publican, republican, Vatican

ICANT
applicant
\ ˈa-pli-kənt\
see
ANT**, ENT**

applicant, communicant, insignificant, lubricant, mendicant, significant, supplicant

ICATE*
dedicate \ ˈde-di-kət\
see
AIGHT, AIT**, ATE*,
EAT**, EIGHT*

abdicate, communicate, complicate, dedicate, domesticate, duplicate, eradicate, excommunicate, extricate, fabricate, fornicate, imbricate, implicate, indelicate, indicate, intoxicate, intricate, lubricate, masticate, pontificate, predicate**, prevaricate, prognosticate, reduplicate, rusticate, supplicate, syndicate**, vindicate

ICATE**
delicate \ ˈde-li-kət\
see
AIT**, AT***, ATE**,
EDIT, EIT**, ERATE**,
ERIT, ET**, ETTE**,
IATE**, IBIT, ICIT,
ICKET, IDGET, IGOT,
IMATE*, INATE**,
IOT**, IT, ITE***,
OLATE*, ORATE**,
OSET, OT***, UET***,
UGGET, UIT*, ULATE**,
URATE*

certificate, delicate, indelicate,
intricate, predicate*, sophisticate,
syndicate*

ICE*
nice \ ˈnīs\
see
EISS, ISE**

advice, allspice, bice, device, dice,
entice, field mice, high price, ice,
interslice, lice, low price, mice,
nice, price, rice, sacrifice, slice,
spice, splice, suffice, thrice, trice,
twice, vice

ICE**
office \ ˈä-fəs\
see
IFICE, IS*, ISE****, ISS

accomplice, apprentice, armistice,
artifice, auspice, avarice, benefice,
box office, cantatrice, caprice,
chalice, cicatrice, cornice,
cowardice, crevice, dentifrice,
hospice, injustice, justice, lattice,
licorice, malice, malpractice,
notice, novice, office, poultice,
practice, precipice, prejudice,
pumice, summer solstice, service,
surplice, winter solstice

ICE***
police \pə- ˈlēs\
see
EASE**, EESE**, ISE***

caprice, police

ICH
rich \ ˈrich\
see
ICHE, ITCH

enrich, Greenwich, Ipswich,
ostrich, rich, sandwich, which

ICHE
niche \ˈnich\ *or*
\ˈnēsh\ *or* \ˈnish\
see
EESH, ICH, ISH, ITCH

microfiche, niche

ICIAL
official \ə-ˈfi-shəl\
see
AL*, IAL***

artificial, beneficial, judicial,
official, prejudicial, sacrificial,
superficial, unofficial

ICIAN
magician
\mə-ˈji-shən\
see
AN**

geometrician, magician,
musician, optician, patrician,
Phoenician, physician, politician,
statistician, technician

ICIDE
suicide \ˈsü-ə-ˌsīd\
see
IDE, IE**+ *ed*, IGH+*ed*,
Y*+*ed*

fratricide, germicide, infanticide,
matricide, parricide, patricide,
regicide, suicide, vermicide

ICISM
criticism
\ˈkri-tə-ˌsi-zəm\
see
ISM

agnosticism, Catholicism,
criticism, didacticism,
empiricism, eroticism,
fanaticism, gnosticism, mysticism,
romanticism, witticism

ICIT
solicit \sə-ˈli-sət\
see
AIT**, AT***, ATE**,
EDIT, EIT**, ERATE**,
ERIT, ET**, ETTE**,
IATE**, IBIT, ICATE**,
ICKET, IDGET, IGOT,
IMATE*, INATE**,
IOT**, IT, ITE***,
OLATE*, ORATE**,
OSET, OT***, UET***,
UGGET, UIT*, ULATE**,
URATE*

deficit, explicit, illicit, implicit,
licit, solicit

ICITY
publicity
\\(ˌ)pə-ˈbli-sə-tē\\
see
E*, EA*, EE*, I**, IE*,
ITY, Y**

authenticity, causticity,
domesticity, duplicity,
eccentricity, electricity, ellipticity,
felicity, lubricity, periodicity,
publicity, rusticity, sphericity,
simplicity

ICK
brick \\ˈbrik\\
see
IC, IK

bailiwick, brick, broomstick,
candlestick, chick, chopstick,
click, cowlick, crick, derrick,
dirty trick, dropkick, drumstick,
fiddlestick, flick, goldbrick,
hayrick, homesick, joss stick, kick,
lick, limerick, lipstick, maulstick,
maverick, Moby Dick, niblick,
nick, pick, Pickwick, pinprick,
pogo stick, prick, quick, rick,
rollick, seasick, sick, slapstick,
slick, swizzle stick, thick, tick,
toothpick, trick, walking stick,
wick, yardstick

ICKER
wicker \\ˈwi-kər\\
see
AR**, ER*, OR*

bicker, dicker, flicker, pricker,
ragpicker, slicker, snicker, sticker,
thicker, wicker

ICKET
picket \\ˈpi-kət\\
see
AIT**, AT***, ATE**,
EDIT, EIT**, ERATE**,
ERIT, ET**, ETTE**,
IATE**, IBIT, ICATE**,
ICIT, ICKET, IDGET,
IGOT, IMATE*,
INATE**, IOT**, IT,
ITE***, OLATE*,
ORATE**, OSET, OT***,
UET***, UGGET, UIT*,
ULATE**, URATE*

cricket, picket, thicket, ticket,
wicket

ICKLE
pickle \ˈpi-kəl\
see
EL, LE

fickle, mickle, pickle, prickle, sickle, tickle, trickle

ICKY
icky \ˈi-kē\
see
E*, EA*, EE*, I**, IE**, Y**

icky, finicky, panicky, sticky, tricky

ICLE
cubicle \ˈkyü-bi-kəl\
see
EL, ICKLE, LE, YCLE

auricle, canticle, chicle, chronicle, conventicle, cubicle, cuticle, icicle, particle, Popsicle, radicle, vehicle, ventricle, versicle, vesicle

ICO
calico \ˈka-li-ˌkō\
see
EAU, EW**, O*, OE*, OT***, OUGH*, OW*, OWE

calico, medico, Mexico, Pimlico, portico, pro bono publico

ICON*
icon \ˈī-ˌkän\
see
ON**

icon

ICON**
lexicon
\ˈlek-sə-ˌkän\
see
ON*

harmonicon, Helicon, irenicon, lexicon, Rubicon, silicon

ICS
politics \ˈpä-lə-ˌtiks\
see
IC+*s*, ICK+*s*

academics, analytics, classics, dynamics, eclectics, empirics, ethics, genetics, kinetics, mathematics, metaphysics, metrics, physics, politics, psychics, statistics, tactics, thermodynamics, topics

ICT
verdict \ ˈvər-(ˌ)dikt\
see
IC+*ed*, ICK+*ed*

addict, afflict, benedict, conflict, constrict, contradict, convict, depict, derelict, district, edit, evict, inflict, interdict, predict, relict, restrict, strict, verdict

ICTION
fiction \ ˈfik-shən\
see
ION*

benediction, diction, fiction, friction, interdiction, jurisdiction, malediction, prediction

ICURE
manicure
\ ˈma-nə-ˌkyûr\
see
URE

epicure, manicure, pedicure

ICY*
spicy \ ˈspī-sē\
see
E*, EA*, EE*, I**, IE*,
ICE+*y*, Y**

icy, spicy

ICY**
policy \ ˈpä-lə-sē\
see
ACY*, E*, EA*, EE*,
I**, ICACY, IE*, Y**

impolicy, policy

ID
acid \ ˈa-səd\
see
ALID*, ED, OD**,
UID*, UID**, UMID,
UPID, YD

acid, acrid, amid, aphid, avid, bicuspid, bid, candid, Cid, coverlid, did, Euclid, fervid, fetid, flaccid, florid, forbid, frigid, gelid, gravid, hid, horrid, hybrid, ibid, id, insipid, intrepid, invalid, katydid, kid, Leonid, lid, limpid, livid, lucid, lurid, Madrid, masjid, mid, morbid, nonskid, orchid, outbid, outdid, Ovid, pallid, pellucid, Perseid, placid, putrid, pyramid, rabid, rancid, rapid, rid, rigid, sayid, skid, slid, solid, sordid, splendid, squalid, stolid, timid, torpid, torrid, turbid, turgid, underbid, undid, valid, vapid, viscid, vivid

YOU SAY POE-TAY-TOE, I SAY POE-TAH-TOE
REGIONAL DIALECT IN RHYME

IN CENTRAL UNITED STATES, *merry* and *marry* are pronounced the same. In New York City and New Jersey, those words are pronounced quite differently: *MEH-REE* and *MAIR-ee*. Likewise with *pour*, *pore*, and *poor*. Though they are single-syllable homonyms in much of the country, New Yorkers add a second syllable to *pour*: *POO-er*. Southerners tend to drop their *g*'s as in, "How about *somethin*' cold, *darlin*'?" On Long Island and New Jersey, those same end sounds are emphasized, as in *Lon-g(eh) Island(eh)*. In New England, particularly on the coast, many locals drop or soften the final *r*'s on words such as *car*. So you might hear Maine, New Hampshire, or Boston folks hop in *cahs* to drive to seafood *bahs* and eat clam *chowduh*. Those dropped *r*'s turn up in funny places: tacked onto the ends of words that end in simple vowels elsewhere. *Idea* becomes *idear* in Massachusetts, and in West Virginia and Ohio, *wash* becomes *warsh*. Pennsylvanians and Ohioans often drop helping verbs: dishes *need washed* rather than *need to be washed*. Midwesterners tend to soften and shorten vowels: *room* sounds like *rum*, *roof* sounds like *ruff*, while West Coasters tend to accentuate, making vowels and consonants sound almost doubled: *That's tootally harrsh!* Even a simple word such as *you* morphs across the continent: *you*, *youse*, *youn's*, *you guys*, and *y'all* all mean the same thing.

Then there are our neighbors to the north. Canadians pronounce many vowels differently. They eat *PA-sta* rather than *PAH-sta*, live in *HOO*ses instead of *HOW*ses, and go *OOT* rather than *OUT*. (Canadian readers, *SOR-ry*, make that, *SORE-y*, no offense intended. We think you're cute!)

In the context of speech or song, all these permutations don't much impede comprehension. But in text, the wrong pronunciation can transform an elegant verse into a real clunker. There's no need to call the whole thing off, as the Gershwin song suggests, however. To avoid sour notes, reach a reasonable compromise:

- Be aware of your own dialect as you write and don't assume the way you speak is standard.
- With questionable words, listen to the standard pronunciation from a reputable online dictionary.
- It's okay to use colloquialisms if your piece has a very regional feel and other supporting words and images to provide context.
- If you need a regional pronunciation to make a piece work, it's easier for readers if the nonstandard usage comes second, as the first rhyme of the couplet will prep them to pronounce the second one as you prefer.

I SOUNDS

IDAL
tidal \ˈtī-dᵊl\
see
AL*, IDLE, ITAL

bridal, cotidal, tidal, suicidal

IDATE
candidate
\ˈkan-də-ˌdāt\
see
AIGHT, AIT*, ATE*,
EAT**, EIGHT*

candidate, delapidate, elucidate,
intimidate, invalidate, lapidate,
liquidate, validate

IDDLE
fiddle \ˈfi-dᵊl\
see
EL, ITTLE, LE

diddle, fiddle, griddle, middle,
riddle, twiddle, unriddle

IDE
hide \ˈhīd\
see
EYE+*ed*, ICIDE, IED*,
UIDE, Y+*ed*

abide, alongside, aside, astride,
backslide, bedside, beside,
betide, bona fide, bride,
broadside, bromide, carbide,
chide, coincide, collide, confide,
countryside, cyanide, decide,
deride, dioxide, divide, ebb tide,
eventide, fireside, flood tide,
glide, hayride, hide, hillside,
homicide, ingleside, inside,
landslide, lopside, noontide,
outride, outside, override, ox
hide, oxide, peroxide, preside,
pride, provide, rawhide,
reside, ride, ringside, roadside,
seaside, set-aside, Shrovetide,
side, slide, stand aside, stride,
subside, sulphide, tide, wayside,
wide, worldwide, yuletide

IDENT*
accident
\ˈak-sə-dᵊnt\
see
ENT**

accident, coincident, confident,
incident, occident, overconfident,
president, provident, resident

IDENT**
strident \\ˈstrī-dᵊnt\\
see
ENT**

strident, trident

IDER
rider \\ˈrī-dər\\
see
AR**, ER*, IDE+*er*, OR*

backslider, cider, circus rider,
divider, glider, outrider, outsider,
provider, rider, roughrider,
spider, wider

IDES
besides \\bi-ˈsīdz\\
see
IDE+*s*

besides, bestrides, coincides,
Ides, Old Ironsides

IDGE
ridge \\ˈrij\\
see
AGE*, EGE

abridge, bridge, cartridge,
covered bridge, drawbridge,
footbridge, partridge,
pepperidge, porridge, ridge, toll
bridge

IDGET
fidget \\ˈfi-jət\\
see
AIT**, AT***, ATE**,
EIT**, EDIT, ERATE**,
ERIT, ET**, ETTE**,
IATE**, IBIT, ICATE**,
ICIT, ICKET, IGOT,
IMATE*, INATE**,
IOT**, IT, ITE***,
OLATE*, ORATE**,
OSET, OT***, UET***,
UGGET, UIT*, ULATE**,
URATE*

fidget, midget, widget

IDIAN
meridian
\\mə-ˈri-dē-ən\\
see
IAN*

antemeridian, meridian,
ophidian, quotidian

I SOUNDS

IDITY
acidity \ə-ˈsi-də-tē\
see
E*, EA*, EE*, I**, IE*,
ITY, Y**

acidity, aridity, avidity, cupidity,
fluidity, humidity, insipidity,
intimity, intrepidity, lucidity,
placidity, rapidity, sapidity,
solidity, stupidity

IDLE
bridle \ˈbrī-dəl\
see
EL, IDAL, LE

bridle, idle, sidle, unbridle

IDLY*
idly \ˈīd-lē\ *or*
\ˈī-dəl-ē\
see
E*, EA*, EE*, I**, IE*,
Y**

idly

IDLY**
vividly \ˈvi-vəd-lē\
see
E*, EA*, EE*, I**, IE*,
Y**

frigidly, languidly, rigidly,
timidly, vividly

IDOR
humidor
\ˈhyü-mə-ˌdȯr\
see
OOR, OR*, ORE, OUR**

corridor, cuspidor, humidor,
Thermidor

IDST
midst \ˈmidst\

amidst, midst

IDTH
width \ˈwidth\

width

IE*
movie \ˈmü-vē\
see
E*, EA*, EE*, ERIE,
I**, Y**

bowie, brie, brownie, calorie,
cappie, collie, coterie, dearie,
Dixie, dominie, eerie, gillie,
girlie, kelpie, kiltie, lassie, lorrie,
mashie, movie, nixie, prairie,
prima facie, rookie, sharpie,
sortie, specie, talkie, Valkyrie

I SOUNDS

IE**
pie \ ˈpī\
see
EYE, I*, IGH, Y*

belie, die, hie, huckleberry pie, humble pie, lie, magpie, mince pie, necktie, pie, potpie, tie, untie, vie

IECE
piece \ ˈpēs\
see
EASE**, EECE, EESE**, ICE***, ISE***

frontispiece, mantelpiece, masterpiece, mouthpiece, niece, piece

IED*
fried \ ˈfrīd\
see
EYE+*d*, IDE, IE**+*ed*, IGH+*ed*

allied, amplified, certified, citified, complied, countryfied, cried, crucified, defied, deified, denied, died, dried, espied, fortified, fried, glorified, gratified, hog-tied, implied, intensified, justified, lied, liquefied, magnified, mortified, multiplied, mummified, occupied, ossified, petrified, pied, preoccupied, pried, purified, qualified, relied, replied, sanctified, satisfied, shied, spied, stupefied, sun-dried, supplied, tongue-tied, tried, unoccupied, unsatisfied, unversified, versified

IED**
buried \ ˈber-ēd\
see
ED, ID

able-bodied, atrophied, buried, candied, dallied, ferried, ivied, levied, married, mutinied, palsied, parodied, serried, studied, taxied, travestied, varied, wearied

IEF*
brief \ ˈbrēf\
see
EAF*, EEF

bas-relief, belief, brief, chief, disbelief, grief, handkerchief, kerchief**, relief, thief, unbelief

IEF**
mischief \ ˈmis-chəf\
see
IF*, IFF

kerchief*, mischief

IEGE
siege \ ˈsēj\
see
IGE*

besiege, liege, siege

IEK
shriek \ ˈshrēk\
see
EAK*, EEK, EKE, IK*,
IQUE

shriek

IELD
yield \ ˈyēld\
see
EAL*+*ed*, EEL+*ed*

afield, cornfield, field, infield,
outfield, shield, stubble field,
wield, windshield, yield

IEN*
alien \ ˈā-lē-ən\
see
EAN**

alien

IEN**
lien \ ˈlēn\ *or* \ ˈlē-ən\
see
EAN*, EEN, EIN***,
ENE, INE**

lien, mien

IENCE*
audience \ ˈȯ-dē-əns\
see
ENCE

audience, convenience,
experience, inconvenience,
inexperience, obedience,
sapience, subservience

IENCE**
patience \ ˈpā-shəns\
see
ENCE

conscience, faience, nescience,
omniscience, patience,
prescience, resilience

IENCE***
science \ ˈsī-ən(t)s\
see
ENCE, ENSE, INCE

science

IENT*
patient \ ˈpā-shənt\
see
ENT**

ambient, ancient, convenient, deficient, desipient, ebullient, efficient, emollient, esurient, expedient, gradient, incipient, inconvenient, inexpedient, ingredient, insufficient, lenient, nescient, obedient, omniscient, orient, patient, percipient, proficient, prurient, recipient, reorient, resilient, salient, sapient, sentient, subservient, sufficient

IENT**
client \ ˈklī-ənt\
see
ENT**, IANT*, INT

client

IER*
barrier \ ˈber-ē-ər\
see
AIRY+er, AR**,
ARRY*+er, ER*, ERE***,
ERRY+er, OR*, Y**+er

barrier, carrier, chillier, collier, courier, courtier, croupier, fancier, farrier, frontier, Montpellier, rapier, terrier

IER**
purifier
\ ˈpyu̇r-ə-ˌfī(ə)r\
see
AR**, ER*, IAR*, IRE*,
OR*, YER

amplifier, brier, crier, flier, magnifier, modifier, plier, purifier, sweetbrier

IER***
pier \ ˈpir\
see
EAR*, ERE*

bier, brigadier, cashier, cavalier, chandelier, chiffonier, financier, grenadier, pier, premier, tier, vizier

IER****
brazier \ ˈbrā-zhər\
see
AR**, ER*, IR*, OR*,
URR

brazier, crosier, glazier, hoosier, osier

I SOUNDS

IERCE
fierce \ˈfirs\

fierce, pierce, tierce

IERE
derriere \ˌder-ē-ˈer\
see
AIR, ARE*, ERE*

boutonniere, derriere, jardiniere, portiere

IES*
cries \ˈkrīz\
see
IE**+*s*, IGH+*s*, ISE*,
IZE, UISE, UY+*s*, Y*+*s*

cries, dragonflies, fireflies, flies, fortifies, lies, pies, plies, ratifies, skies, spies, squash pies, supplies, tries

IES**
arteries \ˈär-tə-rēz\
see
E*+*s*, EASE*, EE*+*s*,
EEZE, ES*, EY*+*s*,
I**+*s*, IE*+*s*, IS***,
Y**+*s*

absurdities, argosies, Aries, arteries, cavities, centuries, charities, cities, comedies, congeries, courtesies, curiosities, derbies, dictionaries, dowries, duties, East Indies, economies, eddies, effigies, exigencies, fairies, fallacies, fantasies, fillies, fisheries, frailties, Furies, gullies, harpies, idolatries, lilies, miseries, monies, obsequies, oddities, orgies, pansies, peonies, pixies, ponies, quandaries, rareties, remedies, reveries, rubies, scurries, series, species, strawberries, superficies, superfluities, theories, trophies

IEST*
funniest \ˈfə-nē-əst\
see
EST, UEST, Y**+*est*

airiest, driest, earliest, flabbiest, funniest, happiest, leakiest, lowliest, prettiest, ricketiest, rustiest, scantiest, sorriest, stateliest, swankiest, tidiest, trickiest, wittiest, worthiest

IEST**
priest \ ˈprēst\
see
EASE**+*d*, EAST*,
EECE+*ed*, ICE***+*ed*,
ISTE

high priest, priest

IET
quiet \ ˈkwī-ət\
see
ET, IOT**

diet, disquiet, quiet

IETY
anxiety \aŋ-ˈzī-ə-tē\
see
I**, E*, EE*, Y**

anxiety, contrariety, impiety,
moiety, notoriety, piety,
propriety, satiety, sobriety,
society, variety

IEU
adieu \ə-ˈdü\
see
EW, IEW, O*, OE**,
OO, OU*, OUGH****,
OUS**, OUT*, OUX, U,
UE*, UT

adieu, lieu, prie-dieu, purlieu

IEVE*
believe \bə-ˈlēv\
see
EAVE, EIVE

achieve, believe, disbelieve,
grieve, make-believe, relieve,
reprieve, retrieve, thieve

IEVE**
sieve \ ˈsiv\
see
IVE**

sieve

IEVES
thieves \ ˈthēvz\
see
EAF*+*s*, EAVE*+*s*,
EVE*+*s*

Forty Thieves, retrieves, thieves

IEW
view \ˈvyü\
see
EW*, IEU, O**, OE**,
OO, OU*, OUGH****,
OUT**, OUX, U, UE*,
UT***

interview, preview, purview,
review, view

IEZE
frieze \ˈfrēz\
see
E*+*s*, EASE*, EE*+*s*,
EESE*, EEZE, EIZE,
ESE*

frieze

IF*
if \ˈif\
see
IFE, IFF, YPH

alif, calif, if, khalif, serif

IF**
motif \mō-ˈtēf\
see
EEF

aperitif, motif

IFE
wife \ˈwīf\

alewife, bowie knife, fife,
housewife, inner life, jackknife,
knife, life, loosestrife, lowlife,
midwife, pocketknife, rife, strife,
wife, wildlife

IFER*
lifer \ˈlī-fər\
see
AR**, ER*, IPHER, OR*

fifer, lifer

IFER**
Lucifer \ˈlü-sə-fər\
see
AR**, ER*, OR*

Lucifer, thurifer

IFF
cliff \ ˈklif\
see
IF*, IPH, YPH

bailiff, biff, caitiff, Cardiff, cliff, hippogriff, jiff, mastiff, midriff, miff, plaintiff, pontiff, sheriff, skiff, sniff, stiff, tariff, tiff, whiff

IFIC
Pacific \pə-ˈsi-fik\
see
IC, ICK

beatific, horrific, omnific, pacific, prolific, scientific, soporific, specific, sudorific, terrific, transpacific, unprolific

IFICE
orifice \ˈȯr-ə-fəs\
see
ICE**

edifice, orifice

IFLE
rifle \ˈrī-fəl\
see
EL, LE

rifle, stifle, trifle

IFORM
uniform
\ˈyü-nə-ˌfȯrm\
see
ARM**, ORM*

anguilliform, cruciform, cuneiform, oviform, triform, uniform, vermiform

IFT
rift \ˈrift\
see
IFF+*ed*

adrift, chimney swift, drift, gift, lift, makeshift, rift, shift, shoplift, sift, snowdrift, spendthrift, swift, thrift, uplift

IFUL
dutiful \ˈdü-ti-fəl\
see
UL*, ULL*

beautiful, bountiful, dutiful, fanciful, merciful, pitiful, plentiful

IFY
modify \ˈmä-də-ˌfī\
see
EFY, I*, IE**, IGH, Y*

aerify, amplify, beautify, calcify, certify, clarify, classify, codify, crucify, deify, dignify, disqualify, diversify, dulcify, edify, electrify, falsify, fortify, fructify, gratify, horrify, identify, indemnify, intensify, justify, lapidify,

IFY

lignify, liquify, magnify, modify, mollify, mortify, mummify, mystify, notify, nullify, ossify, pacify, personify, petrify, purify, qualify, ramify, rarify, ratify, rectify, requalify, revivify, salsify, sanctify, solidify, specify, speechify, stultify, terrify, testify, transmogrify, unify, verify, versify, vilify, vivify

IG
big \ ˈbig\

big, bigwig, brig, cat rig, cig, dig, earwig, fig, gig, guinea pig, jig, periwig, pig, prig, rig, swig, thimblerig, thingamajig, trig, twig, whig, whirligig, wig

IGAN
cardigan
\ ˈkär-di-gən\
see
AN**

cardigan, hooligan, ptarmigan

IGATE
navigate
\ ˈna-və-ˌgāt\
see
AIGHT, AIT*, ATE*,
EAT**, EIGHT*

fumigate, fustigate, instigate, investigate, irrigate, litigate, mitigate, navigate, obligate, profligate

IGE*
prestige \pre-ˈstēzh\
see
IEGE

prestige

IGE**
oblige \ə-ˈblīj\

oblige

IGE***
vestige \ ˈves-tij\
see
IDGE

vestige

IGGER
digger \ ˈdi-gər\
see
AR**, ER*, OR*

bigger, chigger, digger, golddigger, jigger, outrigger, rigger, trigger

IGGLE
wiggle \ ˈwi-gəl\
see
EL, LE

giggle, higgle, jiggle, niggle, wiggle, wriggle

IGH
high \ ˈhī\
see
I*, IE**, Y*

anigh, high, knee-high, nigh, sigh, thigh, well-nigh

IGHT
tight \ ˈtīt\
see
EIGHT**, ITE*, YTE

affright, airtight, alight, all right, alright, aright, bedight, bight, birthright, blight, bright, bullfight, candlelight, copyright, daylight, delight, downright, eyebright, eyesight, fight, flashlight, flight, floodlight, fly-by-night, footlight, foresight, fortnight, fright, gaslight, goodnight, headlight, hindsight, insight, Isle of Wight, knight, light, limelight, midnight, might, moonlight, night, outright, overnight, oversight, pilot light, playwright, plight, prizefight, redlight, right, searchlight, second sight, sidelight, sight, skylight, slight, spotlight, stage fright, starlight, sticktight, sunlight, taillight, tight, tonight, Twelfth Night, twilight, upright, watertight, wheelwright, wight, wright

IGHTY
mighty \ ˈmī-tē\
see
E*, EA*, EE*, I**, IE*, Y**

almighty, blighty, flighty, high and mighty, highty-tighty, mighty, nighty

IGMA
stigma \ ˈstig-mə\
see
A**

enigma, sigma, stigma

IGN
sign \ ˈsīn\
see
INE*, UINE**, YNE

align, assign, benign, condign,
consign, design, ensign, malign,
resign, sign, traffic sign

IGO*
indigo \ ˈin-di-ˌgō\
see
EAU, EW**, O*, OE*,
OT***, OUGH*, OW*,
OWE

indigo, vertigo

IGO**
amigo \ə-ˈmē-(ˌ)gō\
see
EAU, EW**, O*, OE*,
OT***, OUGH*, OW*,
OWE

amigo

IGOT
bigot \ ˈbi-gət\
see
AIT**, AT***, ATE**,
EIT**, EDIT, ERATE**,
ERIT, ET**, ETTE**,
IATE**, IBIT, ICATE**,
ICIT, ICKET, IDGET,
IMATE*, INATE**, IOT**,
IT, ITE***, OLATE*,
ORATE**, OSET, OT***,
UET***, UGGET, UIT*,
ULATE**, URATE*

bigot, spigot

IGREE
pedigree
\ ˈpe-də-ˌgrē\
see
E*, EA*, EE*, I**, IE*,
Y**

filigree, pedigree, perigee

I SOUNDS

IGY
prodigy \ ˈprä-də-jē\
see
E*, EA*, EE*, I**, IE*, Y**

effigy, prodigy

IK*
batik \bə-ˈtēk\
see
EAK*, EEK, EKE, IEK,
IQUE

batik, sheik**

IK**
sheik \ˈshāk\
see
ACHE**, AKE, AQUE**,
EAK**

sheik*

IKE
bike \ˈbīk\
see
AIK

alike, belike, bike, childlike,
dike, dislike, fanlike, ghostlike,
gnomelike, gooselike, hitchhike,
homelike, hunger strike,
ladylike, mike, pike, saintlike,
sphinxlike, spike, sportsmanlike,
strike, suchlike, swanlike, tike,
trancelike, trike, turnpike,
unlike, viselike

IL
civil \ˈsi-vəl\
see
ERIL, ERYL, EVIL,
ILE**, ILL, ILLE*

anvil, April, argil, basil, boll
weevil, Brazil, cavil, cheveril,
civil, codicil, council, daffodil,
devil, distil, evil, fibril, fossil,
fulfil, fusil, instil, lentil, nil,
nostril, pencil, stencil, sweet
basil, tendril, tonsil, tumbril,
uncivil, until, utensil, vigil,
Virgil, weevil

ILANT
vigilant \ ˈvi-jə-lənt\
see
ANT**

jubilant, sibilant, vigilant

ILAR
similar \ ˈsi-mə-lər\
see
AR**, ER*, OR*

dissimilar, similar

ILATE
dilate \ ˈdī- ˌlāt\
see
AIGHT, AIT*, ATE*,
EAT**, EIGHT*

annihilate, dilate, jubilate,
mutilate, ventilate

ILCH
filch \ ˈfilch\

filch, milch

ILD*
gild \ ˈgild\
see
IL+*ed*, ILL+*ed*, UILD

Brunhild, gild, regild

ILD**
child \ ˈchī(-ə)ld\
see
ILE*+*ed*, YLE+*ed*

child, godchild, grandchild, mild,
wild

ILDER
builder \ ˈbil-dər\
see
AR**, ER*, OR*

bewilder, builder, guilder

ILE*
file \ ˈfī(-ə)l\
see
ISLE, UILE, YLE

Anglophile, Anile, awhile,
bibliophile, chamomile***,
compile, crocodile, defile,
domicile, erstwhile, exile,
febrile, file, fluviatile, Gentile,
hostile**, juvenile, meanwhile,
mercantile, mile, Nile, pile,
profile, projectile, reconcile,
red tile, reptile, revile, scissile,
seldomwhile, senile, servile,
single file, smile, stile, textile,
tile, turnstile, versatile**, vile,
volatile**, while, wile, woodpile

ILE**
fragile \ ˈfra-jəl\
see
EL, IL, LE, UL

Castile, docile, ductile, facile,
fertile, flexile, fragile, futile,
hostile*, imbecile, immobile,
missile, mobile***, pensile,
prehensile, puerile, sextile,
sterile, tactile, tensile, virile,
versatile*, volatile*

ILE***
automobile
\ ˈȯ-tə-mō-ˌbēl\
see
EAL, EEL, IEL, ILLE**

automobile, chamomile*,
mobile**

ILE****
simile \ ˈsi-mə-(ˌ)lē\
see
E*, EA*, EE*, I**, IE*,
Y**

facsimile, primum mobile, simile

ILESS
merciless
\ ˈmər-si-ləs\
see
ESS

merciless, penniless, pitiless

ILGE
bilge \ ˈbilj\

bilge

ILION
pavilion \pə-ˈvil-yən\
see
ILL, ION**

pavilion, postilion, vermilion

ILITY
ability \ə-ˈbi-lə-tē\
see
E*, EA*, EE*, I**, IE*,
Y**

ability, anility, applicability,
capability, compatability,
civility, culpability, debility,
dependability, disability,
divisibility, durability, eligibility,
facility, fallibility, fertility,
flexibility, gentility, gullibility,
immutability, impenetrability,
inability, incivility,

ILITY

incompatibility, indefatigability, indefectibility, indelibility, inevitability, infallibility, instability, invisibility, liability, mutability, negligibility, nobility, notability, plausibility, possibility, probability, responsibility, senility, sensibility, servility, stability, susceptibility, tangibility, utility, virility, visibility, volubility, vulnerability

ILK
milk \ˈmilk\

bilk, buttermilk, ilk, milk, silk

ILL
bill \ˈbil\
see
IL, UILL

anthill, bill, Bunker Hill, chill, dill, distill, doorsill, drill, duckbill, dunghill, fill, firedrill, foothill, frill, fulfill, gill, goodwill, frill, gristmill, handbill, hill, hornbill, ill, ill will, kill, krill, mandrill, mill, molehill, pill, playbill, refill, rill, sandhill, sawmill, shrill, sill, skill, spill, spoonbill, standstill, still, swill, thrill, till, treadmill, trill, twill, uphill, whippoorwill, will, windmill, windowsill

ILLA
gorilla \gə-ˈri-lə\
see
A**

camilla, cedilla, chinchilla, flotilla, gorilla, guerilla, mantilla, pulsatilla, sapodilla, sarsaparilla, scintilla, vanilla, villa

ILLE*
vaudeville \ˈvȯd-vəl\
see
ILL

escadrille, espadrille, grille, Hotel de Ville, quadrille, Seville, vaudeville

ILLE**
chenille \shə-ˈnēl\
see
ILE***

Bastille, chenille, dishabille

ILLER
filler \ ˈfi-lər\
see
AR**, ER*, ILL+*er*, OR*

filler, miller, shriller, stiller,
tiller, thriller

ILLION
million \ ˈmi(l)-yən\
see
ION**

billion, cotillion, gazillion,
million, pillion, trillion,
vermillion

ILLO
armadillo
\ ˌär-mə-ˈdi-(ˌ)lō\
see
EAU, EW**, O*, OE*,
OT***, OUGH*, OW*,
OWE

armadillo, Murillo, Negrillo,
peccadillo

ILLY
silly \ ˈsi-lē\
see
E*, EA*, EE*, I**, IE*,
ILL+*y*, Y**

billy, Chantilly, chilly, filly,
hillbilly, hilly, Piccadilly, silly,
stilly, willy nilly

ILM
film \ ˈfilm\

film

ILN
kiln \ ˈkiln\

kiln

ILT
wilt \ ˈwilt\
see
UILT

full tilt, gilt, hilt, jilt, kilt, lilt,
silt, spilt, stilt, tilt, wilt

ILTH
filth \ ˈfilth\

filth, spilth, tilth

ILVER
silver \ ˈsil-vər\
see
AR**, ER*, OR*

quicksilver, silver

I SOUNDS

ILY
lazily \ ˈlā-zə-lē\
see
E*, EA*, EE*, I**, IE*,
Y**

bodily, busily, cannily, clammily,
clumsily, craftily, daintily,
dreamily, drearily, drowsily,
easily, eerily, family, faultily,
gaudily, gloomily, greedily,
guiltily, homily, lazily, luckily,
lustily, merrily, mightily, moodily,
pluckily, primarily, scantily,
shabbily, Sicily, speedily, spunkily,
stealthily, temporarily, uncannily,
unluckily, verily, voluntarily, wittily

ILY**
wily \ ˈwī-lē\
see
E*, EA*, EE*, I**, IE*,
Y**

wily

IM
brim \ ˈbrim\
see
ATIM, ONYM, YMN

bedim, brim, broadbrim,
cherubim, dim, Elohim, grim,
him, interim, maxim, megrim,
passim, pilgrim, prim, Purim,
rim, seraphim, skim, slim, swim,
teraphim, Thummim, trim,
Urim, verbatim, victim, whim

IMAL
decimal \ ˈde-sə-məl\
see
AL*

animal, decimal, infinitesimal,
maximal, millesimal

IMATE*
climate \ ˈklī-mət\
see
AIT**, AT***, ATE**,
EDIT, EIT**, ERATE**,
ERIT, ET**, ETTE**,
IATE**, IBIT, ICATE**,
ICIT, ICKET, IDGET,
IGOT, INATE**, IOT**,
IT, ITE***, OLATE*,
ORATE**, OSET, OT***,
UET***, UGGET, UIT*,
ULATE**, URATE*

animate**, antepenultimate,
approximate, climate, estimate**,
inanimate, intimate**, legitimate,
penultimate, proximate, ultimate

IMATE**
primate \\'prī-ˌmāt\\
see
AIGHT, AIT*, ATE*,
EAT**, EIGHT*

animate*, decimate, estimate*,
intimate*, overestimate, primate,
reanimate, sublimate

IMB*
limb \\'lim\\
see
IM, ONYM, YMN

limb

IMB**
climb \\'klīm\\
see
IME*, YME

climb

IMBER
timber \\'tim-bər\\
see
AR**, ER*, OR*

limber, timber

IMBLE
nimble \\'nim-bəl\\
see
EL, LE

nimble, thimble, wimble

IME*
crime \\'krīm\\
see
YME

aforetime, bedtime, begrime,
chime, Christmastime, class
time, clime, crime, dime,
grime, lifetime, lime, maritime,
mealtime, meantime, mime,
ofttime, overtime, pantomime,
pastime, prime, quicklime,
ragtime, rime, seedtime,
slime, sometime, spare
time, springtime, sublime,
summertime, swing time, time,
wartime, wintertime

IME**
regime \\rā-'zhēm\\
see
EAM, EEM, EME

intime, regime

I SOUNDS

IMEN
specimen
\ˈspe-sə-mən\
see
EN**

regimen, specimen

IMENT
compliment
\ˈkäm-plə-mənt\
see
ENT***, INT

accompaniment, aliment,
compliment, condiment,
detriment, embodiment,
experiment, habiliment,
impediment, liniment,
merriment, nutriment,
orpiment, presentiment,
regiment, rudiment, sediment,
sentiment

IMITY
proximity
\präk-ˈsi-mə-tē\
see
E*, EA*, EE*, IE*, I**,
ITY, Y**

dimity, equanimity, magnanimity,
proximity, sublimity, unanimity

IMMER
simmer \ˈsi-mər\
see
AR**, ER*, OR*

dimmer, glimmer, shimmer,
simmer, slimmer, swimmer,
trimmer

IMP
blimp \ˈblimp\
see
UIMP

blimp, crimp, imp, limp, pimp,
primp, scrimp, shrimp, simp,
skimp

IMPLE
dimple \ˈdim-pəl\
see
EL, LE

dimple, pimple, simple, wimple

IMPSE
glimpse \ˈglim(p)s\

glimpse

IN
bin \ˈbin\
see
AIN**, EN**, INN, UIN

Adrenalin, akin, Aladdin, all-in, antitoxin, assassin, bare skin, basin, bearskin, begin, bin, bobbin, bodkin, bowfin, Brahmin, break-in, buckskin, built-in, bulletin, bumpkin, buskin, cabin, calfskin, Capuchin, catkin, chagrin, chin, chinquapin, clothespin, coffin, cousin, cretin, cumin, Darwin, dauphin, deerskin, din, dobbin, doeskin, dolphin, Dublin, duckpin, dunlin, fin, firkin, florin, gelatin, gherkin, gin, goblin, griffin, grimalkin, grin, herein, highfalutin, hin, hobgoblin, in, insulin, Jacobin, jasmin, javelin, jerkin, kaolin, khamsin, kin, kingpin, Kremlin, lambskin, listen in, log cabin, lupin, lynchpin, mandarin, manikin, margin, martin, matin, maudlin, mechlin, Merlin, metheglin, moccasin, moleskin, muezzin, muffin, muslin, napkin, ninepin, nubbin, Odin, oilskin, origin, paladin, paraffin, Pekin, Pepin, pepsin, pidgin, pigskin, pin, pippin, poplin, puffin, pumpkin, ragamuffin, raisin, ramekin, replevin, resin, rolling pin, round-robin, saccharin, safety pin, Sanhedrin, sculpin, sealskin, sea urchin, sheepskin, shin, sin, skin, sloe gin, spavin, spillikin, spin, tailspin, tannin, tarpaulin, terrapin, therein, theremin, thin, tholepin, tiffin, tocsin, toxin, twin, underpin, urchin, vermin, virgin, washbasin, welkin, wherein, win, within, yin, zeppelin

INA*
china \ˈchī-nə\
see
A**

Agrippina, Carolina, China

INA**
ballerina
\ˌba-lə-ˈrē-nə\
see
A**

ballerina, Catalina, cavatina,
concertina, czarina, farina,
Medina, ocarina, Regina, vina

INA***
stamina
\ˈsta-mə-nə\

lamina, retina, stamina

INAL*
cardinal
\ˈkär-də-nəl\
see
AL, IN+*al*

aboriginal, cardinal, criminal,
germinal, latitudinal, libidinal,
longitudinal, marginal,
matutinal, nominal, original,
paginal, Quirinal, subliminal,
terminal, virginal

INAL**
final \ˈfī-nəl\
see
YNL

final

INARY
imaginary
\i-ˈma-jə-ˌner-ē\
see
AIRY, ARRY*, ARY*, E*,
EA*, EE*, ERRY, ERY**,
I**, IE*, Y**

culinary, extraordinary,
imaginary, luminary, ordinary,
preliminary, sanguinary,
seminary, veterinary

INATE*
terminate
\ˈtər-mə-nət\
see
AIGHT, AIT*, ATE*,
EAT**, EIGHT*

assassinate, culminate,
disseminate, dominate, eliminate,
exterminate, fascinate, fulminate,
germinate, hallucinate,
illuminate, incriminate,
nominate, originate, peregrinate,
predominate, procrastinate,
recriminate, ruminate, terminate,
vaccinate

I SOUNDS

INATE**
obstinate
\ˈäb-stə-nət\
see
AIT**, AT***, ATE**,
EDIT, EIT**, ERATE**,
ERIT, ET**, ETTE**,
IATE**, IBIT, ICATE**,
ICIT, ICKET, IDGET,
IGOT, IMATE*, IOT**,
IT, ITE***, OLATE*,
ORATE**, OSET, OT***,
UET***, UGGET, UIT*,
ULATE**, URATE*

determinate, indeterminate,
insubordinate, obstinate,
subordinate

INC
zinc \ˈziŋk\
see
INK

zinc

INCE
prince \ˈprin(t)s\
see
INT+s

convince, evince, mince, prince,
province, quince, since, wince

INCH
inch \ˈinch\
see
YNCH

bullfinch, chaffinch, cinch,
clinch, finch, flinch, goldfinch,
grinch, inch, pinch, winch

INCT
distinct \di-ˈstiŋ(k)t\
see
INK+ed

distinct, extinct, indistinct,
precinct, succinct

IND*
bind \ˈbīnd\
see
IGN+ed, INE*+d

behind, bind, blind, color-
blind, grind, humankind, kind,
mankind, mastermind, mind,
never mind, purblind, remind,
rind, unkind, unwind, wind**,
window blind

IND**
wind \ ˈwind\
see
IN+*ed*

rescind, second wind, tamarind, tradewind, whirlwind, wind*

INDER*
blinder \ ˈblīn-dər\
see
IND+*er*, AR**, ER*, OR*

binder, blinder, grinder, pathfinder, reminder, sidewinder

INDER**
hinder \ ˈhin-dər\
see
AR**, ER*, OR*

cinder, cylinder, hinder

INDLE
swindle \ ˈswin-dᵊl\
see
EL, LE

brindle, dwindle, kindle, rekindle, spindle, swindle

INE*
vine \ ˈvīn\
see
IGN, UINE**, YNE

airline, alkaline***, Alpine, aquiline, asinine, beguine, bovine, Brandywine, brine, canine, caprine, carmine, chalk line, clothesline, coal mine, columbine, combine, concubine, confine, decline, define, dine, disincline, divine, eglantine, enshrine, entwine, equine, feline, fine, fish line, goldmine, grapevine, headline, incarnadine, incline, intertwine, iodine, kine, lifeline, line, lupine, mine, monkeyshine, moonshine, muscadine***, nine, opaline**, opine, outline, Palatine, Palestine, phocine, pine, pitch pine, plumb line, porcine, porcupine, port wine, rapine, ratline, recline, red wine, refine, repine, Rhine, salt mine, serpentine**, shine, shoreline, shrine, sideline, sine, skyline,

I SOUNDS

INE*

spine, streamline, strychnine, superfine, supine, swine, tape line, thine, tine, transpontine, turbine***, twine, undermine, ursine, valentine, vine, vulpine, waterline, whine, wine, woodbine

INE**
chlorine \ ˈklȯr-ˌēn\
see
EAN*, EEN, EIN***,
ENE, IEN**, INE**

adamantine, Algerine, aquamarine, Argentine, atropine, Benedictine, benzine, bombazine, brigantine, chlorine, Constantine, cuisine, elephantine, Evangeline, figurine, fluorine, gaberdine, gasoline, Ghibelline, grenadine, guillotine, latrine, leporine, levantine***, libertine, limousine, machine, magazine, marine, mezzanine, nectarine, opaline*, ovine, palatine, pelerine***, peregrine***, Philippine, Philistine, praline, pristine, quarantine, ravine, routine, Sabine, saline, serpentine*, Sibylline, Sistine, slot machine, submarine, tambourine, tangerine, tourmaline, ultramarine, undine, vaccine, vaseline

INE***
engine \ ˈen-jən\
see
IN, INN

adrenaline, alexandrine, alkaline*, amaranthine, aniline, clandestine, crinoline, crystalline, destine, determine, discipline, doctrine, engine, ermine, famine, feminine, gamine, heroine, hyaline, illumine, imagine, intestine, jessamine, leonine, leporine, levantine**, margarine, masculine, medicine, muscadine*, pelerine**, peregrine**, predestine, quinine, saccharine, turbine*

INENT
continent
\ˈkän-tə-nənt\
see
ENT*

continent, eminent, imminent,
impertinent, incontinent,
pertinent, preeminent,
prominent

INER*
shiner \ˈshī-nər\
see
AR**, ER*, OR**

diner, finer, forty-niner, liner,
miner, moonshiner, ocean liner,
refiner, shiner, shriner

INER**
mariner \ˈmer-ə-nər\
see
AR**, ER*, OR*

mariner, milliner

INESS
happiness
\ˈha-pē-nəs\
see
ES**, ESS

bulkiness, cloudiness, coziness,
dinginess, dowdiness, emptiness,
fussiness, fustiness, ghastliness,
giddiness, guiltiness, happiness,
haughtiness, headiness, holiness,
loneliness, loveliness, mightiness,
mistiness, pettiness, readiness,
silliness, steadiness, sultriness,
surliness, tidiness, uneasiness,
weariness, wordiness, worthiness

INET
clarinet
\ˌkler-ə-ˈnet\
see
ET

bassinet, bobbinet, cabinet,
clarinet, martinet, spinet

ING
anything \ˈe-nē-thiŋ\
see
ER*+*ing*, ING, PLUS
ADJECTIVES FORMED
BY ADDING —*ing* TO
VERBS, FOR EXAMPLE,
amazing, PLUS VERBS
WITH INFLECTED
ENDING —*ing*, FOR
EXAMPLE, *running*

angling, anything, apron string,
awing, awning, baffling, batting,
beekeeping, belting, bing,
blessing, blueing, bombing,
boring, bowling, bowstring,
boxing, bring, building, bunting,
casing, ceiling, central heating,
chattering, cling, closing,
coming, cunning, darling, do-
nothing, drawing, dressing,
duckling, dumpling, during,

ING

dwelling, easygoing, ending, etching, far-reaching, farthing, feeling, fledgling, fling, foundling, going, good breeding, gosling, grilling, hamstring, hasty pudding, heat lightning, herring, Highland fling, hireling, howling, imposing, incoming, inkling, juggling, key ring, kidding, kindling, king, Kipling, landscaping, lapwing, lashing, lasting, latchstring, law-abiding, leave-taking, lightning, liking, lining, lodging, longing, long-standing, long-suffering, lutestring, mainspring, matting, maying, meeting, merrymaking, mining, mooring, morning, mumbling, Nanking, necking, nestling, never ending, nothing, notwithstanding, nursling, obliging, offing, offspring, oncoming, opening, outbuilding, outlying, outpouring, outstanding, padding, painstaking, painting, paling, parting, pervading, pettifogging, petting, piffling, prevailing, princeling, pudding, ranking, rattling, reckoning, redwing, rigging, ring, ruching, rustling, sapling, scantling, screaming, seafaring, seagoing, seasoning, seedling, sewing, shambling, shelving, shocking, shoestring, shortening, sidesplitting, sightseeing, shilling, simpling, sing, sling, smattering, spring, starling, sterling, stilling, sting, stocking, string, suckling, swaddling, swelling, swing, tantalizing, tap dancing, teething, Thanksgiving, thing, tingling, town meeting, twinkling,

ING

ugly duckling, underling, underpinning, undying, unending, unfeeling, unflinching, unknowing, untiring, upbuilding, uplifting, upstanding, upswing, Viking, wainscoting, warning, webbing, wedding, well-being, wending, whiting, wing, winning, witling, worldling, wring, writing, yearling, yearning

INGE
hinge \ ˈhinj\

astringe, binge, constringe, cringe, fringe, hinge, impinge, infringe, singe, syringe, tinge, twinge, unhinge

INGER*
finger \ ˈfiŋ-gər\
see
AR**, ER*, OR*

finger, ladyfinger, linger, minnesinger, singer, slinger, wringer

INGER**
ginger \ ˈjin-jər\
see
AR**, ER*, OR*

ginger, harbinger, porringer

INGLE
single \ ˈsiŋ-gəl\
see
EL, LE

commingle, ingle, intermingle, jingle, Kris Kringle, mingle, shingle, single, surcingle, tingle

INGO
bingo \ ˈbiŋ-(̣)gō\
see
EAU, EW**, O*, OE*,
OT***, OUGH*, OW*,
OWE

bingo, dingo, flamingo, jingo, lingo, Santo Domingo

INGS
wings \ ˈwiŋz\
see
ING+s

apron strings, bearings, blessings, dwellings, innings, playthings, shillings, stockings, strings, things, wings

I SOUNDS

INGUE
meringue \mə-ˈraŋ\
see
ANG

meringue

INI
martini \mär-ˈtē-nē\
see
E*, EA*, EE*, I**, IE*,
Y**

Anno Domini, bikini, martini,
Mussolini

INIC
clinic \ˈkli-nik\
see
IC, ICK

actinic, clinic

INION
opinion \ə-ˈpin-yən\
see
ION**

dominion, minion, opinion,
pinion

INITY
infinity \in-ˈfi-nə-tē\
see
E*, EA*, EE*, I**, IE*,
ITY, Y**

consanguinity, femininity,
infinity, masculinity, trinity,
vicinity, virginity

INK
pink \ˈpiŋk\
see
INC

bethink, blink, bobolink, brink,
chewink, chink, clink, drink,
fink, hoodwink, India ink,
interlink, jink, kink, link, mink,
pen and ink, pink, prink, rink,
rinky-dink, shell shrink, sink,
slink, stink, think, wink

INKER
tinker \ˈtiŋ-kər\
see
AR**, ER*, OR*

blinker, diesinker, drinker,
pinker, stinker, thinker, tinker

INKLE
wrinkle \ˈriŋ-kəl\
see
EL, LE

crinkle, periwinkle, Rip van
Winkle, sprinkle, twinkle, wrinkle

INKS
links \ˈliŋ(k)s\
see
INK+*s*

cuff links, golf links, methinks

INKY
dinky \ˈdiŋ-kē\
see
E*, EA*, EE*, I**, IE*,
Y**

dinky, hinky, inky, kinky, pinky,
stinky

INN
inn \ˈin\
see
IN

Finn, inn

INNER
winner \ˈwi-nər\
see
AR**, ER*, OR*

dinner, inner, sinner, spinner,
thinner, tinner, winner

INNY
tinny \ˈti-nē\
see
E*, EA*, EE*, I**, IE*,
Y**

finny, hinny, ninny, shinny,
tinny, whinny

INO*
casino \kə-ˈsē-(ˌ)nō\
see
EAU, EW**, O*, OE*,
OT***, OUGH*, OW*,
OWE

bambino, casino, Filipino,
maraschino, merino, solferino

INO**
albino \al-ˈbī-(ˌ)nō\
see
EAU, EW**, O*, OE*,
OT***, OUGH*, OW*,
OWE

albino

INOUS
ominous \ˈä-mə-nəs\
see
OUS*

bituminous, libidinous,
luminous, mucilaginous,
multitudinous, mutinous,
ominous, platitudinous, resinous,
ruinous, villainous, voluminous

INSE
rinse \ˈrin(t)s\
see
INCE

rinse

INT
mint \ˈmint\

blueprint, cuckoopint, dint,
fingerprint, flint, footprint, glint,
hint, hoofprint, imprint, lint,
mezzotint, mint, peppermint,
print, reprint, Septuagint,
skinflint, spearmint, splint,
sprint, squint, stint, tint, varmint

INTER*
winter \ˈwin-tər\
see
AR**, ER*, OR*

printer, splinter, sprinter, winter

INTER**
inter \in-ˈtər\
see
ER**, URR

inter

INTH
hyacinth
\ˈhī-ə-(ˌ)sin(t)th\

absinth, Corinth, hyacinth,
jacinth, labyrinth, plinth,
terebinth

INTZ
chintz \ˈchin(t)s\
see
INCE, INT+s

blintz, chintz

INUS
minus \ˈmī-nəs\
see
US

Linus, minus, Plotinus, sinus

INX
jinx \ ˈjiŋ(k)s\
see
INK+*s*, YNX

jinx, minx, sphinx, syrinx

INY*
mutiny \ ˈmyü-tə-nē\
see
E*, EA*, EE*, I**, IE*,
Y**

destiny, hominy, ignominy,
mutiny, scrutiny

INY**
shiny \ ˈshī-nē\
see
E*, EA*, EE*, I**, IE*,
Y**

briny, Pliny, shiny, tiny

IO
curio \ ˈkyu̇r-ē- ˌō\
see
ARIO, EAU, EW**, O*,
OE*, OLIO, OT***,
OUGH*, OW*, OWE

adagio, agio, arpeggio, Bellagio,
braggadocio, cheerio, curio,
ex officio, Horatio, imbroglio,
impresario, intaglio, internuncio,
lothario, nuncio, oratorio, patio,
pistachio, presidio, punctilio,
radio, ratio, Rio, scenario,
Scipio, Scorpio, seraglio,
solfeggio, studio, tertio, trio

IOD
period \ ˈpir-ē-əd\
see
UD

Hesiod, period

IOL
vitriol \ ˈvi-trē-əl\
see
OL, OLE

viol, vitriol

IOM
axiom \ ˈak-sē-əm\
see
OM*, OME*

axiom, idiom

ION*
action \ˈak-shən\
see
ASION, ATION,
EGION, EON, ESSION,
IATION, ICTION,
ILION, ILLION, INION,
ISION, ISSION, ITION,
ON*, OSION, OTION,
UCTION, UN, UNION,
USION, UTION

abjection, abortion, absorption,
action, adhesion, adjunction,
affection, air-condition,
anthelion, ascension, assertion,
assumption, attention,
benefaction, bisection, bullion,
caution, circumscription,
circumspection, coercion,
collection, companion,
compulsion, conception,
concoction, concretion,
concussion, confection,
congestion, conjunction,
connection, contagion,
contortion, contraction,
contraption, convention,
conversion, correction,
corruption, counteraction,
crucifixion, cushion, deception,
decoction, defection, dejection,
description, dimension,
discretion, discussion,
disruption, distention,
distortion, diversion, election,
emotion, emulsion, erection,
exception, excursion,
expansion, extension, extortion,
extroversion, faction, fashion,
film version, fourth dimension,
function, gumption, inaction,
inattention, incorruption,
incursion, indigestion,
indiscretion, induction,
infraction, inhesion, injunction,
inquisition, insertion,
insurrection, intention,
interjection, interruption,
intervention, introspection,
introversion, invention,
inversion, irruption, junction,
lesion, maladaption, mansion,
medallion, mention, mullion,

ION*

objection, onion, oppression, option, passion, pension, perception, percussion, perfection, perihelion, perversion, petrifaction, pincushion, portion, precaution, predilection, prelection, presumption, prevention, proportion, proscription, protection, putrefaction, question, reaction, recollection, redaction, redemption, reflection, reflexion, refraction, rejection, religion, repercussion, resumption, resurrection, revulsion, sanction, scullion, section, selection, stallion, stanchion, subjection, subscription, suggestion, suspension, suspicion, tension, traction, transaction, transfixion, unction, version, vivisection

ION**
scorpion
\ ˈ skȯr-pē-ən\
see
IAN*, UN

accordion, Albion, battalion, carrion, centurion, champion, collodion, criterion, Endymion, enchiridion, gammadion, ganglion, Hyperion, Ixion, oblivion, orchestrion, Pygmalion, quaternion, rapscallion, scorpion

ION***
lion \ ˈ lī-ən\
see
UN

ant lion, dandelion, ion, lion, Orion, scion

IONAL
emotional
\i- ˈ mō-shə-nᵊl\
see
AL*

confessional, conventional, dimensional, emotional, exceptional, fractional, functional, intentional, international, irrational, national, notional, occasional, optional, precessional,

IONAL

professional, proportional, rational, recessional, sectional, sensational, traditional, transitional, vocational

IOR*
inferior \in-ˈfir-ē-ər\
see
AR**, ER*, OR*

anterior, excelsior, exterior, inferior, interior, mother superior, posterior, superior, ulterior, warrior

IOR**
senior \ˈsē-nyər\
see
AR**, ER*, OR*

behavior, junior, senior

IOR***
prior \ˈprī(-ə)r\
see
AR**, ER*, EYER, OR*,
UYER, Y*+*er*

prior

IORI
a priori
\ˌä-prē-ˈȯr-ē\
see
E*, EA*, EE*, I**, IE*,
Y**

a fortiori, a posteriori, a priori

IOS
adios \ˌä-dē-ˈōs\
see
OSE*

adios, Helios

IOSE
grandiose
\ˈgran-dē-ˌōs\
see
OSE*

grandiose, otiose

IOT**
patriot \ˈpā-trē-ət\
see
OT***

chariot, cheviot, compatriot, idiot, Judas Iscariot, patriot

I SOUNDS

IOT**
riot \ ˈrī-ət\
see
AIT**, AT***,
ATE**, EDIT, EIT**,
ERATE**, ERIT, ET**,
ETTE**, IATE**,
IBIT, ICATE**, ICIT,
ICKET, IDGET, IGOT,
IMATE*, INATE**,
IT, ITE***, OLATE*,
ORATE**, OSET, OT***,
UET***, UGGET, UIT*,
ULATE**, URATE*

riot

IOUS
cautious \ ˈkȯ-shəs\
see
ACIOUS, AMUS, EUS*,
OUS*, UOUS, US

adscititious, adventitious,
anxious, atrocious, auspicious,
bumptious, capricious, captious,
cautious, conscientious,
conscious, contagious,
contentious, delicious,
disputatious, egregious,
expeditious, ferocious, fictitious,
flagitious, inauspicious,
infectious, injudicious,
injurious, irreligious, judicious,
licentious, lugubrious, luscious,
malicious, meretricious, noxious,
nutritious, obnoxious, officious,
ostentatious, pernicious,
precious, precocious, pretentious,
prodigious, propitious, religious,
sacrilegious, scrumptious,
seditious, self-conscious,
subconscious, superstitious,
surreptitious, suspicious,
unconscious, vexatious, vicious

IOUS**
previous \ ˈprē-vē-əs\
see
ISS, OUS*

abstemious, acrimonious, amphibious, bilious, calumnious, ceremonious, commodious, compendious, copious, curious, delirious, dubious, envious, fastidious, felonious, furious, glorious, gregarious, harmonious, hilarious, ignominious, impecunious, imperious, impervious, industrious, ingenious, inglorious, inharmonious, insidious, invidious, laborious, luxurious, melodious, meritorious, multifarious, mysterious, nefarious, notorious, oblivious, obsequious, obvious, odious, opprobrious, parsimonious, penurious, perfidious, pluvious, precarious, previous, punctilious, rebellious, salubrious, sanctimonious, serious, specious, spurious, studious, supercilious, tedious, unceremonious, uxorious, vainglorious, various, vicarious, victorious

IP
clip \ ˈklip\

apostleship, battleship, buggy whip, catnip, censorship, championship, chip, clip, companionship, courtship, cowslip, dictatorship, dip, drip, equip, fellowship, fingertip, flip, gossip, grip, guardianship, harelip, hardship, hero-worship, hip, horsewhip, kinship, ladyship, leadership, lip, lordship, marksmanship, midship, nip, outstrip, ownership, parsnip, partnership, penmanship, phantom ship, pillow slip, pleasure trip, potato chip, quip, rocketship, round-trip, scholarship, scrip, ship,

IP
showmanship, sip, skip, slip, snip, spaceship, strip, tallow dip, trip, tulip, turnip, warship, whale ship, whip, worship, zip

IPAL
principal
\ ˈprin(t)-s(ə-)pəl\
see
AL*

municipal, principal

IPATE
anticipate
\an-ˈti-sə-ˌpāt\
see
AIGHT, AIT*, ATE*,
EAT**, EIGHT*

anticipate, dissipate, emancipate, participate

IPE
ripe \ ˈrīp\
see
YPE

bagpipe, blowpipe, gripe, guttersnipe, hornpipe, organ pipe, overripe, pipe, pitchpipe, rareripe, reed pipe, ripe, sideswipe, snipe, stovepipe, stripe, swipe, tripe, unripe, windpipe, wipe

IPER
piper \ ˈpī-pər\
see
AR**, ER*, OR*

piper, sandpiper, sniper, swiper, viper

IPH
caliph \ ˈkā-ləf\ *or*
\ ˈka-ləf\
see
IF*, IFF

caliph

IPLE
triple \ ˈtri-pəl\
see
EL, IPPLE, LE

multiple, participle, principle, triple

I SOUNDS

IPPER
dipper \ˈdi-pər\
see
AR**, ER*, OR*

Big Dipper, clipper, dipper, flipper, gallinipper, lady's slipper, ripper, shipper, skipper, slipper, tripper, worshipper, zipper

IPPLE
ripple \ˈri-pəl\
see
EL, IPLE, LE

cripple, nipple, ripple, stipple, tipple

IPSE
eclipse \i-ˈklips\
see
IP+s

eclipse, ellipse

IPSY
tipsy \ˈtip-sē\
see
E*, EA*, EE*, I**, IE*, Y**

Gipsy, tipsy

IPT
script \ˈskript\
see
IP+ed, YP+ed, YPT

conscript, manuscript, nondescript, postscript, script, transcript

IQUE
antique \(ˌ)an-ˈtēk\
see
EAK*, EEK, EKE, IEK, IK*

antique, bezique, cacique, clique, critique, Mozambique, oblique, perique, physique, pique, pratique, technique, unique

IR*
fir \ˈfər\
see
AR**, ARTYR, ER*, ERE***, IRR, OR*, URR, YRRH

astir, bestir, decemvir, elixir, fir, nadir**, Ophir, sir, stir, tapir, triumvir

IR**
souvenir
\ ˈsü-və-ˌnir\
see
EAR*, EER, ERE*,
IER***

emir, fakir, Kashmir, Mimir,
nadir*, souvenir, Vladimir, Ymir

IRCH
birch \ ˈbərch\
see
ERCH, URCH

besmirch, birch, smirch

IRCLE
circle \ ˈsər-kəl\
see
EL, LE

circle, encircle, semicircle

IRD
bird \ ˈbərd\
see
EARD*, ERD, IR*+*ed*,
ORD**, URD

bird, blackbird, catbird, gird,
jailbird, jaybird, lovebird,
mockingbird, railbird, third

IRE*
fire \ ˈfi(-ə)r\
see
IAR*, IER**, OIR*,
UIRE, Y**+*er*, YRE

admire, afire, aspire, attire,
backfire, barbwire, bonfire,
campfire, conspire, crossfire,
crosswire, desire, Devonshire,
dire, empire, expire, fire,
for hire, grandsire, gunfire,
haywire, hire, inspire, ire, live
wire, mire, misfire, perspire,
pismire, quagmire, respire,
retire, samphire, sapphire, satire,
shire, spare tire, spitfire, suspire,
tire, transpire, umpire, vampire,
wildfire, wire

IRE**
Worcestershire
\ ˈwˋus-tər-shir\
see
EAR*, EER, ERE*,
IER***, IR**, IRR

Ayrshire, Worcestershire

IRGE
dirge \ ˈdərj\
see
ERGE, OURGE

dirge

IRK
shirk \ ˈshərk\
see
ERK, ORK**

dirk, irk, kirk, quirk, shirk, smirk

IRL
girl \ ˈgər(-ə)l\
see
EARL, URL

flower girl, girl, skirl, swirl, twirl, whirl

IRM
firm \ ˈfərm\
see
ERM, IRM, ORM**

affirm, confirm, firm, infirm, squirm

IRON*
iron \ ˈī(-ə)rn\
see
EARN, ERN, IRN, URN

andiron, cast-iron, curling iron, flatiron, grappling iron, gridiron, iron, midiron, sadiron, wrought-iron

IRON**
environ \in-ˈvī-rən\
see
ON*, UN

Chiron, environ

IRST
first \ ˈfərst\
see
ORST, URST

first, thirst

IRT
dirt \ ˈdərt\
see
ERT, UIRT, URT

dirt, flirt, girt, hoopskirt, outskirt, redshirt, seagirt, shirt, skirt, stuffed shirt, undershirt

IRTH
birth \ ˈbərth\
see
EARTH, ORTH**

birth, firth, girth, mirth, rebirth

I SOUNDS

IRY
wiry \ ˈwī(-ə)r-ē\
see
E*, EA*, EE*, I**, IE*,
IRE*+*y*, Y**

miry, spiry, wiry

IS*
iris \ ˈī-rəs\
see
AIS, ALIS, ARIS, ASIS,
ATIS, ESIS, ICE**,
ISE****, ISS, OLIS,
ONIS, OPSIS, OSIS,
UCE**

aegis, amaryllis, ambergris,
analepsis, analysis, Annus
Mirabilis, Anubis, aphis,
apodosis, Artemis, Atlantis, axis,
caddis, Charybdis, clematis,
Clovis, crisis, de profundis, dis,
ephemeris, epidermis, finis,
gratis, ibis, ichthyornis, iris, Isis,
laryngitis, mantis, Memphis,
metamorphosis, morris,
myosotis, non compos mentis,
orris, Osiris, Paris, parvis, pelvis,
portcullis, proboscis, prognosis,
psychoanalysis, rara avis, sacred
ibis, salpiglossis, semper fidelis,
stephanotis, tennis, thesis,
Thetis, this, Tigris, trellis, Tunis,
verdigris

IS**
his \ˈhiz\
see
IZ

his, is, 'tis

IS***
chassis \ ˈcha-sē\
see
E*, EA*, EE*, I**, IE*,
Y**

Chablis, chamois, chassis,
marquis

ISAN
artisan \ ˈär-tə-zən\
see
AN**

artisan, Nisan, nonpartisan,
partisan

ISC
disc \ ˈdisk\
see
ISK

disc

ISE*
wise \ ˈwīz\
see
EYE+*s*, IE**+*s*, IGH+*s*,
IZE, Y+*s*

advise, anywise, apprise, arise,
catechise, chastise, circumcise,
coastwise, comprise, compromise,
contrariwise, crosswise, demise,
despise, devise, edgewise, enterprise,
exercise, exorcise, franchise,
improvise, incise, leastwise,
lengthwise, likewise, merchandise**,
moonrise, nowise, otherwise,
pennywise, revise, rise, sunrise,
supervise, surmise, surprise,
thuswise, unwise, weatherwise, wise

ISE**
precise \pri- ˈsīs\
see
ICE*

concise, merchandise, Paradise,
precise

ISE***
chemise \shə- ˈmēz\
see
EACE, EASE**, EESE**,
ESE**, ICE***, IECE

cerise, chemise, marquise, valise

ISE****
premise \ ˈpre-məs\
see
ISS

anise, mortise, practise, premise,
promise, treatise

ISER
miser \ ˈmī-zər\
see
AR*, ER*, IZE+*er*, OR*

appetiser, despiser, Kaiser, miser,
wiser

ISH
fish \ ˈfish\
see
EESH, ERISH, OLISH,
UISH

accomplish, admonish, apish, astonish, banish, blemish, bluefish, bookish, boorish, boyish, brackish, brandish, British, brutish, bulldoggish, burnish, butter dish, catfish, cattish, chafing dish, churlish, cloddish, clownish, coltish, Cornish, crawfish, dervish, devilish, elfish, embellish, English, establish, famish, fetish, finish, fish, Flemish, flourish, foolish, freakish, furbish, furnish, garish, garnish, girlish, goldfish, grayish, greenish, hashish, heathenish, hellish, hoggish, horseradish, impish, Irish, jellyfish, Jewish, knavish, lavish, loutish, mannish, mawkish, modish, monkish, Moorish, mulish, oafish, offish, ogreish, outlandish, paganish, parish, peevish, pound-foolish, priggish, prudish, publish, punish, radish, rakish, ravish, reddish, relish, replenish, rubbish, sawfish, selfish, sheepish, shellfish, shrewish, skirmish, skittish, slavish, sluggish, snobbish, Spanish, squeamish, starfish, stiffish, sunfish, swish, swordfish, tarnish, ticklish, undiminish, vanish, varnish, waggish, waspish, whirling dervish, whitish, wish, Yiddish

ISHER
fisher \ ˈfi-shər\
see
AR*, ER*, OR*

fisher, garnisher, kingfisher, publisher, well-wisher

ISION
vision \ ˈvi-zhən\
see
ION*

decision, derision, division, elision, envision, incision, indecision, precision, prevision, provision, revision, supervision, television, vision

ISK
risk \ ˈrisk\
see
ISQUE

asterisk, basilisk, brisk, disk, frisk, obelisk, risk, tamarisk, whisk

ISKY
frisky \ ˈfris-kē\
see
E*, EA*, EE*, I**, IE*,
Y**

frisky, risky, whisky

ISLE
aisle \ ˈī(-ə)l\
see
ILE*

aisle, Carlisle, Emerald Isle, Fair Isle, lisle

ISM
organism
\ ˈȯr-gə-ˌni-zəm\
see
AISM, ALISM, ICISM,
ONISM, UISM, YSM

actinism, altruism, analogism, anthropomorphism, aphorism, archaism, asterism, atavism, baptism, barbarism, Bolshevism, Brahmanism, Buddhism, catechism, chauvinism, chrism, collectivism, conservatism, despotism, dynamism, egoism, egotism, empiricism, epicurism, exorcism, Fascism, galvanism, Hebraism, henotheism, heroism, hyperbolism, incendiarism, Islamism, Judaism, Lamaism, magnetism, mannerism, mechanism, mesmerism, metabolism, microorganism, modernism, monotheism, Nazism, nepotism, nihilism, occultism, optimism, organism, ostracism, pacifism, paganism, pantheism, pessimism, phallicism, polytheism, prism,

I SOUNDS

ISM
proletarianism, propagandism, pugilism, purism, quietism, recidivism, republicanism, rheumatism, rowdyism, sabbatism, sadism, schism, Shiism, skepticism, solecism, somnambulism, sophism, surrealism, sybaritism, syllogism, symbolism, theism, tokenism, totemism, vandalism, voodooism, witticism

ISON*
unison \ˈyü-nə-sən\
see
ON*

caparison, comparison, garrison, imprison, jettison, orison, prison, unison, venison

ISON**
bison \ˈbī-sən\
see
ON*

bison

ISP
crisp \ˈkrisp\

crisp, lisp, will-o'-the-wisp, wisp

ISQUE
bisque \ˈbisk\
see
ESQUE, ISK

bisque, odalisque

ISS
miss \ˈmis\
see
ICE**, IS*, ISE****,
YSS

amiss, bliss, dismiss, hiss, kiss, miss, Swiss, remiss

ISSION
mission \ˈmi-shən\
see
ION*

admission, emission, intermission, mission, omission, permission, remission, submission, transmission

IST*
artist \ ˈär-tist\
see
OGIST, ONIST, UIST,
YST*

alarmist, alchemist, apiculturist, artist, atheist, atomist, atwist, balladist, banjoist, Baptist, bicyclist, bigamist, Bonapartist, caricaturist, cartoonist, chemist, cist, colonist, columnist, Communist, conformist, consist, copyist, cubist, cyclist, deist, dentist, desist, druggist, egoist, egotist, equilibrist, enlist, eucharist, evangelist, exist, exorcist, fabulist, Fascist, fatalist, feminist, fist, florist, futurist, gist, glossarist, grist, herbalist, hist, hobbyist, homilist, humorist, insist, journalist, jurist, leftist, list, lobbyist, loyalist, Methodist, miniaturist, mist, moralist, motorist, naturalist, nihilist, nonconformist, novelist, nudist, obscurantist, occultist, Oliver Twist, opportunist, optimist, optometrist, organist, orientalist, pacifist, palmist, parodist, Paulist, persist, pessimist, pharmacist, philatelist, physicist, physiognomist, physiologist, pianist, plagiarist, polytheist, propagandist, psalmist, psychist, pugilist, purist, pyramidologist, quietist, realist, resist, revivalist, rhapsodist, rightist, ritualist, Romanist, royalist, sadist, satirist, scientist, shortist, soloist, somnambulist, sophist, specialist, strategist, stylist, subsist, surrealist, taxlist, theist, theurgist, tourist, Trappist, twist, violinist, vocalist, whist, wrist, wist

I SOUNDS

IST**
Christ \ˈkrīst\
see
ICE+*ed*

Christ

ISTA
vista \ˈvis-tə\
see
A**

ballista, genista, vista

ISTE
artiste \är-ˈtēst\
see
EAST*, EECE+*ed*,
IECE+*ed*, IEST**, YST**

artiste, batiste, modiste

ISTER
mister \ˈmis-tər\
see
AR**, ER*, OR*

administer, barrister, blister,
canister, minister, mister,
register, sinister, sister

ISTIC
statistic \stə-ˈtis-tik\
see
IC, ICK

altruistic, anachronistic, animistic,
anomalistic, artistic, cabalistic,
Calvinistic, casuistic, characteristic,
deistic, egoistic, egotistic,
euphuistic, fatalistic, inartistic,
Jehovistic, linguistic, militaristic,
modernistic, optimistic,
pantheistic, pessimistic, phlogistic,
realistic, ritualistic, sadistic,
spiritistic, statistic

ISTLE
bristle \ˈbri-səl\
see
EL, ISSILE, LE

bristle, epistle, gristle, thistle,
whistle

ISTRY
chemistry
\ˈke-mə-strē\
see
E*, EA*, EE*, I**, IE*,
Y**

artistry, chemistry, ministry,
palmistry, papistry, registry,
sophistry

I SOUNDS

IT
bit \ ˈbit\
see
AIT**, AT***, ATE**,
EDIT, EIT**, ERATE**,
ERIT, ET**, ETTE**,
IATE**, IBIT, ICATE**,
ICIT, ICKET, IDGET,
IGOT, IMATE*,
INATE**, IOT**,
ITE***, OLATE*,
ORATE**, OSET, OT***,
UET***, UGGET, UIT*,
ULATE**, URATE*

accredit, adit, admit, affidavit,
audit, bandit, befit, benefit,
bit, bottomless pit, bowsprit,
chit, coal pit, cockpit, comfit,
commit, cubit, culprit, davit,
debit, decrepit, deposit, digit,
discomfit, dispirit, emit, exit,
explicit, fit, flit, grit, habit, half-
wit, hermit, hit, Holy Writ, illicit,
inhabit, intermit, ipse dixit, it,
jack-in-the-pulpit, kit, knit,
lamplit, licit, lickety-split, limit,
lit, makeup kit, manumit, misfit,
moonlit, nimble-wit, nit, nitwit,
no-hit, obit, omit, orbit, outfit,
outwit, permit, pit, plaudit, posit,
preterit, profit, prohibit, prosit,
pulpit, pundit, rabbit, rarebit,
refit, remit, revisit, Sanskrit, sit,
skit, slit, so be it, spirit, spit,
split, sprit, starlit, stone pit,
submit, summit, tidbit, tit, to
wit, transit, twit, unfit, unit, visit,
vomit, Welsh rabbit, whit, wit,
writ

ITABLE
charitable
\ ˈcher-a-ta-bəl\
see
ABLE*, IBAL*

charitable, habitable, hospitable,
illimitable, indubitable,
inevitable, inhospitable,
inimitable, profitable, veritable

ITAL
vital \ ˈvī-tᵊl\
see
AL*

recital, requital, vital

ITAL
capital \ ˈka-pə-tᵊl\
see
AL*

capital, hospital, marital, non-
commital, orbital

I SOUNDS

ITAN
puritan \ˈpyu̇r-ə-tən\
see
AN**

cosmopolitan, metropolitan,
Neapolitan, puritan, Samaritan

ITANT
militant \ˈmil-i-tənt\
see
ANT**, ENT**

annuitant, concomitant,
exorbitant, habitant, inhabitant,
irritant, militant, visitant

ITATE
meditate
\ˈme-də-ˌtāt\
see
AIGHT, AIT*, ATE*,
EAT**, EIGHT*

agitate, cogitate, felicitate,
gravitate, gurgitate, hesitate,
imitate, incapacitate, irritate,
meditate, necessitate, precipitate,
premeditate, regurgitate,
rehabilitate, solicitate

ITCH
pitch \ˈpich\
see
ICH

backstitch, bewitch, bitch, ditch,
featherstitch, flitch, hemstitch,
hitch, itch, lockstitch, low pitch,
pitch, stitch, switch, twitch,
tzarevitch, whipstitch, witch

ITE*
kite \ˈkīt\
see
EIGHT**, IGHT, YTE

aconite, Adamite, aerolite,
Ammonite, anchorite,
anthracite, appetite, apposite,
ashy white, backbite, bite,
blatherskite, bobwhite, box
kite, Canaanite, Carmelite,
cenobite, cite, contrite, cyanite,
despite, dolomite, dynamite,
ebonite, Edomite, eremite,
erudite, excite, expedite, finite,
frostbite, graphite, Hepplewhite,
hermaphrodite, hoplite, incite,
indite, invite, Israelite, Jacobite,
kite, labradorite, lazulite, lignite,
lyddite, malachite, meteorite,
milk white, mite, Muscovite,
Nazarite, niccolite, parasite,
phosphite, plebiscite, polite,
quite, recite, recondite, requite,
rite, satellite, Semite, Shiite, site,
smite, socialite, spite, sprite,

ITE*

stalactite, stalagmite, suburbanite, sulphite, Sybarite, termite, thalmite, theodolite, trite, underwrite, unite, vulcanite, white, write

ITE**
infinite \ ˈin-fə-nət\
see
AIT**, AT***,
ATE**, EDIT, EIT**,
ERATE**, ERIT, ET**,
ETTE**, IATE**,
IBIT, ICATE**, ICIT,
ICKET, IDGET, IGOT,
IMATE*, INATE**,
IOT**, IT, OLATE*,
ORATE**, OSET, OT***,
UET***, UGGET, UIT*,
ULATE**, URATE*

definite, exquisite, favorite, granite, indefinite, infinite, opposite, perquisite, prerequisite, requisite

ITE***
marguerite
\ ˌmär-gə-ˈrēt\
see
EAT*, EET, ETE

marguerite, petite

ITER*
arbiter \ ˈär-bə-tər\
see
AR**, ER*, OR*

arbiter, Jupiter, scimiter

ITER**
liter \ ˈlē-tər\
see
AR**, EAT*+*er*, EET+*er*,
ER*, ETER**, ETRE*,
OR*

liter

ITER***
writer \ ˈrī-tər\
see
AR**, IGHT+*er*, ITE*+*er*,
ER*, OR*

niter*, miter, typewriter, writer

I SOUNDS

ITH
with \ˈwi<u>th</u>\
see
YTH

aerolith, blacksmith, forthwith, frith, goldsmith, kith, Lilith, locksmith, megalith, monolith, neolith, pith, silversmith, smith, with, zenith

ITHE
tithe \ˈtī<u>th</u>\
see
YTHE

blithe, lithe, tithe, writhe

ITHER
wither \ˈwi-<u>th</u>ər\
see
AR**, ER*, OR*

dither, hither, nowhither, slither, thither, whither, wither, zither

ITHM
logarithm
\ˈlȯ-gə-ˌri-<u>th</u>əm\
see
YTHM

logarithm

ITI
Tahiti \tə-ˈhē-tē\
see
E*, EA*, EE*, I**, IE*,
Y**

Tahiti, wapiti

ITIC
critic \ˈkri-tik\
see
IC, ICK

critic, mephitic, parasitic

ITION
edition \i-ˈdi-shən\
see
ION*

abolition, admonition, air-condition, ambition, apparition, apposition, attrition, audition, coalition, cognition, coition, competition, composition, condition, contrition, decomposition, disposition, ebullition, edition, exhibition, expedition, exposition, extradition, fruition, ignition,

ITION

imposition, inhibition, Inquisition, intuition, juxtaposition, munition, nutrition, opposition, partition, perdition, petition, position, predisposition, premonition, prohibition, recognition, recondition, rendition, repetition, requisition, sedition, special edition, superstition, supposition, tradition, tuition, volition

ITIVE
fugitive \ˈfyü-jə-tiv\
see
IVE**

auditive, competitive, fugitive, genitive, infinitive, inquisitive, intransitive, partitive, primitive, prohibitive, punitive, sensitive, transitive, volitive

ITO
mosquito
\mə-ˈskē-(ˌ)tō\
see
EAU, EW**, O*, OE*,
OT***, OUGH*, OW*,
OWE

incognito, mosquito, Quito

ITOR
visitor \ˈvi-zə-tər\
see
AR**, ER*, OR*

auditor, competitor, creditor, depositor, editor, inquisitor, janitor, monitor, progenitor, servitor, solicitor, suitor, traitor, visitor

ITOUS
calamitous
\kə-ˈla-mə-təs\
see
OUS*, US

calamitous, circuitous, felicitous, gratuitous, iniquitous, solicitous, ubiquitous

ITTER
bitter \ˈbi-tər\
see
AR**, ER*, OR*

bitter, flitter, fritter, glitter, jitter, litter, outfitter, quitter, sitter, titter, transmitter, twitter

I SOUNDS

ITTLE
little \ ˈli-tᵊl\
see
EL, IDDLE, LE

belittle, brittle, lickspittle, little, spittle, tittle, vittle, whittle

ITTY
witty \ ˈwi-tē\
see
E*, EA*, EE*, I**, IE**,
Y**

ditty, gritty, kitty, nitty-gritty, witty

ITUDE
attitude \ ˈa-tə-ˌtüd\
see
UDE, UE*+*ed*

altitude, amplitude, aptitude, attitude, beatitude, certitude, decreptitude, exactitude, fortitude, gratitude, habitude, inaptitude, incertitude, ineptitude, infinitude, ingratitude, lassitude, latitude, longitude, magnitude, multitude, negritude, platitude, plenitude, promptitude, rectitude, servitude, similitude, solicitude, solitude, turpitude, verisimilitude, vicissitude

ITUM
ad infinitum
\ad-ˌin-fə-ˈnī-təm\
see
AM**, UM

ad infinitum, ad libitum

ITURE
furniture
\ ˈfər-ni-chər\
see
AR**, ER**, IR*, OR*,
URR

discomfiture, expenditure, forfeiture, furniture, garniture, geniture, investiture, portraiture, primogeniture

ITUTE
institute
\ ˈin(t)-stə-ˌtüt\
see
OOT, UTE

constitute, destitute, institute, prostitute, substitute

ITY
city \ ˈsi-tē\
see
ACITY, ALITY, ANITY,
ARITY, E*, EA*, EE**,
EITY, ENITY, ERITY,
EVITY, I**, ICITY,
IDITY, IE*, ILITY,
IMITY, INITY, IVITY,
OCITY, ORITY, OSITY,
UITY, UNITY, URITY,
Y**

absurdity, alacrity, amity,
anonymity, benignity, caducity,
calamity, cavity, celebrity,
chastity, city, comity, complexity,
concavity, conformity, corporeity,
credulity, deformity, density,
depravity, dignity, enmity,
enormity, entity, equality,
eternity, fatality, fecundity,
fidelity, fraternity, frivolity,
gravity, heredity, identity,
immensity, indemnity, indignity,
inequality, infidelity, infirmity,
integrity, intensity, jollity, laity,
laxity, maternity, necessity,
nonconformity, nonentity,
nudity, nullity, obesity, oddity,
paucity, perplexity, perversity,
pity, polity, probity, profundity,
prolixity, propensity, quality,
quantity, Radio City, rotundity,
salubrity, sanctity, sanity, scarcity,
self-pity, solemnity, spontaneity,
suavity, taciturnity, tensity,
uniformity, university, varsity,
velocity

ITZ
fritz \ ˈfrits\
see
IT+*s*, UIT*+*s*

fritz, sitz

ITZER
howitzer
\ ˈhau̇-ət-sər\
see
AR**, ER*, OR*

howitzer, kibitzer, spritzer

IUM*
atrium \ˈā-trē-əm\
see
AM**, EUM, OM*,
OME*, ORIUM, UM

alluvium, aquarium, atrium,
bdellium, Byzantium, calcium,
chromium, compendium,
cranium, decennium, delirium,
delphinium, diluvium, effluvium,
elysium, encomium, eulogium,
euphorbium, exordium,
geranium, gymnasium,
harmonium, helium, herbarium,
iridium, magnesium, medium,
millennium, odium, opium,
opprobrium, osmium, palladium,
pandemonium, peculium,
pericranium, planetarium,
polonium, potassium, premium,
principium, proscenium,
protevangelium, radium,
scholium, selenium, sodium,
stadium, stramonium,
symposium, tedium, trifolium,
trillium, trivium, uranium

IUM**
Belgium \ˈbel-jəm\
see
AM**, OM*, OME*, UM

Belgium, nasturtium

IUS*
radius \ˈrā-dē-əs\
see
US

Aquarius, Athanasius, Boëthius,
Cassius, Confucius, Dionysius,
expurgatorius, genius, Marcus
Aurelius, nisi prius, Pluvius,
Polonius, radius, Sagittarius,
Sirius, Stradivarius, Tiberius,
Titus Vesuvius

IVAL*
rival \ˈrī-vəl\
see
AL*

arrival, outrival, revival, rival,
survival

IVAL**
carnival \ˈkär-nə-vəl\
see
AL*

carnival, festival

IVATE
activate \ ˈak-tə-ˌvāt
see
AIGHT, AIT*, ATE*,
EAT**, EIGHT*

activate, cultivate, motivate,
recidivate, titivate

IVE*
alive \ə-ˈlīv
see
YVE

alive, archive, arrive, beehive,
chive, connive, contrive, deprive,
dive, endive, five, hive, live**,
ogive, revive, rive, skive, strive,
survive, thrive

IVE**
active \ ˈak-tiv
see
ATIVE, IEVE**, ITIVE,
OSIVE, OTIVE, USIVE

active, adhesive, aggressive,
attentive, captive, cohesive,
collective, compressive,
consumptive, convective,
convictive, cursive, decisive,
defective, descriptive, destructive,
detective, diminutive, directive,
elective, endive, eruptive,
executive, exhaustive, expansive,
expensive, expressive, extensive,
festive, forgive, furtive, give,
impassive, inactive, incentive,
inexpensive, inoffensive,
instinctive, intensive, invective,
inventive, irrespective, Khedive,
live*, massive, misgive, missive,
objective, obstructive, offensive,
olive, oppressive, outlive, passive,
pendentive, pensive, perceptive,
perspective, persuasive,
pervasive, perversive, plaintive,
presumptive, progressive,
projective, prospective,
radioactive, receptive,
reflective, respective, restive,
retentive, retrogressive, rive,
secretive, selective, sportive,
suasive, subjective, submissive,
substantive, subversive,
suggestive, susceptive, vindictive,
votive

IVEL
swivel \ ˈswi-vəl\
see
AL*, EL, LE

drivel, shrìvel, snivel, swivel

IVER*
diver \ ˈdī-vər\
see
ER*, OR*

diver, driver, screwdriver, slave driver

IVER**
liver \ ˈli-vər\
see
AR**, ER*, IVE**+*er*,
OR*

deliver, giver, lawgiver, liver, quiver, river, shiver, sliver

IVERY
delivery
\di- ˈli-v(ə-)rē\
see
E*, EA*, EE*, I**, IE*,
Y**

delivery, livery

IVES
hives \ ˈhīvz\
see
IVE*+*s*

archives, hives, housewives, pocketknives

IVET
trivet \ ˈtri-vət\
see
ET, IVOT

civet, privet, rivet, trivet

IVITY
activity \ak- ˈti-və-tē\
see
E*, EA*, EE*, I**, IE*,
ITY, Y**

acclivity, activity, captivity, declivity, festivity, inactivity, nativity, objectivity, passivity, proclivity, receptivity, relativity, selectivity

IX
six \ˈsiks\
see
IC+s, ICK+s, YX

administratrix, affix, Aix,
appendix, betwixt, calix, cicatrix,
crucifix, dominatrix, fix,
intermix, janitrix, matrix, mix,
nix, Phoenix, prefix, prolix,
radix, semper felix, six, spadix,
suffix, testatrix, transfix

IXT
betwixt \bi-ˈtwikst\
see
IX+ed

betwixt, 'twixt

IZ
whiz \ˈwiz\
see
IS**, IZZ, UIZ

biz, hafiz, phiz, quiz, rheumatiz,
whiz

IZE
prize \ˈprīz\
see
ALIZE, EYE+s, IES*,
ISE*, ONIZE, UISE*

advertize, anathematize, anglicize,
apologize, apotheosize, assize,
atomize, attitudinize, authorize,
baptize, barbarize, botanize,
capsize, cauterize, centralize,
civilize, criticize, crystallize,
demobilize, demoralize,
deodorize, emphasize, energize,
epitomize, eulogize, evangelize,
extemporize, familiarize, fertilize,
fossilize, fraternize, galvanize,
gormandize, hybridize, idolize,
itemize, jeopardize, latinize,
lionize, memorize, mercerize,
mesmerize, minimize, mobilize,
modernize, monopolize,
neutralize, Nobel prize, organize,
ostracize, overemphasize, oxidize,
particularize, plagiarize, polarize,
popularize, prize, proselytize,
pulverize, rhapsodize, recognize,
satirize, scandalize, scrutinize,
sensitize, size, solemnize,
soliloquize, stabilize, sterilize,
stigmatize, syllogize, sympathize,

IZE

synchronize, temporize, terrorize, theorize, tranquilize, undersize, utilize, vaporize, victimize

IZEN*
citizen \ˈsi-tə-zən\
see
EN**

citizen, denizen

IZEN**
wizen \ˈwi-zᵊn\
see
EN**

bedizen, wizen

IZER
appetizer
\ˈa-pə-ˌtī-zər\
see
AR**, ER*, OR*

appetizer, atomizer, criticizer, fertilizer, organizer, vocalizer

IZZ
fizz \ˈfiz\
see
IS**, IZ

fizz, gin fizz

IZZLE
sizzle \ˈsi-zəl\
see
EL, LE

drizzle, fizzle, frizzle, grizzle, sizzle, swizzle

SOUNDS

O*
bravo \ ' brä-( )vō\
see
ADO*, ADO**, AGO*,
AGO**, AGO***, ALO,
ANGO, ANO, ANTO,
AO, ARGO, ATO*,
ATO**, EAU, EDO,
EGO, ELLO, ENDO,
ENTO, EO, ERO, ESTO,
ETO, ETTO, EW**, ICO,
ILLO, IMO, INGO, INO,
IO, ITO, OE*, OLO,
OSO, OT***, OTTO,
OUGH*, OW*, OWE

accelerando, afro, akimbo,
Alamo, alfresco, allegro, alterego,
ambo, antipasto, Apollo, Aquilo,
arroyo, auto, autogiro, banjo,
basso, basso profundo, basso
relievo, bilbo, bravo, broncho,
buffalo, burro, Cairo, Callisto,
Calypso, centimo, chiaroscuro,
chromo, Colombo, concerto,
cui bono, de facto, Dido,
ditto, dodo, domino, Draco,
dynamo, echo, ego, embryo,
ergo, Eskimo, fiasco, forego,
fresco, fro, gaucho, gazebo,
ginkgo, go, guano, gusto, halo,
hidalgo, hobo, indigo, inferno,
in toto, ipso facto, Jericho, jocko,
junco, Juno, kilo, kimono, lasso,
libido, Lido, limbo, llano, lo,
maestro, majordomo, manifesto,
mestizo, Michaelangelo, Milano,
Monaco, Monte Carlo, Monte
Cristo, Morocco, mumbo-
jumbo, Navajo, no, octavo, oho,
Orinoco, Palermo, papagayo,
perfecto, peso, photo, piano,
pianissimo, pico, Pizarro,
placebo, Pluto, Po, poncho,
prestissimo, primo, pro,
proviso, proximo, pueblo,
quarto, Quasimodo, rancho,
recto, righto, rococo, Salerno,
salvo, San Diego, San Francisco,
Sappho, Sargasso, secundo,
shako, Shinto, silo, sirocco, so,
so-and-so, soho, soprano, so-so,
status quo, stucco, Tabasco,

O*

tallyho, tardo, taro, tempo, Terra del Fuego, testudo, theorbo, to and fro, tobacco, Tokyo, torso, tyro, ultimo, undergo, verso, veto, Virgo, volcano, water buffalo, yo-yo, Zeno

O**
do \ ˈdü\
see
EW*, IEU, IEW, OE**,
OO, OU*, OUGH****,
OUS**, OUT**, OUX,
U, UE*, UT

ado, came to, do, heave to, hitherto, how do you do, lean-to, outdo, overdo, that will do, thereunto, to, to-do, two, underdo, undo, unto, well-to-do, we two, who

OA*
boa \ ˈbō-ə\
see
A**

Balboa, boa, goa, proa, protozoa, Samoa

OA**
whoa \ ˈwō\
see
EAU, EW**, O*, OE*,
OT***, OUGH*, OW*,
OWE

cocoa, whoa

OACH
coach \ ˈkōch\
see
OCHE

approach, broach, coach, cockroach, encroach, poach, reproach, roach, slow coach, stagecoach

OAD*
toad \ ˈtōd\
see
ODE, OW*+*ed*, OWE+*ed*

carload, crossroad, goad, high road, horned toad, inroad, load, overload, railroad, road, shipload, toad, tree toad, unload, woad

OAD**
broad \ ˈbrȯd\
see
AW+*ed*

abroad, broad

OAF
loaf \ ˈlōf\

loaf, oaf

OAK
soak \ ˈsōk\
see
OKE

bath cloak, cloak, croak, oak,
soak, uncloak

OAL
coal \ ˈkōl\
see
OL*, OLE, OUL**

charcoal, coal, foal, goal, shoal

OAM
foam \ ˈfōm\
see
OMB**, OME**

foam, gloam, loam, roam,
Siloam, sea foam

OAN
loan \ ˈlōn\
see
ONE*

bemoan, groan, loan, moan, roan

OAP
soap \ ˈsōp\
see
OPE*

soap

OAR
boar \ ˈbȯr\
see
OOR, ORE

bezoar, boar, hoar, roar, soar,
uproar, wild boar

OARD*
board \ ˈbȯrd\
see
OAR+*ed*, OR+*ed*, ORD*,
ORE+*ed*

aboard, aboveboard, all aboard,
baseboard, billboard, blackboard,
board, buckboard, cardboard,
checkerboard, chessboard,
dashboard, hoard, inboard,
keyboard, lapboard, larboard,
mortarboard, Ouija board,
outboard, overboard, pasteboard,
school board, shipboard,
shuffleboard, sideboard, signboard,
sounding board, switchboard

OARD**
cupboard \\ˈkə-bərd\\
see
EARD*, ERD, IRD,
ORD**, URD

clapboard, cupboard, starboard

OAST
toast \\ˈtōst\\
see
OST**

boast, cinnamon toast, coast, dry toast, pot roast, roast, toast

OAT
boat \\ˈbōt\\
see
OTE

afloat, bloat, bluecoat, boat, bumboat, coat, cutthroat, ferryboat, float, fur coat, gloat, goat, gunboat, lifeboat, moat, motorboat, nanny goat, oat, overcoat, petticoat, redcoat, rowboat, sailboat, scapegoat, shoat, speedboat, steamboat, surcoat, throat, topcoat, turncoat, U-boat, waistcoat, whaleboat

OATH
oath \\ˈōth\\
see
OTH*

loath, oath

OAX**
see
OAK+*s*, OKE+*s*

coax, hoax

OB
mob \\ˈmäb\\
see
AB**, UAB

blob, bob, cob, corncob, fob, gob, heartthrob, hob, hobnob, job, knob, lob, mob, nabob, rob, slob, snob, sob, thingamabob, throb

OBATE
probate \\ˈprō-ˌbāt\\
see
AIGHT, AIT*, ATE*,
EAT**, EIGHT*

approbate, probate, reprobate

OBBER
robber \ ˈrä-bər\
see
AR**, ER*, OR*

clobber, dobber, jobber, robber, slobber

OBBLE
gobble \ ˈgä-bəl\
see
ABBLE**, EL, LE

bobble, cobble, gobble, hobble, wobble

OBBY
hobby \ ˈhä-bē\
see
E*, EA*, EE*, I**, IE*, Y**

blobby, bobby, hobby, knobby, lobby

OBE
robe \ ˈrōb\

disrobe, globe, lap robe, lobe, microbe, nightrobe, probe, robe, wardrobe

OBER
sober \ ˈsō-bər\
see
AR**, ER*, OR*

October, sober

OBLE
noble \ ˈnō-bəl\
see
EL, LE

ennoble, ignoble, noble

OC
croc \ ˈkräk\
see
OCH

croc, roc

OCAL*
local \ ˈlō-kəl\
see
AL*

bifocal, focal, local, vocal

OCAL**
equivocal
\i-ˈkwi-və-kəl\
see
AL*

equivocal, reciprocal

OCATE
locate \ˈlō-ˌkāt\
see
AIGHT, AIT*, ATE*,
EAT**, EIGHT*

allocate, dislocate, equivocate,
invocate, locate, reciprocate,
suffocate

OCH
loch \ˈläk\
see
OC, OCK*

antioch, epoch, loch, pibroch

OCHRE
ochre \ˈō-kər\
see
AR**, ER*, OAK+*er*,
OKE+*er*, OR*

ochre

OCITY*
velocity \və-ˈlä-sə-tē\
see
E*, EA*, EE*, I**, IE*,
ITY, Y**

atrocity, ferocity, reciprocity,
velocity

OCITY**
precocity
\pri-ˈkä-sə-tē\
see
E*, EA*, EE*, I**, IE*,
ITY, Y**

precocity

OCK*
block \ˈbläk\
see
OC, OCH

alpenstock, bedrock, block, bock,
bullock, burdock, chockablock,
chopping block, clock, cock,
crock, deadlock, dock, fetlock,

OCK*

firelock, flintlock, flock, forelock, frock, gamecock, grandfather clock, haycock, hemlock, hock, hollyhock, interlock, jabberwock, joint stock, knock, laughing-stock, livestock, lock, lovelock, mock, moss-grown rock, oarlock, o'clock, overstock, padlock, peacock, pock, poppycock, Plymouth Rock, rowlock, shamrock, shell shock, shock, shuttlecock, smock, sock, stock, stopcock, stumbling block, ticktock, traprock, unfrock, unlock, warlock, weathercock, wedlock, woodcock

OCK**
hammock \ˈha-mək\
see
ECK, IC, ICK

buttock, cassock, haddock, hammock, hassock, hillock, hummock, mattock, paddock, tussock, shaddock, Pollock

OCKER
locker \ˈlä-kər\
see
AR**, ER*, OR*

knickerbocker, knocker, locker, rocker, shocker

OCKET
pocket \ˈpä-kət\
see
ET

crocket, docket, locket, pickpocket, pocket, rocket, skyrocket, socket, sprocket

OCRE
mediocre
\ˌmē-dē-ˈō-kər\
see
AR**, ER*, OAK+er,
OCHRE, OKE+er, OR*

mediocre

OCT
concoct \kən-ˈkäkt\
see
OCK*+*ed*

concoct, decoct

OCUS
focus \ˈfō-kəs\
see
US

crocus, focus, hocus-pocus, locus

OD*
cod \ˈkäd\
see
AD**, ADE***, ODD,
UAD

bod, Cape Cod, clod, cod,
decapod, demigod, divining rod,
downtrod, dry-shod, ephod,
gastropod, God, goldenrod,
hexapod, hod, Land of Nod,
lightning rod, megapod, Nimrod,
nod, pea pod, plod, pod, prod,
ramrod, rod, roughshod, shod,
slipshod, sod, synod, tripod,
trod, unshod, well-shod

OD**
method \ˈme-thəd\
see
ID

method

ODA
soda \ˈsō-də\
see
A**

bicarbonate of soda, coda,
pagoda, soda

ODD
odd \ˈäd\
see
AD**, ADE***, OD*,
UAD*

odd

NOTHING RHYMES WITH ORANGE
NEAR RHYMES VS. NON-RHYMES

NOTHING RHYMES WITH orange . . . not in common American English, anyway. It's pronounced \ˈȯr(-ə)nj\, or "ornj." In some parts of the country, orange has two syllables: \ˈär-inj\. There are those who might argue that this version of *orange* rhymes with *door hinge* but it's a stretch, and what good does *that* pair of words do anyone?

Orange is not alone in its stubborn refusal to play nice with other words: there's an elite but powerful group of these stand-aloners, able to bring poets and songwriters to their knees with a single syllable or two. To name a few: *angry, bilge, chaos, circle, citrus, cudgel, cusp, dirndl, film, galaxy, gulf, hungry, igloo, kiln, monster, month, nothing, oink, pint, purple, silver, talc, tonsils,* and *wasp.*

Now it *is* true that you might be able to scour the globe and come up with mates for these independents. *Chilver* is an English dialect word that means ewe lamb. But if you used it in a poem or song, would most people know what you were talking about? No. It's also true that you can find *angry* and *hungry* listed in this dictionary under Y**, along with a few hundred other words that end with –*y* and share that sound. Beware! They're **near rhymes**, handy in a pinch but not nearly good enough for fine poetry. If you do happen to write yourself into a corner with a wily word like *orange*, don't despair. "Close, But No Cigar" (on page 46) will help you bring your stuff up to snuff.

ODE
code \ ˈkōd\
see
EW**+*ed*, OAD*,
OW*+*ed*, OWE+*ed*

abode, à la mode, anode, bode,
cathode, code, commode,
corrode, decode, discommode,
episode, epode, erode, explode,
forebode, incommode, lode,
mode, monopode, node, ode,
outmode, rode, strode

ODGE
dodge \ ˈdäj\

dislodge, dodge, hodgepodge,
lodge

ODIC
periodic \ ˈdäj\
see
IC, ICK

anodic, episodic, melodic, odic,
parodic, periodic, prosodic,
spasmodic

ODOX
orthodox
\ ˈȯr-thə- ˌdäks\
see
OCK+*s*, OX

heterodox, orthodox

ODY*
anybody
\ ˈe-nē -bə-dē \ *or*
\ ˈe-nē-bä-dē\
see
UDDY, UDY, E*, EA*,
EE*, I**, IE*, Y**

anybody, everybody, nobody,
somebody

ODY**
body \ ˈbä-dē\
see
E*, EA*, EE**, I**, IE*,
ODDY, Y**

body, disembody, embody

ODY***
custody \ ˈkəs-tə-dē\
see
E*, EA*, EE*, I**, IE*,
Y**

chiropody, custody, melody,
monody, parody, prosody,
psalmody, rhapsody, threnody

OE*
doe \ ˈdō\
see
EAU, EW**, O*, OT***,
OUGH*, OW*, OWE

aloe, Arapahoe, Crusoe, Defoe, doe, floe, foe, John Doe, mistletoe, oboe, pekoe, roe, sloe, throe, tiptoe, toe, woe

OE**
shoe \ ˈshü\
see
EW*, IEU, IEW, O**,
OO, OU*, OUGH****,
OUS**, OUT**, OUX,
U, UE*, UT***

canoe, horseshoe, overshoe, shoe, snowshoe, Tippecanoe

OEM
poem \ ˈpō-əm\
see
EM**

poem, proem

OER*
churchgoer
\ ˈchərch- ˌgō-ər\
see
ER*, OR*, OW*+*er*

churchgoer, o'er

OER**
doer \ ˈdü-ər\
see
ER*, EWER, IEW+*er*,
OR*, UE*+*er*

doer, evildoer, shoer

OF
of \ ˈəv\
see
OVE**

of, unheard of, thereof, whereof

OFF
off \ ˈȯf\
see
OUGH*****

cast-off, cutoff, doff, far-off, kick off, off, palm off, ring off, Romanoff, scoff, send-off, show-off, standoff, takeoff, tee off, toff

O SOUNDS

OFFER
offer \ ˈȯ-fər\
see
AR**, ER*, OR*

coffer, offer, proffer, scoffer

OFT
soft \ ˈsȯft\
see
OFF+*ed*, OUGH*****+*ed*

aloft, croft, hayloft, loft, oft, soft

OG
log \ ˈlȯg\
see
OGUE*

agog, backlog, befog, bog,
bullfrog, clog, cog, cranberry
bog, dog, eggnog, firedog, flog,
fog, frog, grog, groundhog, guide
dog, hedgehog, hog, hot dog, jog,
lapdog, leapfrog, log, peat bog,
polliwog, prairie dog, quahog,
road hog, seadog, sea hog, slog,
underdog, watchdog

OGA
yoga \ ˈyō-gə\
see
A**

Saratoga, toga, yoga

OGATE
interrogate
\in- ˈter-ə- ˌgāt\
see
AIGHT, AIT*, ATE*,
EAT**, EIGHT*

abrogate, arrogate, interrogate

OGE
doge \ ˈdōj\

doge, horologe, gamboge

OGEN
hydrogen
\ ˈhī-drə-jən\
see
EN**

cyanogen, estrogen, hydrogen,
nitrogen, oxyhydrogen

OGGLE
goggle \ ˈgä-gᵊl\
see
EL, LE

boggle, boondoggle, goggle, hornswoggle, joggle, toggle, woggle

OGGY
soggy \ ˈsä-gē\
see
E*, EA*, EE**, I**, IE*,
Y**

boggy, doggy, foggy, groggy, soggy

OGIC
logic \ ˈlä-jik\
see
IC, ICK

geologic, logic, pedagogic, philologic

OGIST
biologist
\bī-ˈä-lə-jist\
see
IST

anthologist, apologist, bacteriologist, biologist, craniologist, entomologist, etymologist, geologist, graphologist, neonatologist, neurologist, oncologist, ontologist, ornithologist, philologist, phrenologist, physiologist, psychologist, sinologist, teratologist

OGNE
cologne \kə-ˈlōn\
see
EWN**, OAN, ONE*,
OWN*

Boulogne, Bourgogne, cologne

OGRAM
kilogram
\ ˈkil-ə-ˌgram\
see
AGM, AM*, AMB,
AME**, AMN

ideogram, kilogram, monogram, parallelogram, program, radiogram, seismogram

OGRE
ogre \ ˈō-gər\
see
AR**, ER*, OR*

ogre

OGUE*
prologue \ˈprō-ˌlóg\
see
OG

analogue, apologue, catalogue,
Decalogue, demagogue, dialogue,
duologue, eclogue, epilogue,
monologue, mystagogue,
pedagogue, prologue, prorogue,
sinologue, theologue, travelogue

OGUE**
vogue \ˈvōg\

brogue, rogue, vogue

OGY
analogy \ə-ˈna-lə-jē\
see
E*, EA*, EE*, I**, IE*,
OLOGY, Y**

amphilogy, analogy, eulogy,
genealogy, logy, mineralogy,
pedagogy, stogy, tetralogy, trilogy

OH
oh \(ˈ)ō\
see
EAU, EW**, O*, OE*,
OT***, OUGH*, OW*,
OWE

oh, Pharaoh, Shiloh

OHL
kohl \ˈkōl\
see
OAL, OL*, OLE, OUL**

kohl

OI
hoi polloi
\ˌhói-pə-ˈlói\
see
OY

hoi polloi, borzoi

OICE
voice \ˈvóis\

choice, invoice, joice, rejoice,
voice

OID
void \ˈvóid\
see
OY+*ed*

alkaloid, aneroid, anthropoid,
asteroid, avoid, celluloid, deltoid,
devoid, ichthyoid, mattoid,
ornithoid, paranoid, planetoid,
rhomboid, spheroid, tabloid,
thyroid, typhoid, void

OIGN
coign \koin\
see
OIN

coign

OIF
coif \ ' kwäf\
see
OFF, OUGH*****

coif

OIL
boil \ ' bòi(-ə)l\
see
OYLE

boil, broil, cinquefoil, coil, despoil, embroil, foil, free-soil, hard-boil, midnight oil, oil, panbroil, parboil, quatrefoil, recoil, roil, salad oil, soil, spark coil, spoil, subsoil, tinfoil, toil, trefoil, turmoil, uncoil

OIN*
coin \ ' kòin\
see
OIGN

benzoin**, coin, disjoin, enjoin, groin, join, loin, purloin, rejoin, sirloin, subjoin, tenderloin

OIN**
see
OIGN

benzoin*, heroin

OINT
joint \ ' jòint\

anoint, appoint, dew point, disappoint, flash point, finger point, joint, needlepoint, point, standpoint, starting point, vanishing point, viewpoint, West Point

OIR*
choir \ ' kwī(-ə)r\
see
AR**, ER*, IER**, IRE*,
OR*, UIRE, Y*+*er*, YRE

choir

OIR**
memoir \ ' mem- wär\
see
AR*, ARE**

boudoir, memoir, noir, peignoir, reservoir

OIRE
armoire \ärm-ˈwär\
see
ARE**, OIR**

armoire, escritoire, pourboire, repertoire

OIS
patois \ˈpa-ˌtwä\
see
AH

chamois, patois

OISE*
noise \ˈnȯiz\
see
OY+s

counterpoise, equipoise, noise, poise, turquoise

OISE**
tortoise \ˈtȯr-təs\
see
ISS

porpoise, tortoise

OIST
hoist \ˈhȯist\
see
OICE+d

foist, hoist, joist, moist

OIT
adroit \ə-ˈdrȯit\

adroit, exploit, maladroit, quoit

OK
amok \ə-ˈmək\
see
UCK

amok

OKE
poke \ˈpōk\
see
OAK, OLK, OQUE

artichoke, awoke, bespoke, bloke, broke, choke, coke, convoke, downstroke, evoke, fog smoke, invoke, joke, moke, poke, provoke, revoke, Roanoke, smoke, spoke, stoke, stroke, sunstroke, upstroke, woke, yoke

OKEN
token \ ˈtō-kən\
see
EN**

bespoken, betoken, broken, Hoboken, outspoken, plainspoken, spoken, token, unspoken

OKER
joker \ ˈjō-kər\
see
AR**, ER*, OAK+*er*,
OCHRE, OCRE, OKE+*er*,
OR*

broker, choker, croker, joker, pawnbroker, poker, smoker, stockbroker, stoker

OL*
control \kən-ˈtrōl\
see
IOL, OLE

control, extol, frijol, idol, patrol, petrol, self-control, Tyrol

OL**
alcohol \ ˈal-kə-ˌhȯl\
see
ALL*, AUL, AWL, IOL

aerosol, alcohol, folderol, entresol, Lysol, menthol, parasol, protocol

OL***
carol \ ˈker-əl\
see
AL*

carol, gambol, idol, pistol, symbol

OLA*
gondola \ ˈgän-də-lə\
see
A**

cupola, gondola, parabola, pergola

OLA**
victrola \vik-ˈtrō-lə\
see
A**

carambola, cola, gorgonzola, Loyola, pianola, victrola, viola, Zola

OLATE*
desolate \ ˈde-sə-lət\
see
AIT**, AT***,
ATE**, EDIT, EIT**,
ERATE**, ERIT, ET**,
ETTE**, IATE**,
IBIT, ICATE**, ICIT,
ICKET, IDGET, IGOT,
IMATE*, INATE**,
IOT**, IT, ITE***,
ORATE**, OSET, OT***,
UET***, UGGET, UIT*,
ULATE**, URATE*

chocolate, desolate, disconsolate,
inviolate

OLATE**
violate \ ˈvī-ə- ˌlāt\
see
AIGHT, AIT*, ATE*,
EAT**, EIGHT*

etiolate, isolate, percolate, violate

OLD
cold \ ˈkōld\
see
OAL+*ed*, OL*+*ed*,
OLE+*ed*

age-old, behold, blindfold,
bold, cold, cuckold, enfold, fine
gold, fold, foothold, foretold,
fourfold, gold, hold, household,
hundredfold, kobold, manifold,
marigold, mold, ninefold,
old, scaffold, scold, sevenfold,
sheepfold, sold, stone-cold,
stranglehold, stronghold,
tenfold, thousandfold, threefold,
threshold, told, unfold, untold,
uphold, withhold, wold

OLDER
folder \ ˈfōl-dər\
see
AR**, ER*, OR*,
OULDER

bolder, colder, folder, holder,
landholder, older, shareholder,
smolder

OLE*
hole \\ ˈhōl\\
see
OAL, OL*, OLL*, OUL**

airhole, aureole, barber pole, barcarole, blowhole, bunghole, cajole, camisole, casserole, cole, condole, console, Creole, cubbyhole, dole, girandole, glory hole, ground mole, hole, keyhole, loophole, manhole, mole, North Pole, Old King Cole, oriole, parole, peephole, pigeonhole, pinhole, pistole, pole, ridgepole, rigmarole, role, Seminole, sole, South Pole, tadpole, tent pole, thole, totem pole, whole

OLE**
hyperbole
\\hī-ˈpər-bə-(̣)lē\\
see
E*, EA*, EE*, I**, IE*,
Y**

hyperbole

OLENT
violent \\ ˈvī-ə-lənt\\
see
ENT**

indolent, insolent, malevolent, redolent, somnolent, violent

OLF*
wolf \\ ˈwu̇lf\\

werewolf, wolf

OLF**
golf \\ ˈgälf\\

golf, rolf

OLI
broccoli \\ ˈbrä-kə-lē\\
see
E*, EA*, EE*, I**, IE*,
Y**

broccoli, Gallipoli, tivoli

OLIA
magnolia
\\mag-ˈnōl-yə\\
see
IA

Anatolia, magnolia, melancholia, Mongolia

OLIC*
frolic \ ˈfrä-lik\
see
IC, ICK

alcoholic, bucolic, carbolic, colic,
diabolic, frolic, nonalcoholic,
parabolic, symbolic

OLIC**
Catholic \ ˈkath-lik\ *or*
\ ˈka-thə- lik\
see
IC, ICK

Catholic

OLID
solid \ ˈsä-ləd\
see
ID, OD**

semisolid, solid, stolid

OLIN
lanolin \ ˈla-nə-lən\
see
IN, INE***

lanolin, mandolin, violin

OLIO
folio \ ˈfō-lē- ˌō\
see
EAU, EW**, IO, O*,
OE*, OT***, OUGH*,
OW*, OWE

folio, olio, portfolio

OLIS
metropolis
\mə- ˈträ-p(ə-)ləs\
see
ICE**, IS*, ISE****

acropolis, Annapolis, Heliopolis,
metropolis, necropolis, Persepolis

OLISH
abolish \ə- ˈbä-lish\
see
ISH

abolish, demolish, polish

OLK
folk \ ˈfōk\
see
OAK, OKE, OQUE

folk, kinsfolk, yolk

OLL*
roll \ˈrōl\
see
OL*, OLE, OUL**

boll, enroll, knoll, payroll, poll, roll, scroll, stroll, toll, troll, unroll

OLL**
doll \ˈdäl\

doll, loll, moll

OLLAR
dollar \ˈdä-lər\
see
AR**, ER*, OR*

collar, dollar

OLLY
jolly \ˈjä-lē\
see
E*, EA*, EE*, I**, IE*,
Y**

dolly, folly, golly, holly, jolly, molly, polly

OLO
solo \ˈsō-(ˌ)lō\
see
EAU, EW**, O*, OE*,
OT***, OUGH*, OW*,
OWE

Diavolo, gigolo, Marco Polo, piccolo, polo, solo, water polo

OLOGY
biology \bī-ˈä-lə-jē\
see
E*, EA*, EE*, I**, IE*,
OGY, Y**

anthology, apology, archaeology, astrology, biology, bryology, Christology, chronology, cryptology, dactylology, demonology, dermatology, doxology, ecology, Egyptology, eschatology, ethnology, etymology, geology, glossology, graphology, hagiology, homology, horology, ichthyology, ideology, lexicology, martyrology, meteorology, metrology, morphology, mythology, neology, nephology, nostology, numerology, odontology, oncology, ontology, ornithology, orthology, osteology, otology, pathology, penology,

OLOGY

philology, phonology, phraseology, phrenology, physiology, psychology, seismology, sinology, tautology, technology, teleology, teratology, terminology, theology, toxicology, zoology

OLT
bolt \ ˈbōlt\

bolt, colt, dolt, jolt, microvolt, molt, revolt, thunderbolt, volt

OLUTE
absolute \ ˈab-sə- ˌlüt\
see
UTE

absolute, dissolute, irresolute, resolute, volute

OLVE
solve \ ˈsälv\

absolve, devolve, dissolve, evolve, involve, resolve, revolve, solve

OLVER
revolver \ri- ˈväl-vər\
see
AR**, ER*, OR*

absolver, dissolver, resolver, revolver

OLY*
holy \ ˈhō-lē\
see
E*, EA*, EE*, I**, IE*,
Y**

holy, holy moly, melancholy***, moly, roly-poly, unholy

OLY**
monopoly
\mə- ˈnä-p(ə-)lē\
see
E*, EA*, EE*, I**, IE*,
Y**

monopoly

OLY***
melancholy
\ ˈme-lən- ˌkä-lē\
see
E*, EA*, EE*, I**, IE*,
Y**

melancholy

OM*
bottom \ ˈbä-təm\
see
AM**, EUM, IUM,
OME*, OSM, UM, UMB

accustom, besom, blossom,
boredom, bosom, bottom,
buxom, cardamom, carom,
Christendom, custom, embosom,
envenom, Epsom, fathom,
freedom, from, hansom,
heathendom, kingdom, lissom,
maelstrom, martyrdom,
officialdom, phantom, pogrom,
random, ransom, rock-bottom,
serfdom, Sodom, stardom,
symptom, unbosom, venom,
whilom, wisdom

OM**
whom \ ˈhüm\
see
OOM, UME

whom

OM***
mom \ ˈmäm\
see
AM***, OMB*

mom, tom-tom

OMA
coma \ ˈkō-mə\
see
A**

aroma, coma, diploma, La
Paloma, Oklahoma, soma, stoma

OMB*
bomb \ ˈbäm\
see
AM***, OM***

aplomb, bomb, rhomb

OMB**
comb \ ˈkōm\
see
OME**, UMB

catacomb, comb, coxcomb,
currycomb, hecatomb,
honeycomb, uncomb

OMB***
tomb \ ˈtüm\
see
OM**, OOM, UME

tomb, womb

OME*
come \ˈkəm\
see
AM**, IUM, UM, UMB,
UMN

become, blithesome,
burdensome, come, cumbersome,
fearsome, foursome, frolicsome,
gladsome, gruesome,
handsome, income, irksome,
lissome, loathsome, lonesome,
meddlesome, mettlesome,
noisome, outcome, overcome,
quarrelsome, rollicksome, some,
tiresome, toilsome, toothsome,
troublesome, venturesome,
wearisome, welcome, wholesome,
winsome

OME**
dome \ˈdōm\
see
OAM

chrome, chromosome, dome,
gnome, hippodrome, home,
metronome, monochrome,
palindrome, polychrome, Rome,
tome

OMEN
omen \ˈō-mən\
see
EN**

cognomen, omen

OMER*
customer
\ˈkəs-tə-mər\
see
AR**, ER*, OR*

astronomer, customer, incomer,
newcomer

OMER**
omer \ˈō-mər\
see
AR**, ER*, OR*

Homer, misnomer, omer

OMIC
comic \ˈkä-mik\
see
IC, ICK

atomic, comic, economic,
gastronomic, seriocomic,
tragicomic

OMING*
coming \ ˈkə-miŋ\
see
ING

blossoming, coming, incoming, oncoming

OMING**
homing \ ˈhō-miŋ\
see
ING

homing, Wyoming

OMO
chromo \ ˈkrō-(ˌ)mō\
see
EAU, EW**, O*, OE*,
OT***, OUGH*, OW*,
OWE

chromo, majordomo

OMP
stomp \ ˈstämp\
see
AMP**

pomp, romp, stomp, tromp

OMPT
prompt \ ˈpräm(p)t\
see
AMP**+*ed*, OMP+*ed*

prompt

OMY
economy
\i-ˈkä-nə-mē\
see
E*, EA*, EE*, I**, IE*,
Y**

anatomy, antinomy, economy, phlebotomy, physiognomy, zootomy

ON*
bacon \ ˈbā-kən\
see
AN**, ASON, AZON,
EACON, EASON, ELON,
EMON*, EMON**, ERON,
ETON, ICON**, ION*,
ISON, ODON, OHN,
OPHON, UN, UTTON

abandon, Anglo-Saxon, apron, Armageddon, backgammon, bacon, baron, beckon, beribbon, blazon, blue-ribbon, bouillon, Bourbon, bunion, cannon, canon, canton, canyon, carbon, cauldron, Charon, chevron, chiton, cinnamon, citron, colon, common, cordon, cotillion,

ON*

cotton, crimson, damson, Devon,
dodecahedron, donjon, eidolon,
emblazon, Emerson, falcon,
gallon, gibbon, gnomon, Gorgon,
grandson, griffon, gryphon,
guerdon, guncotton, halcyon,
horizon, jargon, Klaxon, liaison,
Lisbon, London, Mammon,
matron, mastodon, Mormon,
pardon, parson, patron,
pennon, person, phaeton,
piston, plastron, poison,
Poseidon, Princeton, reckon,
rhododendron, ribbon, salmon,
Samson, Saxon, semicolon,
sermon, sexton, Sheraton, Simple
Simon, simpleton, siphon,
Solomon, Solon, son, squadron,
summon, talon, tarpon, tendon,
triathlon, triton, uncommon,
wagon, wanton, Washington,
weapon, Welsh mutton

ON**
con \ ˈkän\

Agamemnon, Amazon, anon,
antiphon, Audubon, automaton,
Avalon, Babylon, bonbon, bon
ton, boustrophedon, caisson,
call upon, capon, carillon, carry-
on, Celadon, Ceylon, chanson,
chiffon, coupon, crouton,
don, egg on, electron, epsilon,
goings-on, hanger-on, head-on,
Huron, marathon, Memnon,
mignon, moron, myrmidon,
neuron, nylon, Oberon, on,
phenomenon, pompon, pro
and con, prolegomenon,
pylon, python, rayon, saffron,
salon, soupçon, tampon,
tetragrammaton, thereupon,
triathlon, trogon, upon,
whereon, yon, Yukon, zircon

ONA
corona
\kə-ˈrō-nə\
see
A**

Arizona, Barcelona, Bellona, cinchona, corona, Cremona, Desdemona, Latona, Pomona, Verona

ONAL
diagonal
\dī-ˈa-gə-nᵊl\
see
AL*

conditional, confessional, congressional, denominational, devotional, diagonal, dimensional, emotional, functional, gravitational, hexagonal, impersonal, international, national, notional, occasional, octagonal, optional, precessional, processional, prohibitional, rational, recessional, regional, seasonal, traditional, unconditional, vegetational, veronal, visional

ONARY
dictionary
\ˈdik-shə-ˌner-ē\
see
AIRY, ARRY*, ARY*, E*, EA*, EE*, ERY**, I**, IE*, Y**

dictionary, legionary, missionary, pulmonary, reactionary, revolutionary, stationary, visionary

ONATE
detonate
\ˈde-tə-ˌnāt\
see
AIGHT, AIT*, ATE*, EAT**, EIGHT*

detonate, impersonate, intonate, pulmonate

ONCE*
once \ˈwən(t)s\
see
UNCE

once

ONCE**
sconce \ˈskän(t)s\
see
ONSE

ensconce, nonce, sconce

ONCH
conch \ ˈkäŋk\
see
ONK

conch

OND*
bond \ ˈbänd\
see
AND***

abscond, beyond, blond, bond, correspond, despond, fond, frond, pond, respond, second, vagabond

OND**
diamond
\ ˈdī-(ə-)mənd\
see
AND**, END**

almond, diamond, Richmond, second, split-second

ONDA
anaconda
\ˌa-nə-ˈkän-də\
see
A**

anaconda, Gioconda, Golconda

ONDER*
ponder \ ˈpän-dər\
see
AR**, ER*, OR*

fonder, ponder, yonder

ONDER**
wonder \ ˈwən-dər\
see
AR**, ER*, OR*, UNDER

wonder

ONE*
alone \ə-ˈlōn\
see
EWN**, OAN, OGNE, OWN*

alone, anticyclone, atone, backbone, baritone, bloodstone, bone, breastbone, brimstone, brownstone, capstone, chaperone, cheekbone, cobblestone, condone, cone, cornerstone, crone, cross bone, curbstone, cyclone, dethrone, dictaphone, door stone, drone, fish bone, freestone, funny bone,

ONE*

gramophone, graphophone, gravestone, grindstone, halftone, headstone, hearthstone, herringbone, hone, intone, jackstone, jawbone, keystone, knucklebone, limestone, megaphone, microphone, milestone, millstone, monotone, moonstone, oilstone, outshone, overtone, ozone, paroxytone, philosopher's stone, pinecone, phone, postpone, prone, rawbone, rolling stone, Rosetta stone, sandstone, saxophone, scone, semitone, shinbone, shone, soapstone, stepping-stone, stone, telephone, throne, tombstone, tone, trombone, undertone, whalebone, whetstone, xylophone, Yellowstone, zone

ONE**
gone \ ˈgȯn\
see
AWN

agone, begone, bygone, gone, woebegone

ONE***
done \ ˈdən\
see
UN

done, none, one, outdone, overdone, someone, underdone, undone, well-done

ONENT
opponent
\ə-ˈpō-nənt\
see
ENT**

component, exponent, opponent

ONER
falconer \ ˈfal-kə-nər\
see
AR**, ER*, OR*, UN+*er*

almoner, executioner, falconer, practitioner, wagoner

ONES
Nones \ˈnōnz\
see
ONE*+*s*, OWN*+*s*

Nones, sawbones

ONET
bayonet \ˈbā-ə-nət\
see
ET

baronet, bayonet, canzonet, coronet

ONEY
honey \ˈhə-nē\
see
E*, EE*, EY*, I**, IE*,
Y**

honey, money, paper money, pin money

ONG*
long \ˈlȯɳ\

agelong, along, belong, cradlesong, ding-dong, evensong, folk song, furlong, gong, headlong, headstrong, Hong Kong, livelong, long, mahjong, oblong, oolong, ping-pong, prolong, prong, sarong, sidelong, singsong, siren song, song, strong, swan song, thong, throng, tong, war song, wrong

ONG**
among \ə-ˈməɳ\
see
ONGUE, UNG

among

ONGE
sponge \ˈspənj\
see
UNGE

sponge

ONGUE
tongue \ˈtəɳ\
see
ONG**, UNG

mother tongue, oxtongue, sacred tongue, silver tongue, tongue

O SOUNDS

ONI
macaroni
\ˌma-kə-ˈrō-nē\
see
E*, EA*, EE*, EY*, I**,
IE*, Y**

macaroni, Zamboni, yoni

ONIA
begonia \bi-ˈgōn-yə\
see
IA

ammonia, begonia, Caledonia,
Franconia, Harmonia,
Macedonia, Patagonia,
pneumonia

ONIC
tonic \ˈtä-nik\
see
IC, ICK

bubonic, chronic, cyclonic,
demonic, diatonic, electronic,
harmonic, histrionic, iconic,
Ionic, ironic, laconic, mnemonic,
moronic, Platonic, philharmonic,
polyphonic, sardonic, Slavonic,
symphonic, telephonic, Teutonic,
tonic

ONIS
Adonis \ə-ˈdä-nəs\
see
ICE**, IS*, ISE****, ISS

Adonis

ONISM
hedonism
\ˈhē-də-ˌni-zəm\
see
ISM

anachronism, antagonism,
exhibitionism, hedonism,
reactionism, synchronism,
unionism

ONIST
antagonist
\an-ˈtag-ə-nist\
see
IST

abolitionist, antagonist, hedonist,
impressionist, protagonist

ONIZE
agonize \ˈa-gə-ˌnīz\
see
EYE+*s*, IE**+*s*, IGH+*s*,
IZE, Y*+*s*

agonize, canonize, carbonize,
colonize, harmonize, lionize,
patronize

ONK*
honk \ˈhäŋk\
see
ONCH

bonk, conk, honk, zonk

ONK**
monk \ˈməŋk\
see
UNK

monk

ONLY*
commonly
\ˈkä-mən-lē\
see
E*, EA*, EE*, I**, IE*, Y**

commonly, matronly, wantonly

ONLY**
see
ONE*+ *ly*

only

ONNA
madonna
\mə-ˈdä-nə\
see
A**

belladonna, Madonna, prima donna

ONOUS
synchronous
\ˈsiŋ-krə-nəs\
see
OUS*

anachronous, autochthonous, cacophonous, gluttonous, poisonous, synchronous

ONRY
masonry
\ˈmā-sⁿn-rē\
see
E*, EA*, EE*, I**, IE*, Y**

blazonry, falconry, freemasonry, masonry

ONSE
response
\ri-ˈspän(t)s\
see
ONCE*

response

ONT*
front \ˈfrənt\
see
ANT***, UNT

confront, front, shirtfront,
waterfront

ONT**
don't \ˈdōnt\

don't, won't

ONT***
font \ˈfänt\
see
AUNT**

font, wont

ONTH*
millionth
\ˈmi(l)-yən(t)th\

billionth, millionth, trillionth

ONTH**
month \ˈmən(t)th\

month

ONY*
balcony \ˈbal-kə-nē\
see
E*, EA*, EE*, I**, IE*,
Y**

agony, antiphony, balcony,
betony, bryony, cacophony,
colony, disharmony, ebony,
euphony, felony, gluttony,
harmony, hegemony, monotony,
patrimony, peony, scammony,
theogony

ONY**
ceremony
\ˈser-ə-ˌmō-nē\
see
E*, EA*, EE*, I**, IE*,
Y**

acrimony, agrimony, alimony,
antimony, bony, bryony,
cacophony, ceremony,
chalcedony, crony, parsimony,
patrimony, phony, pony,
testimony

ONYM
synonym
\ˈsi-nə-ˌnim\
see
IM, IMB*, YMN

acronym, anonym, antonym,
homonym, pseudonym, synonym

ONZE
bronze \ˈbränz\

bonze, bronze

O SOUNDS

OO
bamboo \\( )bam-ˈbü\\
see
ABOO, EW*, O**,
OUGH****, U, UE*

ballyhoo, bamboo, bazoo, boo,
boo-hoo, cockatoo, coo, cuckoo,
goo, halloo, hoodoo, hullabaloo,
igloo, kangaroo, karoo, kazoo,
moo, shampoo, shoo, skidoo,
tattoo, too, toodle-oo, voodoo,
Waterloo, woo, yoo-hoo, zoo

OOB
boob \\ˈbüb\\
see
UBE

boob

OOCH*
mooch \\ˈmüch\\

hooch, mooch, pooch, scooch,
smooch

OOCH**
brooch \\ˈbrōch\\
see
OACH

brooch

OOD*
hood \\ˈhu̇d\\
see
OULD

basswood, boxwood, briar
wood, brushwood, candlewood,
childhood, cottonwood, deadwood,
dogwood, driftwood, falsehood,
fatherhood, firewood, good,
greenwood, hardihood, hood,
ironwood, knighthood, likelihood,
livelihood, logwood, matchwood,
misunderstood, monkhood,
motherhood, neighborhood, no
good, parenthood, priesthood,
Red Riding Hood, redwood, Robin
Hood, rosewood, sandalwood,
selfhood, stood, understood,
Wedgwood, wildwood, withstood,
wood

OOD**
flood \\ˈfləd\\
see
UD

blood, blue blood, cold blood,
flood

OOD***
brood \ ˈbrüd\
see
UDE

brood, food, mood, rood, snood

OODY*
moody \ ˈmü-dē\
see
E*, EA*, EE*, I**, IE*,
UTY, Y**

broody, moody

OODY*
goody \ ˈgu̇-dē\
see
E*, EA*, EE*, I**, IE*,
Y**

goody, woody

OOF*
aloof \ ˈgu̇-dē\

aloof, bombproof, bulletproof,
disproof, fireproof, foolproof,
galley proof, gas-proof, high
proof, hoof**, poof, proof,
rainproof, reproof, roof**,
shadoof, spoof, waterproof,
woof**

OOF**
hoof \ ˈhu̇f\

hoof*, roof*, woof*

OOGE
stooge \ ˈstüj\
see
OUGE*, UGE

scrooge, stooge

OOH
pooh-pooh
\ ˈpü-(ˌ)pü\
see
EW*, OO, UE*

pooh-pooh

OOK*
book \ ˈbu̇k\

betook, book, brook, buttonhook, cook, crook, fishhook, forsook, hook, inglenook, look, mistook, nook, outlook, overlook, pocketbook, pothook, scrapbook, shepherd's crook, shook, sketchbook, storybook, tenterhook, textbook, took, undertook, unhook

OOK**
spook \ ˈspük\
see
UKE

kook, spook

OOKS
gadzooks \gad-ˈzüks\

gadzooks

OOL*
drool \ ˈdrül\
see
OUL***, UEL, ULE

April fool, camp stool, cool, drool, faldstool, finishing school, fool, footstool, Liverpool, pool, school, spool, stool, toadstool, tool, whirlpool, wool

OOL**
wool \ ˈwu̇l\
see
ULL*

wool

OOLISH
see
OUL***+*ish*

coolish, foolish

OOM
bloom \ ˈblüm\
see
OM**, OMB***, UME

anteroom, barroom, bloom, boom, bridegroom, broadloom, broom, doom, elbow room, foredoom, gloom, greenroom, grillroom, groom, guestroom, heirloom, jib boom, loom, mushroom, showroom, stateroom, taproom, waiting room, zoom

O SOUNDS

OOMER
bloomer \ˈblü-mər\
see
AR**, ER*, OR*

bloomer, boomer, roomer

OON
baboon \ba-ˈbün\
see
EWN*, UNE

afternoon, aswoon, baboon,
balloon, bassoon, boon,
Brigadoon, buffoon, cartoon,
cocoon, coon, croon, doubloon,
dragoon, festoon, forenoon,
galloon, half-moon, harpoon,
harvest moon, honeymoon,
lagoon, lampoon, loon,
macaroon, maroon, monsoon,
moon, new moon, noon,
pantaloon, picaroon, platoon,
poltroon, pontoon, raccoon,
Rangoon, rigadoon, saloon,
shalloon, shoon, silver spoon,
simoon, soon, spittoon, spoon,
swoon, teaspoon, typhoon,
wooden spoon

OONER
crooner \ˈkrü-nər\
see
AR**, ER*, OR*

crooner, honeymooner,
schooner, spooner

OOP
coop \ˈküp\
see
OUP, OUPE**, UPE

coop, droop, goop, hoop, loop,
nincompoop, poop, scoop,
scroop, sloop, snoop, stoop,
swoop, troop, whoop

OOR
door \ˈdȯr\
see
OR**, ORE

barn door, boor, door, floor,
indoor, next door, moor, poor,
stage door, spoor, trapdoor

OOSE*
caboose \kə-ˈbüs\
see
UCE*, USE*

burnoose, caboose, calaboose,
goose, loose, mongoose, moose,
Mother Goose, noose, papoose,
unloose, vamoose

O SOUNDS

OOSE**
choose \\ˈchüz\
see
EW+*s*, IEW+*s*, OE**+*s*,
OOZE, OSE***, UE*+*s*,
USE**

choose

OOSH
tarboosh \tär–ˈbüsh\

tarboosh, whoosh

OOST
boost \\ˈbüst\
see
OOSE*+*ed*, UICE+*ed*

boost, roost

OOT*
boot \\ˈbüt\
see
EWT, UIT**, UTE*

alumroot, arrowroot, bandicoot,
bitterroot, bloodroot, boot,
cahoot, cheroot, coot, crowfoot,
hoot, loot, moot, offshoot,
overshoot, pussyfoot, root**,
scoot, shoot, snakeroot, snoot,
square root, taproot, toot, uproot

OOT**
foot \\ˈfût\
see
UT****

afoot, barefoot, flatfoot, forefoot,
hotfoot, light-foot, presser
foot, pussyfoot, root*, soot,
tenderfoot, underfoot, webfoot

OOTH**
booth \\ˈbüth\
see
OUTH*

booth, bucktooth, eyetooth,
forsooth, sooth, tooth, walrus
tooth

OOTH**
smooth \\ˈsmü<u>th</u>\

smooth

OOTY*
booty \\ˈbü-tē\
see
E*, EA*, EE*, I**, IE*,
UTE+*y*, Y**

booty, snooty

O SOUNDS

OOTY**
sooty \ ˈsu̇-tē\
see
E*, EA*, EE*, I**, IE*,
Y**

sooty

OOVE
groove \ ˈgrüv\
see
OVE***

behoove, groove

OOZE
ooze \ ˈüz\
see
EW+*s*, IEW+*s*, OE**+*s*,
OO+*s*, OOSE**, OSE***,
USE**

booze, ooze, snooze

OP*
crop \ ˈkräp\
see
AP**, UP

Aesop, bucket shop, chimney
top, chop, cop, crop, dewdrop,
drop, eardrop, eavesdrop,
flop, grogshop, gumdrop, hop,
housetop, lollipop, lop, milksop,
mop, Mrs. Malaprop, nonstop,
organ stop, overtop, pawnshop,
peg-top, plop, pop, porkchop,
prop, raindrop, rooftop,
shop, shortstop, slipslop, slop,
snowdrop, stop, strop, sweatshop,
sweetsop, teardrop, tip-top, top,
treetop, wallop, whop, workshop

OP**
bishop \ ˈbi-shəp\
see
UP

archbishop, bishop, develop,
gallop, hyssop, scallop, shallop,
wallop

OPAL
opal \ ˈō-pəl\
see
AL*

copal, opal

OPATH
sociopath
\ˈsō-sē-ə-ˌpath\
see
ATH*

homeopath, neuropath, osteopath, psychopath, sociopath

OPE*
cope \ˈkōp\
see
OAP

antelope, bell rope, Cape of Good Hope, chromoscope, cope, dope, electroscope, elope, envelope, grope, guy rope, gyroscope, heliotrope, hope, horoscope, interlope, kaleidoscope, kinetoscope, microscope, misanthrope, mope, movie scope, myope, ope, periscope, pope, pyrope, rope, scope, slope, stanhope, spectroscope, telescope, tightrope, trope

OPE**
calliope
\kə-ˈlī-ə-(ˌ)pē\
see
E*, EA*, EE*, I**, IE*, Y**

calliope, Merope, Parthenope, Penelope, syncope

OPHE
apostrophe
\ə-ˈpäs-trə-(ˌ)fē\
see
E*, EA*, EE*, I**, IE*, Y**

apostrophe, catastrophe, strophe

OPHER
philosopher
\fə-ˈlä-s(ə-)fər\
see
AR**, ER*, OR*

philosopher, St. Christopher

OPHON
colophon \ˈkä-lə-fən\
see
ON*

Bellerophon, colophon, Xenophon

OPHY*
atrophy \ˈa-trə-fē\
see
E*, EA*, EE*, I**, IE*,
Y**

anthroposophy, atrophy,
philosophy, theosophy

OPHY**
trophy \ˈtrō-fē\
see
E*, EA*, EE*, I**, IE*,
Y**

trophy

OPIA
utopia \yu̇-ˈtō-pē-ə\
see
IA

cornucopia, Ethiopia, Utopia

OPIC
topic \ˈtä-pik\
see
IC, ICK

kaleidoscopic, myopic,
microscopic, philanthropic,
telescopic, topic, tropic

OPPER
copper \ˈkä-pər\
see
AR**, ER*, OR*

chopper, clodhopper, copper,
cropper, grasshopper, hopper,
popper, topper, whopper,
woodchopper

OPPY
poppy \ˈpä-pē\
see
E*, EA*, EE*, I**, IE*,
Y**

choppy, floppy, poppy, sloppy,
soppy

OPS
Cyclops \ˈsī-ˌkläps\
see
OP*+s

Cyclops, ops, Pelops

OPSE
copse \ˈkäps\
see
OP+s, OPS

copse

O SOUNDS

OPSIS
synopsis
\sə-ˈnäp-səs\
see
ICE**, IS*, ISE****

ampelopsis, calliopsis, coreopsis, synopsis

OPT
opt \ˈäpt\
see
OP*+*ed*

adopt, co-opt, Copt, opt

OPUS
opus \ˈō-pəs\
see
US

Canopus, magnum opus, opus

OQUE
baroque \bə-ˈrōk\
see
OAK, OKE

baroque, toque

OQUY
soliloquy
\sə-ˈli-lə-kwē\
see
E*, EA*, EE*, I**, IE*,
Y**

colloquy, obloquy, soliloquy

OR*
censor \ˈsen(t)-sər\
see
ACTOR, ADOR*, AMOR,
AR**, ATOR, AUR,
ECTOR, ER*, IOR,
ITOR, UTOR

abettor, ancestor, anchor, antecessor, arbor, armor, Asia Minor, author, bachelor, boa constrictor, camphor, candor, cantor, captor, carburetor, Castor, censor, chancellor, clangor, color, condor, conductor, confessor, councilor, counselor, conveyor, demeanor, discolor, doctor, donor, dor, endeavor, ephor, error, favor, fervor, flavor, governor, honor, horror, humor, ichor, impostor, instructor, inventor, labor, languor, liquor, major, manor, mayor, meteor, minor, mirror,

OR*

misdemeanor, motor, neighbor, nonconductor, odor, off-color, oppressor, pallor, parlor, pastor, phosphor, preceptor, predecessor, proctor, professor, proprietor, protestor, purveyor, rancor, razor, rector, reflector, rigor, rumor, sailor, savor, sculptor, sector, sheet anchor, social error, splendor, sponsor, squalor, stupor, successor, succor, suitor, supervisor, surveyor, survivor, technicolor, tenor, terror, tormentor, tremor, tricolor, Tudor, Ursa Major, Ursa Minor, valor, vapor, vendor, victor, vigor, visor, watercolor, Windsor

OR**
mentor \ ˈmen-ˌtȯr\
see
ADOR**, IDOR, OOR,
ORE, OUR**

abhor, for, mentor, metaphor, nor, or, señor, Thor, tor

ORA*
flora \ ˈflȯr-ə\
see
A**

angora, aurora, diaspora, fedora, flora, mandragora, Pandora, señora, signora, sora

ORA**
plethora \ ˈple-thə-rə\
see
A**

agora, amphora, plethora

ORAGE
storage \ ˈstȯr-ij\
see
AGE*

anchorage, borage, forage, harborage, storage

ORAL*
floral \ ˈflȯr-əl\
see
AL*

balmoral, chloral, choral, coral, floral, immoral, moral, oral, pastoral, pectoral

ORAL**
temporal
\ˈtem-p(ə-)rəl\
see
AL*

caporal, corporal, littoral,
temporal

ORATE*
orate \ȯ-ˈrāt\
see
AIGHT, AIT*, ATE*,
EAT**, EIGHT*

ameliorate, commemorate,
corroborate, decorate,
deteriorate, elaborate**,
evaporate, expectorate,
incorporate, invigorate,
meliorate, orate, percolate,
perforate, perorate, reinvigorate

ORATE**
corporate
\ˈkȯr-p(ə-)rət\
see
AIT**, AT***,
ATE**, EDIT, EIT**,
ERATE**, ERIT, ET**,
ETTE**, IATE**,
IBIT, ICATE**, ICIT,
ICKET, IDGET, IGOT,
IMATE*, INATE**,
IOT**, IT, ITE***,
OLATE*, OSET, OT***,
UET***, UGGET, UIT*,
ULATE**, URATE*

corporate, directorate, elaborate*,
pastorate, protectorate

ORB
orb \ˈȯrb\

absorb, orb, resorb, sorb

ORCE
force \ˈfȯrs\
see
ORSE*, OURSE

divorce, enforce, force, perforce,
reinforce, tour de force

ORCH
porch \ˈpȯrch\

blowtorch, porch, scorch, torch

ORD*
cord \ ˈkȯrd\
see
OARD, ORDE, ORE+*ed*,
OURD

accord, afford, broadsword,
chord, clavichord, concord,
cord, discord, ford, harpsichord,
hexachord, lord, monochord,
Norwegian fjord, overlord,
record**, sword, warlord,
whipcord

ORD**
word \ ˈwərd\
see
EARD*, ERD, IRD, URD

byword, catchword, crossword,
foreword, Hartford, Oxford,
password, record*, watchword,
word

ORDE
horde \ ˈhȯrd\
see
ORD*

horde

ORDER
order \ ˈȯr-dər\
see
AR**, ER*, OR*

border, corder, disorder, order,
recorder

ORE
bore \ ˈbȯr\
see
ADOR**, IDOR, OAR,
OOR, OR**, OUR**

adore, afore, alongshore,
ashore, battledore, before, bore,
chain store, chore, coldsore,
commodore, core, deplore,
drugstore, encore, evermore,
explore, folklore, fore, foreshore,
fourscore, furthermore, galore,
gore, hellebore, heretofore,
ignore, implore, inshore, lore,
more, nevermore, offshore, ore,
pinafore, pore, restore, score,
semaphore, shore, Singapore,
snore, sophomore, sore, spore,
stevedore, store, sycamore,
herefore, threescore, tore,
underscore, wherefore, whore,
wore, yore

OREM
theorem \ ˈthē-ə-rəm\
see
EM**

ad valorem, theorem

ORG
cyborg \ ˈsī-ˌbȯrg\

cyborg, Swedenborg

ORGE
forge \ ˈfȯrj\
see
OURGE

disgorge, drop forge, forge, gorge

ORGUE
morgue \ ˈmȯrg\
see
ORG

morgue

ORIA
gloria \ ˈglȯr-ē-ə\
see
IA

gloria, noria, phantasmagoria,
Victoria

ORIAL
memorial
\mə-ˈmȯr-ē-əl\
see
IAL**

armorial, consistorial,
dictatorial, editorial, gladiatorial,
gubernatorial, immemorial,
inspectorial, memorial,
phantasmagorial, pictorial,
piscatorial, purgatorial, sartorial,
senatorial, sensorial, territorial,
tonsorial

ORIAN
historian
\hi-ˈstȯr-ē-ən\
see
IAN*, IN, UN

Dorian, gregorian, historian,
salutatorian, stentorian,
valedictorian, Victorian

ORIC
historic \hi-ˈstȯr-ik\
see
IC, ICK

allegoric, amphoric, boric,
caloric, Doric, historic,
paregoric, plethoric, prehistoric,
toric

ORITY
majority
\mə-ˈjȯr-ə-tē\
see
E*, EA**, EE*, I**, IE*,
ITY, Y**

anteriority, authority, inferiority,
majority, minority, priority,
sonority, sorority, superiority

ORIUM
emporium
\im-ˈpȯr-ē-əm\
see
AM**, IUM, OM*,
OME*, UM, UMB

auditorium, emporium,
moratorium, sanatorium,
scriptorium

ORK*
cork \ˈkȯrk\

cork, fork, New York, pitchfork,
pork, stork, tuning fork, York

ORK**
work \ˈwərk\
see
ERK, IRK, URK

basketwork, brickwork,
clockwork, earthwork, fancywork,
fieldwork, framework, fretwork,
frostwork, groundwork,
guesswork, handiwork,
needlework, network, openwork,
overwork, schoolwork, scrollwork,
stonework, trestlework, waxwork,
wickerwork, work

ORL
whorl \ˈhwȯr(-ə)l\
see
IRL, URL

schorl, whorl

ORLD
world \ˈwər(-ə)ld\
see
IRL+*ed*, URL+*ed*

netherworld, underworld, world

ORM
form \ˈfȯrm\
see
ARM**, IFORM

barnstorm, chloroform, conform,
cuneiform, deform, dust storm,
form, inform, iodoform,
misinform, norm, perform,
platform, reform, sandstorm,
snowstorm, thunderstorm,
transform

ORM**
worm \ˈwərm\
see
ERM, IRM

angleworm, armyworm,
bookworm, earthworm,
glowworm, grub worm,
inchworm, silkworm

ORMAL
normal \ˈnôr-məl\
see
AL*

formal, informal, normal,
subnormal, supernormal

ORN*
corn \ˈkôrn\
see
ARN**, OURN**

acorn, adorn, barleycorn,
baseborn, bicorn, bighorn,
blackthorn, born, broomcorn,
buckthorn, bugle horn, Cape
Horn, Capricorn, careworn,
corn, earthborn, firstborn,
foghorn, footworn, forlorn,
forsworn, freeborn, greenhorn,
hawthorn, horn, inborn,
Leghorn, longhorn, lorn, manor
born, morn, newborn, Norn,
outworn, overworn, popcorn,
pronghorn, saxhorn, scorn,
seaborne, shoehorn, shopworn,
shorn, shorthorn, staghorn,
suborn, sweet corn, sworn,
thorn, twice-born, unborn,
unicorn, unshorn, waterborn,
war-torn, wayworn, worn

ORN**
stubborn \ˈstə-bərn\
see
ERN, OURN*, URN

stubborn

OROUS
vigorous
\ˈvi-g(ə-)rəs\
see
OUS*

amorous, carnivorous, dolorous,
glamorous, humorous,
languorous, malodorous,
odorous, omnivorous,
phosphorous, porous, rancorous,
rigorous, sonorous, stertorous,
vigorous

ORP
thorp \ˈthȯrp\
see
ARP**

dorp, gorp, thorp

ORPSE
corpse \ˈkȯrps\
see
ORP+*s*

corpse

ORRY*
lorry \ˈlȯr-ē\
see
E*, EA*, EE*, I**, IE*,
Y**

lorry, sorry**

ORRY**
sorry \ˈsär-ē\
see
E*, EA*, EE*, I**, IE*,
Y**

sorry*

ORRY***
worry \ˈwər-ē\
see
URRY

worry

ORS
scissors \ˈsi-zərz\
see
OR**+*s*, UR+*s*

scissors

ORSE*
horse \ˈhȯrs\
see
OARSE, ORCE, OURCE,
OURSE

clotheshorse, cockhorse, endorse,
gorse, hobbyhorse, horse, Norse,
racehorse, remorse, rocking
horse, sawhorse, sea horse

ORSE**
worse \ˈwərs\
see
EARSE, ERCE, ERSE

worse

ORST
worst \ ˈwərst\
see
ERST, IRST, URST

worst

ORT*
contort \kən-ˈtȯrt\
see
ART**, OURT, UART

abort, assort, bellwort, cavort,
cohort, colewort, comport,
consort, contort, davenport,
deport, discomfort, disport,
distort, escort, exhort, export,
extort, figwort, fort, gypsywort,
import, liverwort, mugwort,
passport, port, purport, report,
resort, retort, ribwort, seaport,
short, snort, sort, spiderwort,
sport, support, transport, what
sort

ORT**
comfort
\ˈkəm(p)-fərt\
see
IRT, URT

comfort, discomfort

ORTAL
mortal \ˈmȯr-tᵊl\
see
AL*

immortal, mortal, portal

ORTER
porter \ˈpȯr-tər\
see
AR**, ER*, OR*

exporter, importer, porter,
reporter, shorter, sorter,
supporter

ORTH*
north \ˈnȯrth\
see
OURTH

forth, go forth, henceforth,
north, thenceforth

ORTH**
worth \ˈwərth\
see
IRTH

worth

O SOUNDS

ORUM
forum \ ˈfȯr-əm\
see
AM**, OM*, OME*,
UM, UMB

decorum, forum, quorum,
sanctum sanctorum

ORUS
chorus \ ˈkȯr-əs\
see
ICE**, IS*, ISE****, US

Apollodorus, chorus, helleborus,
Horus

ORY*
factory \ ˈfak-t(ə-)rē\
see
E*, EA*, EE*, I**, IE*,
URRY, Y**

accessory, armory, chicory,
compulsory, cursory, desultory,
directory, factory, hickory,
history, illusory, introductory,
ivory, memory, noncompulsory,
offertory, olfactory, peremptory,
perfunctory, pillory, priory,
rectory, refectory, refractory,
satisfactory, savory, sensory,
succory, theory, valedictory,
vapory, victory

ORY**
story \ ˈstȯr-ē\
see
E*, EA*, EE*, I**, IE*,
ORRY**, Y**

allegory, auditory, category,
dormitory, dory, fish story, ghost
story, glory, gory, inventory,
invocatory, lory, morning glory,
Old Glory, pre-inventory,
promissory, promontory,
repository, short story, story,
territory, tory, transitory,
vainglory

OS*
pathos \ ˈpā-thōs\
see
IOS, OSS

Atropos, Barbados, bathos,
caballeros, Chronos, cosmos, Eos,
Eros, Galapagos, Hyksos, Hypnos,
logos, pathos, pueblos, reredos

OS**
thermos \ ˈthər-məs\
see
ICE**, IS*, ISE****, ISS

asbestos, Patmos, rhinoceros,
Tantalos, thermos

OS***
chaos \ˈkā-ˌäs\
see
OSS

chaos, naos, omphalos, os,
Pharos, Thanatos

OSA
mimosa \mə-ˈmō-sə\
see
A**

Formosa, mimosa, scabiosa, sub-
rosa, via dolorosa

OSE*
hose \ˈhōz\
see
EW+s, IOSE, O*+es,
OE*+s, OTHE+s,
OUGH+s, OW*+s, OWE+s
OWS, OZE

appose, arose, bottlenose, chose,
close**, compose, damask rose,
decompose, depose, disclose,
dispose, enclose, expose,
foreclose, hook nose, hose,
impose, interpose, juxtapose,
metamorphose, nose, oppose,
overexpose, pose, predispose,
presuppose, primrose, propose,
prose, repose, rose, suppose, tea
rose, those, transpose, tuberose,
unclose, wild rose

OSE**
dose \ˈdōs\
see
OSS**

adipose, bellicose, cellulose,
close*, comatose, crystalose,
dose, equipose, glucose, jocose,
lachrymose, morose, overdose,
plumose, pruinose, verbose

OSE***
lose \ˈlüz\
see
EW+s, IEW+s, OE**+s,
OOSE**, OOZE, UE*+s,
USE**

lose, whose

OSE****
purpose \ˈpər-pəs\
see
ACE**, ICE**, IS*,
ISE****, ISS, OISE**

purpose

OSET
closet \ ˈklä-zət\
see
AIT**, AT***, ATE**,
EDIT, EIT**, ERATE**,
ERIT, ET**, ETTE**,
IATE**, IBIT, ICATE**,
ICIT, ICKET, IDGET,
IGOT, IMATE*, INATE**,
IOT**, IT, ITE***,
OLATE*, ORATE**,
OT***, UET***, UGGET,
UIT*, ULATE**, URATE*

closet

OSH
gosh \ ˈgäsh\
see
ASH**, UASH

bosh, cohosh, galosh, gosh, josh,
kibosh, mackintosh, Oshkosh,
slosh

OSION
erosion \i- ˈrō-zhən\
see
ION*, UN

corrosion, erosion, explosion

OSIS
hypnosis
\hip- ˈnō-səs\
see
ICE**, IS*, ISE****, ISS

apotheosis, diagnosis, halitosis,
hypnosis, kenosis, ketosis,
etempsychosis, necrosis, neurosis,
osmosis, prognosis, psychosis,
tuberculosis

OSITY
curiosity
\ˌkyu̇r-ē- ˈä-s(ə-)tē\
see
E*, EA*, EE*, I**, IE*,
ITY, Y**

anfractuosity, curiosity,
generosity, gibbosity, impetuosity,
jocosity, luminosity, monstrosity,
nebulosity, pomposity, sinuosity,
tortuosity, verbosity, virtuosity

OSIVE
explosive
\ik- ˈsplō-siv\
see
IVE**

corrosive, erosive, explosive

OSK
bosk \ ˈbäsk\
see
OSQUE

bosk, kiosk

OSM
microcosm
\ ˈmī-krə- ˌkä-zəm\
see
ISM, OM*

macrocosm, microcosm

OSO
virtuoso
\ ˈvər-chü- ˈō-(ˌ)sō\
see
EAU, EW**, O*, OE*,
OT***, OUGH*, OW*,
OWE

amoroso, capriccioso, virtuoso

OSQUE
mosque \ ˈmäsk\
see
OSK

mosque

OSS*
boss \ ˈbäs\
see
AUCE, OS, OSSE**

across, albatross, boss, bugloss,
Charing Cross, crisscross, cross,
double-cross, dross, emboss,
engross, floss, gloss, hoss, joss,
loss, moss, Red Cross, toss

OSS**
gross \ ˈgrōs\
see
OSE**

gross

OSSE*
posse \ ˈpä-sē\
see
E*, EA*, EE*, I**, IE*,
Y**

posse

OSSE**
lacrosse \lə-ˈkrȯs\
see
OSS

fosse, lacrosse

OSSY
glossy \ˈglä-sē\
see
E*, EA*, EE*, I**, IE*, Y**

bossy, flossy, glossy, mossy

OST*
cost \ˈkȯst\
see
AUST

accost, cost, defrost, frost, hoarfrost, Jack Frost, long-lost, lost, Pentecost

OST**
host \ˈhōst\
see
OAST

almost, easternmost, foremost, ghost, hindmost, host, impost, inmost, innermost, middlemost, milepost, most, nethermost, northernmost, outpost, parcel post, post, provost, signpost, southernmost, topmost, uppermost, utmost, westernmost, whipping post

OSTLE
apostle \ə-ˈpä-səl\
see
EL, LE

apostle, jostle, throstle

OSURE
closure \ˈklō-zhər\
see
AR**, ER*, OR*, URE

closure, composure, disclosure, enclosure, exposure, foreclosure, inclosure, overexposure, underexposure

OSY*
rosy \ˈrō-zē\
see
E*, EA*, EE*, I**, IE*, Y**

nosy, posy, prosy, rosy

OSY**
leprosy \ˈle-prə-sē\
see
E*, EA*, EE*, I**, IE*, Y**

argosy, leprosy

OT*
blot \ ˙ blät\
see
ACHT, AT****, ATT,
OTT, OTTE

allot, apricot, begot, bergamot,
bloodshot, blot, bowknot,
bow-shot, buckshot, Camelot,
coffeepot, copilot, cot, diglot, dot,
dry rot, earshot, ergot, fleshpot,
flowerpot, forget-me-not, forgot,
foxtrot, gallipot, got, grapeshot,
grot, hot, hot spot, Hottentot,
jackpot, jot, knot, lot, love knot,
mascot, monoglot, not, ocelot,
piping hot, plot, polyglot, pot,
red-hot, rot, Scot, shot, slingshot,
slot, snapshot, sot, spot, teapot,
tender spot, tommyrot, tot, touch-
me-not, trot, turkey trot, upshot,
wainscot, watering pot, whatnot,
wot

OT**
depot \ ˙ dē-(ˌ)pō\
see
EAU, EW**, O*, OE*,
OUGH*, OW*, OWE

argot, bon mot, depot, Huguenot,
jabot, matelot, Pierrot, robot,
sabot, tarot

OT***
carrot \ ˙ ker-ət\
see
AIT**, AT***, ATE**,
EDIT, EIT**, ERATE**,
ERIT, ET**, ETTE**,
IATE**, IBIT, ICATE**,
ICIT, ICKET, IDGET,
IGOT, IMATE*,
INATE**, IOT**, IT,
ITE***, OLATE*,
ORATE**, OSET,
UET***, UGGET, UIT*,
ULATE**, URATE*

ballot, carrot, despot, divot,
fagot, harlot, helot, ingot,
maggot, marmot, parrot, pilot,
pivot, riot, turbot, zealot

OTA
quota \ ˙ kwō-tə\
see
A**

Dakota, iota, Minnesota, quota,
rota

BLINDED BY THE LIGHT
AVOIDING MISHEARD SONG LYRICS

SOMETIMES MISHEARD SONG lyrics (known as "mondegreens" to people who study these things) are all about the listener, as with this overheard version of the Beatles' song, "Michelle": *Michelle, ma belle, some say monkeys play piano well, my Michelle.* The person who belted out that doozy might have "heard" the song for very personal reasons: perhaps he plays piano, admires monkeys, or needs to do a better job with the cotton swabs. The blame for other perpetually mangled songs lies with vocalists who enunciate poorly and songwriters who compose lyrics that are hard to sing.

Writers aren't always the best judge of their own work. It behooves songwriters and poets to listen as others sing or read their work aloud. Hearing your work in someone else's voice provides a more objective perspective. When a third party reads your words cold turkey, it's easier to hear if the phrasing makes sense, whether any near rhymes are close enough, if the alliteration is too much of a mouthful, and if you've got the stresses in all the right places.

Resist the temptation to coach your reader or singer to get it right. If you have to say, "But it works if you do it *this* way," you, the writer, haven't quite finished your homework. You may be in love with your lyrics, but if listeners or readers can't understand them, you might find yourself like the poor fellows from Manfred Man: *Blinded by the light, wrapped up like a douche, another Roman in the night.*

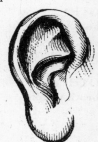

O SOUNDS

OTAGE
dotage \ˈdō-tij\
see
AGE*

dotage, flotage

OTATE
rotate \ˈrō-ˌtāt\
see
AIT, AIGHT, ATE*,
EAT**, EIGHT*

annotate, connotate, rotate

OTCH
botch \ˈbäch\
see
ATCH**

blotch, botch, crotch, hopscotch,
notch, Scotch, splotch, top-notch

OTE
rote \ˈrōt\
see
OAT

anecdote, antidote, banknote,
capote, connote, cote, coyote,
creosote, demote, denote, devote,
dote, dovecote, footnote, keynote,
misquote, mote, note, quote,
promote, redingote, remote, rote,
sheepcote, smote, straw vote, tote,
treasury note, vote, wrote

OTH*
both \ˈbōth\
see
OATH, OWTH

betroth, both, quoth, troth

OTH**
broth \ˈbróth\

azoth, broadcloth, broth,
cheesecloth, cloth, fish broth,
froth, Goth, moth, neckcloth,
oilcloth, sackcloth, sloth, troth,
Visigoth, wroth

OTH***
mammoth
\ˈma-məth\
see
ITH

behemoth, mammoth

OTHE
clothe \ˈklōth\
see
OATHE

clothe

OTHER*
other \ˈə-thər\
see
AR**, ER*, OR*

another, brother, foster mother,
grandmother, half-brother,
mother, other, smother,
stepmother, tother

OTHER**
bother \ˈbä-thər\
see
AR**, ER*, OR*

bother, pother

OTIC
exotic \ig-ˈzä-tik\
see
IC, ICK

chaotic, demotic, despotic,
exotic, hypnotic, idiotic, narcotic,
neurotic, patriotic, quixotic

OTION
notion \ˈnō-shən\
see
ION*

commotion, devotion, emotion,
locomotion, lotion, love potion,
motion, notion, perpetual
motion, potion, promotion,
slow-motion

OTIVE
motive \ˈmō-tiv\
see
IVE**

automotive, locomotive, motive,
promotive, votive

OTT
boycott \ˈbȯi-ˌkät\
see
OT*, OTTE

boycott

OTTE
gavotte \gə-ˈvät\
see
OT*, OTT

calotte, cocotte, culotte, gavotte,
Wyandotte

OTTLE
bottle \\ ˈbä-tᵊl\\
see
EL, LE, ODDLE

bluebottle, bottle, mottle, throttle

OTTO
lotto \\ ˈlä-(ˌ)tō\\
see
EAU, EW**, O*, OE*,
OT***, OUGH*, OW*,
OWE

blotto, grotto, lotto, motto, Otto,
risotto

OU*
you \\ ˈyü\\
see
EW*, IEU, IEW, O**,
OE**, OO, OU*,
OUGH****, OUT*,
OUX, U, UE*, UT***

Anjou, bayou, bijou, caribou,
froufrou, marabou, sou, you

OU**
thou \\ ˈthau̇\\
see
OUGH**, OW**

thou

OUBT
doubt \\ ˈdau̇t\\
see
OUT*

doubt, misdoubt, redoubt

OUCH*
couch \\ ˈkau̇ch\\

avouch, couch, crouch, grouch,
ouch, pouch, slouch, vouch

OUCH**
touch \\ ˈtəch\\
see
UCH*

retouch, touch

OUCHE
douche \\ ˈdüsh\\

barouche, cartouche, douche,
Scaramouche

OUD
loud \ˈlaủd\
see
OWD, OW**+*ed*

aloud, becloud, cloud, enshroud, loud, overcloud, overloud, proud, shroud, stroud, thundercloud

OUGE*
rouge \ˈrüzh\
see
OOGE, UGE

rouge

OUGE**
gouge \ˈgaủj\

gouge

OUGH*
dough \ˈdō\
see
EAU, EW**, O*, OE*,
OT***, OW*, OWE

although, borough, dough, furlough, though, thorough

OUGH**
bough \ˈbaủ\
see
AU, OW**

bough, plough, slough***, sough***

OUGH***
rough \ˈrəf\
see
UFF

enough, rough, slough**, tough, sough**

OUGH***
through \ˈthrü\
see
EW*, IEU, IEW, O**,
OE**, OO, OU*, OUS**,
OUT**, OUX, U, UE*,
UT

through

OUGH****
cough \ˈkòf\
see
OFF

cough, trough

OUGHT*
fought \ ˈfôt\
see
AUGHT*, AUT

afterthought, besought, bethought, bought, brought, forethought, fought, nought, ought, overwrought, sought, thought, unsought, well-fought, wrought

OUGHT**
drought \ ˈdraût\
see
AUT, OUT*

drought

OUIN
bedouin
\ ˈbe-də-wən\
see
IN, INE***, UIN

bedouin

OUL*
foul \ ˈfaû(-ə)l\
see
OWL

afoul, befoul, foul

OUL**
soul \ ˈsōl\
see
OL*, OLE, OWL*

soul

OUL***
ghoul \ ˈgül\
see
OOL*, ULE

ghoul

OULD**
could \ ˈkûd\
see
OOD*

could, should, would

OULDER
boulder \ ˈbōl-dər\
see
AR**, ER*, OR*

boulder, shoulder

OUN
noun \ˈna*ů*n\
see
OWN**

noun, pronoun

OUNCE
bounce \ˈba*ů*n(t)s\

announce, bounce, denounce, flounce, jounce, ounce, pounce, pronounce, renounce, trounce

OUND
bound \ˈba*ů*nd\
see
OWN**+*ed*

abound, aground, around, astound, background, bloodhound, bound, camping ground, compound, dumbfound, expound, found, greyhound, harehound, hidebound, homeward-bound, horehound, hound, impound, ironbound, merry-go-round, mound, musclebound, outward bound, playground, pound, profound, propound, rebound, redound, resound, round, sleuthhound, snowbound, sound, spellbound, staghound, stamping ground, surround, underground, vantage ground, wound**

OUND**
wound \ˈwünd\
see
OON+*ed*

wound*

OUNDER
flounder \ˈfla*ů*n-dər\
see
AR**, ER*, OR*

bounder, flounder, founder, grounder, rounder, sounder

OUNDS
grounds \ˈgra*ů*ndz\
see
OUND+*s*

coffee grounds, zounds

OUNG
young \ˈyəŋ\
see
ONG**, ONGUE, UNG

young

OUNGE
lounge \ˈlau̇nj\

lounge, scrounge

OUNT
count \ˈkau̇nt\

account, amount, catamount, count, discount, dismount, fount, miscount, mount, paramount, recount, surmount, tantamount, viscount

OUNTY
bounty \ˈbau̇n-tē\
see
E*, EA*, EE*, I**, IE*,
Y**

bounty, county, mounty

OUP*
soup \ˈsüp\
see
OOP, OUPE**, UPE

croup, group, recoup, soup, troup

OUP**
coup \ˈkü\
see
OU*, UE*

coup

OUPE*
cantaloupe
\ˈkan-tə-ˌlōp\
see
OPE*

cantaloupe

OUPE**
troupe \ˈtrüp\
see
OOP, OUP*, UPE

troupe

OUR*
colour \ˈkə-lər\
see
AR**, ER*, EUR, OR*,
URR

armour, belabour, colour, favour,
flavour, glamour, honour, ill-
favour, labour, parlour, rumour,
saviour, splendour, succour,
vigour, your**

OUR**
four \fȯr\
see
OAR, OOR, OR**, ORE,
URE

amour, detour, downpour, four,
outpour, paramour, Pompadour,
pour, tambour, tour, troubadour,
your*

OUR***
sour \ˈsau̇(-ə)r\
see
OWER

devour, dour, flour, giaour, half
hour, hour, our, scour, sour

OURCE
source \ˈsȯrs\
see
OURSE

resource, source

OURD
gourd \ˈgȯrd\
see
ORD

gourd

OURGE
scourge \ˈskərj\ *or*
\ˈskōrj\
see
ERGE, IRGE, URGE

scourge

OURN*
adjourn \ə-ˈjərn\
see
EARN, ERN, URN

adjourn, sojourn

OURN**
mourn \ˈmȯrn\
see
ORN*

bourn, mourn

OURS
ours \ˈau̇(-ə)rz\
see
OUR***+s, OWER+s

hours, ours, velours, yours

OURSE
course \ˈkȯrs\
see
ORCE, ORSE, OURCE

bourse, concourse, course, discourse, intercourse, of course, racecourse, recourse

OURT
court \ˈkȯrt\
see
ORT*

court

OURTH
fourth \ˈfȯrth\
see
ORTH

fourth

OUS*
famous \ˈfā-məs\
see
ALOUS, EOUS, EROUS, INOUS, IOUS, ITOUS, ONOUS, OROUS, ULOUS, UOUS, US

adventurous, ambidextrous, analogous, androgynous, anonymous, barbarous, bibulous, blasphemous, bulbous, callous, chivalrous, cumbrous, declivitous, desirous, diaphanous, disastrous, enormous, famous, frivolous, gibbous, gluttonous, hazardous, heinous, homologous, idolatrous, infamous, impious, jealous, joyous, ludicrous, magnanimous, mischievous, momentous, monstrous, multifidous, murderous, nervous, nitrous, nubilous, ominous, parlous, pendulous, perilous, pious, pompous, portentous, posthumous, prognathous, pusillanimous, rapturous, raucous, ravenous, rigorous, riotous, scurrilous, stupendous, synonymous, torturous, tremendous, troublous,

OUS*

tyrannous, unanimous, venomous, venous, venturous, viscious, viscous, wondrous, zealous

OUS**
rendezvous
\ˈrän-di-ˌvü\
see
EW*, IEU, IEW, O**,
OE**, OO, OU*,
OUGH****, OUT**,
OUX, U, UE*, UT***

entre nous, rendezvous

OUSE*
house \ˈhaùs\

blouse**, chophouse, coach house, dormouse, douse, farmhouse, flitter mouse, full house, greenhouse, grouse, hothouse, house, lighthouse, louse, mouse, penthouse, playhouse, poorhouse, powerhouse, roughhouse, roundhouse, schoolhouse, spouse, souse, state house, storehouse, summerhouse, titmouse, workhouse

OUSE**
rouse \ˈraùz\
see
OW**+S, OWSE

arouse, blouse*, carouse, espouse, rouse

OUSLY
joyously \ˈjòi-əs-lē\
see
E*, EA*, EE*, I**, IE*,
IOUS+*ly*, OUS*+*ly*, Y**

assiduously, continuously, copiously, curiously, furiously, instantaneously, joyously, previously, simultaneously, viciously

OUST
oust \ˈaùst\

joust, oust, roust

OUT*
bout \ˈbaùt\
see
AUT, OUBT, OUGHT**

about, blowout, bout, boy scout, clout, cutout, devout, dugout, eke out, flout, gadabout, gout, hereabout, in and out, knockout,

OUT*

knout, layout, lookout, lout, mahout, out, out and out, pig's snout, pout, right about, root out, roundabout, rout, salmon trout, scout, shout, snout, spout, sprout, stout, thereabout, throughout, tout, trout, tryout, turnout, walkout, washout, waterspout, whereabout, without, worn-out

OUT**
ragout \ra-ˈgü\
see
EW*, IEU, IEW, O**,
OE**, OO, OU*,
OUGH****, OUS**,
OUT**, U, UE*, UT***

marabout, passe partout, ragout

OUTE*
route \ˈraut\
see
OUT*

route**

OUTE**
route \ˈrüt\
see
OOT, UTE

route

OUTH*
youth \ˈyüth\
see
OOTH, UTH

couth, uncouth, vermouth, Yarmouth, youth

OUTH**
south \ˈsauth\

drouth, mouth, south

OUTH***
plymouth \ˈpli-məth\
see
ITH, UTH

plymouth

OUX
Sioux \\ˈsü\\
see
EW*, IEU, IEW, O**,
OE**, OO, OU*,
OUGH****, OUS**,
OUT**, U, UE*, UT***

billet-doux, roux, Sioux

OVAL*
removal \\ri-ˈmü-vəl\\
see
AL*

approval, disapproval, removal

OVAL**
oval \\ˈō-vəl\\
see
AL*

oval

OVATE
ovate \\ˈō-ˌvāt\\
see
AIGHT, AIT*, ATE*,
EAT**, EIGHT*

innovate, ovate, renovate

OVE*
cove \\ˈkōv\\
see
AUVE

alcove, clove, cove, drove, grove,
hove, interwove, Jove, mangrove,
rove, shrove, stove, strove,
throve, trove, wove

OVE**
love \\ˈləv\\
see
OF

above, belove, boxing glove, dove,
foxglove, glove, ringdove, self-
love, shove, turtledove, unglove

OVE***
prove \\ˈprüv\\
see
OOVE

approve, disapprove, disprove,
improve, move, prove, remove,
reprove

OVEL**
novel \\ˈnä-vəl\\
see
EL, LE

grovel, hovel**, novel

OVEL**
shovel \\´shə-vəl\\
see
EL, LE

hovel*, shovel

OVEN*
oven \\´ə-vən\\
see
EN**

coven, oven, sloven

OVEN**
proven \\´prü-vən\\
see
EN**

disproven, proven

OVEN*
woven \\´wō-vən\\
see
EN**

cloven, interwoven, woven

OVER*
clover \\´klō-vər\\
see
AR**, ER*, OR*

clover, four-leaf clover, hangover, Hanover, moreover, over, Passover, plover**, popover, rover, runover, stopover, turnover

OVER**
hover \\´hə-vər\\
see
AR**, ER*, OR*

cover, discover, hover, lover, plover*, recover, uncover, undercover

OW*
flow \\´flō\\
see
ARROW, EAU, ELLOW, EW**, O*, OE*, OT***, OUGH*, OWE, URROW

afterglow, aglow, backflow, bellow, below, bestow, billow, blow, borrow, bow**, bungalow, burrow, crossbow, crow, elbow, fiddle bow, flow, follow, foreshadow, furbelow, Glasgow, glow, grass widow, hedgerow, inflow, know, low, meadow, minnow, morrow, mow, outgrow, overflow, overshadow, overthrow, peep show, pillow, pussy willow, rainbow, road show, row**,

OW*

saddlebow, scarecrow, shadow, show, slow, snow, sorrow, stone's throw, stow, throw, tomorrow, tow, undertow, widow, willow, window, winnow

OW**
cow \ ˈkau̇\
see
AU, OUGH**

allow, anyhow, avow, bow*, bowwow, brow, chow, chowchow, cow, dhow, disavow, endow, enow, erenow, eyebrow, highbrow, how, kowtow, Moscow, Nankow, now, plow, powwow, row*, scow, snowplow, somehow, sow, trow, vow, wow

OWD
crowd \ ˈkrau̇d\
see
OW**+*ed*, OUD

crowd, overcrowd

OWDER
powder \ ˈpau̇-dər\
see
AR**, ER*, OR*

chowder, gunpowder, powder

OWDY
howdy \ ˈhau̇-dē\
see
E*, EA*, EE*, I**, IE*, Y**

dowdy, howdy, rowdy

OWE
owe \ ˈō\
see
EAU, EW**, O*, OE*, OT***, OUGH*, OW*

owe

OWEL
towel \ ˈtau̇(-ə)l\
see
EL, OWL**

bowel, dowel, paper towel, towel, trowel, vowel

OWER*
power \ ˈpau̇(-ə)r\
see
AR**, ER*, OR*,
OUR**, OUR***,
OW**+er

bower, candlepower, cauliflower, cornflower, cower, dower, embower, empower, flower, gilliflower, glower, horsepower, Leaning Tower, mayflower, overpower, power, shower, sunflower, tower, wallflower, watchtower

OWER**
follower \ ˈfä-lə-wər\
see
AR**, ER*, OR*

borrower, follower, lower, ower, widower

OWERY
bowery \ ˈbau̇(-ə)r-ē\
see
E*, EA*, EE*, ERY*,
I**, IE*, Y**

bowery, flowery, lowery

OWL*
bowl \ ˈbōl\
see
OAL, OLE, OUL**

bowl, finger bowl, pipe bowl, wassail bowl

OWL**
fowl \ ˈfau̇(-ə)l\
see
OUL*, OWEL

cowl, fowl, growl, howl, jowl, night owl, prowl, scowl, yowl

OWLY
slowly \ ˈslō-lē\
see
E*, EA*, EE*, I**, IE*,
Y**

lowly, narrowly, slowly

OWN*
blown \ ˈblōn\
see
EWN**, OAN, OGNE,
ONE*

blown, disown, flown, full-blown, full-grown, grown, high-flown, known, mown, new-mown, outgrown, overblown, overthrown, own, self-sown, shown, sown, strown, thrown, unblown, unknown, unsown, well-known

OWN**
down \ ˙daůn\
see
OUN

brown, Cape Town, Chinatown, clown, comedown, crown, down, downtown, dressing gown, drown, frown, gown, knockdown, letdown, lowdown, marked down, nightgown, renown, shakedown, showdown, shutdown, sit-down, sundown, swansdown, thistledown, throw down, touchdown, town, tumbledown, uncrown, upside-down, uptown

OWS
bellows \ ˙be-(ˌ)lōz\
see
O*+s, OE*+s, OSE*,
OW*+s, OWE+s

bellows, gallows, overgrows, who knows

OWSE
browse \ ˙braůz\
see
OUSE**, OW**+s

browse, dowse, drowse

OWTH
growth \ ˙grōth\
see
OATH, OTH*

growth, overgrowth, undergrowth

OWY
billowy \ ˙bi-lə-wē\
see
E*, EA*, EE*, I**, IE*,
Y**

billowy, pillowy, shadowy, willowy

OX
box \ ˙bäks\
see
OCK*+s, ODOX

ballot box, bandbox, box, chatterbox, cowpox, deposit box, equinox, fox, letterbox, music box, muskox, ox, paddle box, Pandora's box, paradox, phlox, pillbox, shooting box, smallpox, snuffbox, soapbox, strongbox, tinderbox

OXY
foxy \ ´fäk-sē\
see
E*, EA*, EE*, I**, IE*,
Y**

doxy, foxy, heterodoxy,
orthodoxy, proxy

OY
boy \ ´bȯi\
see
OI

ahoy, alloy, altar boy, annoy, boy,
busboy, charpoy, cloy, convoy,
corduroy, coy, decoy, destroy,
employ, enjoy, envoy, errand
boy, goy, hautboy, Helen of Troy,
highboy, joy, killjoy, lowboy,
newsboy, overjoy, playboy, Rob
Roy, savoy, sepoy, teapoy, tomboy,
toy, viceroy

OYAL
royal \ ´rȯi(-ə)l\
see
AL*

disloyal, loyal, pennyroyal, royal,
unloyal

OYLE
gargoyle
\ ´gär-ˌgȯi(-ə)l\
see
OIL

gargoyle, hoyle

OZE
doze \ ´dōz\
see
O*+s, OE*+s, OSE*,
OW*+s, OWE*+s

bulldoze, doze, froze

– U –
SOUNDS

U
Zulu \ ˈzü-(ˌ)lü\
see
EW*, IEU, IEW, O**,
OE**, OO, OU*,
OUGH****, OUS**,
OUT**, OUX, U, UE*,
UT***

babu, Bantu, Danu, emu, fichu,
gnu, guru, Hindu, Honolulu,
impromptu, IOU, Jehu, jujitsu,
juju, menu, mumu, ormolu, pari
passu, parvenu, perdu, Peru,
poilu, tofu, Timbuktu, Vishnu,
zebu, Zulu

UA
aqua \ ˈä-kwə\
see
A**

aqua, Chatauqua, Gargantua,
Nicaragua, Padua, Papua

UAD
quad \ ˈkwäd\
see
AD**, ADE***, OD*,
ODD

quad, squad

UADE
persuade \pər-ˈswäd\
see
ADE*, UEDE

dissuade, overpersuade, persuade

UAFF
quaff \ ˈkwäf\

quaff

UAL
actual \ ˈak-ch(ə-w)əl\
see
AL*

actual, annual, biannual,
bilingual, casual, coequal,
contextual, continual, conventual,
dual, effectual, eventual,
gradual, habitual, heterosexual,
homosexual, individual,
ineffectual, intellectual, lingual,
manual, mutual, perpetual,
punctual, residual, ritual, sensual,
sexual, spiritual, unusual, usual,
victual, virtual, visual

U SOUNDS

UALLY
usually
\ˈyü-zhə-wə-lē\
see
ALLY, E*, EA*, EE*,
I**, IE*, Y**

casually, eventually, habitually,
mutually, perpetually, punctually,
spiritually, unusually, usually,
virtually

UANT
truant \ˈtrü-ənt\
see
ANT**

piquant, pursuant, truant

UARD
guard \ˈgärd\
see
ARD**

blackguard, bodyguard,
coastguard, guard, lifeguard,
safeguard, vanguard

UARRY
quarry \ˈkwȯr-ē\
see
E*, EA*, EE*, I**, IE*,
ORRY, ORY, Y**

quarry

UART
quart \ˈkwȯrt\
see
ART***, ORT*, OURT

quart

UARTZ
quartz \ˈkwȯrts\
see
ORT*+s, OURT+s,
UART+s

quartz

UARY
actuary
\ˈak-chə-ˌwer-ē\
see
AIRY, ARRY*, ARY*, E*,
EA*, EE*, ERRY, ERY**,
I**, IE*, Y**

actuary, antiquary, electuary,
estuary, February, January,
mortuary, obituary, ossuary,
reliquary, residuary, sanctuary,
statuary, voluptuary

UASH
squash \ˈskwäsh\
see
ASH**, OSH

quash, musquash, squash

UAT
kumquat
\ˈkəm-ˌkwät\
see
AT****, OT*, OTT,
OTTE

kumquat

UATE
evaluate
\i-ˈval-yə-ˌwāt\
see
AIGHT, AIT*, ATE*,
EAT**, EIGHT*

accentuate, actuate, antiquate,
attenuate, devaluate, evacuate,
evaluate, extenuate, fluctuate,
graduate, individuate, infatuate,
insinuate, perpetuate, punctuate,
sinuate, situate, superannuate

UAVE
suave \ˈswäv\

suave, Zouave

UAY
quay \ˈkē\ *or* \ˈkā\
see
A*, AY, E*, EA*, EE*,
I**, IE*, Y**

Paraguay, quay, Uruguay

UB
club \ˈkləb\

bathtub, Beelzebub, club, cub,
dub, grub, hub, hubbub, pub,
rub, rub-a-dub, scrub, shrub,
syllabub, slub, snub, stub, sub,
tub, yacht club

UBBER
rubber \ˈrə-bər\
see
AR**, ER*, OR*

blubber, India rubber,
landlubber, rubber, snubber

UBBY
tubby \ˈtə-bē\
see
E*, EA*, EE*, I*, IE*,
Y**

chubby, cubby, grubby, hubby,
nubby, scrubby, snubby, tubby

UBE
tube \ˈtüb\
see
OOB

cube, inner tube, jujube, rube, tube

UBLE*
double \ˈdə-bəl\
see
EL, LE, UBBLE

double, redouble, trouble

UBLE**
soluble \ˈsäl-yə-bəl\
see
ABLE*, EL, LE

dissoluble, insoluble, resoluble, soluble, voluble

UCE
reduce \ri-ˈdüs\
see
EUS, OOSE*, UICE,
USE*

adduce, Bruce, conduce, deuce, educe, induce, introduce, lettuce, produce, puce, reduce, reproduce, seduce, spruce, superinduce, traduce, truce

UCH*
much \ˈməch\
see
OUCH**, UTCH

forasmuch, inasmuch, much, nonesuch, overmuch, such

UCH*
eunuch \ˈyü-nək\
see
ICK

eunuch

UCH**
Pentateuch
\ˈpen-tə-ˌtük\
see
OOK

Pentateuch

UCHE
ruche \ˈrüsh\
see
OOSH, OUCHE

ruche

UCK
buck \ ˈbək\
see
OK

amuck, awestruck, bestruck, buck, Canuck, chuck, cluck, duck, good luck, horror-struck, luck, moonstruck, muck, pluck, potluck, Puck, roebuck, sawbuck, shuck, struck, stuck, suck, tuck, truck, woodchuck

UCKLE
buckle \ ˈbə-kəl\
see
EL, LE

buckle, chuckle, honeysuckle, knuckle, muckle, shoe buckle, suckle

UCRE
lucre \ ˈlü-kər\
see
AR**, ER*, OR*

lucre

UCT
duct \ ˈdəkt\
see
EDUCT, UCK+*ed*

abduct, aqueduct, conduct, construct, deduct, duct, induct, instruct, misconduct, obstruct, product, reconstruct, safe conduct, viaduct

UCTION
suction \ ˈsək-shən\
see
ION*

auction, deduction, destruction, instruction, obstruction, overproduction, production, reduction, reproduction, ruction, seduction, suction

UD
mud \ ˈməd\
see
OOD**

bud, collar stud, cud, dud, mud, rosebud, scud, spud, stud, Talmud, thud

UDDER
udder \ ˈə-dər\
see
AR**, ER*, OR*, UTTER

rudder, shudder, udder

UDDLE
puddle \ ˈpə-dᵊl\
see
EL, LE, UTTLE

befuddle, fuddle, huddle, muddle, puddle

UDE
rude \ ˈrüd\
see
EUD, IEW+*ed*, ITUDE,
OOD***, UE*+*ed*

allude, collude, conclude, crude,
delude, desuetude, dude, elude,
etude, exclude, exude, include,
inquietude, interlude, intrude,
mansuetude, nude, obtrude,
preclude, prelude, protrude,
prude, quietude, rude, seclude

UDGE
fudge \ ˈfəj\

begrudge, budge, drudge, fudge,
grudge, judge, misjudge, nudge,
sludge, smudge, trudge

UDS
suds \ ˈsədz\
see
UD+*s*

soapsuds, suds

UE*
true \ ˈtrü\
see
EW*, IEU, IEW, O**,
OE**, OO, OU*,
OUGH****, OUS**,
OUT**, OUX, U, UT***

accrue, ague, argue, avenue,
barbecue, blue, clue, construe,
continue, cue, curlicue, due,
ensue, flue, glue, hue, imbue,
ingenue, issue, misconstrue,
overdue, pursue, queue, rescue,
retinue, revenue, revue, rue, slue,
statue, subdue, sue, tissue, true,
true-blue, undervalue, undue,
untrue, value, vendue, virtue

UE**
fatigue \fə-ˈtēg\
see
AGUE**

fatigue, intrigue, overfatigue

UEDE**
suede \ ˈswād\
see
ADE*, AID*, AY+*ed*,
UADE

suede

UEL
duel \ ˈdü-əl\
see
EL, ELL

cruel, duel, fuel, gruel

U SOUNDS

UEL**
sequel \ ˈsē-kwəl\
see
EL, LE

sequel

UENCE*
affluence
\ˈa-(ˌ)flü-ən(t)s\
see
ENCE, ENSE, ENT**+*s*

affluence, congruence, effluence

UENCE**
sequence \ˈsē-
kwən(t)s\
see
ENCE, ENT**+*s*

consequence, eloquence,
sequence

UENT*
affluent \ˈaf-lü-ənt\
see
ENT**

affluent, confluent, constituent,
effluent, fluent, influent,
refluent, unguent

UENT**
eloquent
\ˈel-ō-kwənt\
see
ANT**, ENT**

delinquent, eloquent, frequent,
grandiloquent, inconsequent,
infrequent, sequent, subsequent

UEST
quest \ˈkwest\
see
EAST**, ESS+*ed*, EST,
IEST**, UESS+*ed*

bequest, conquest, guest, inquest,
quest, request

UET*
duet \dü-ˈet\
see
ET

cruet, duet, minuet

UET**
croquet \krō-ˈkā\
see
A*, AY, EIGH*, UAY

croquet, piquet, parquet,
sobriquet***

UET***
banquet \ ˈ **baŋ-kwət**\
see
AIT**, AT***, ATE**,
EDIT, EIT**, ERATE**,
ERIT, ET**, ETTE**,
IATE**, IBIT, ICATE**,
ICIT, ICKET, IDGET,
IGOT, IMATE*,
INATE**, IOT**, IT,
ITE***, OLATE*,
ORATE**, OSET,
OT***, UGGET, UIT*,
ULATE**, URATE*

banquet, sobriquet**, tourniquet

UFF
buff \ ˈ **bəf**\
see
OUGH***

bluff, buff, cuff, dandruff,
duff, fisticuff, fluff, gruff, guff,
handcuff, huff, luff, muff, puff,
rebuff, ruff, scruff, scuff, snuff,
stuff

UFT
tuft \ ˈ **təft**\
see
OUGH***+*ed*, UFF+*ed*

candytuft, tuft

UG
bug \ ˈ **bəg**\

bug, chug, drug, dug, firebug,
fireplug, fug, glug, hug, humbug,
jug, ladybug, lightning bug, lug,
mealy bug, mug, plug, potato bug,
pug, rug, shrug, slug, smug, snug,
sparkplug, thug, tug

UGAL*
centrifugal
\ **sen-** ˈ **tri-fyə-gəl**\
see
AL*

centrifugal, Portugal

UGAL**
frugal \ ˈ **frü-gəl**\
see
AL*

frugal, fugal

UGE
huge \ˈhyüj\
see
OOGE, OUGE*

deluge, huge, luge, refuge, subterfuge

UGGET
nugget \ˈnə-gət\
see
AIT**, AT***, ATE**,
EDIT, EIT**, ERATE**,
ERIT, ET**, ETTE**,
IATE**, IBIT, ICATE**,
ICIT, ICKET, IDGET,
IGOT, IMATE*,
INATE**, IOT**, IT,
ITE***, OLATE*,
ORATE**, OSET,
OT***, UET***, UIT*,
ULATE**, URATE*

drugget, nugget

UGGLE
juggle \ˈjə-gəl\
see
EL, LE

juggle, smuggle, snuggle, struggle

UGGY
buggy \ˈbə-gē\
see
E*, EA*, EE*, I**, IE*,
Y**

buggy, muggy, puggy, sluggy

UGN
impugn \im-ˈpyün\
see
EWN*, OON, UNE

impugn, oppugn

UICE
juice \ˈjüs\
see
OOSE*, UCE, USE*

juice, sluice

UID*
squid \ˈskwid\
see
ID

languid, liquid, quid, squid

UID**
fluid \ˈflü-əd\
see
ID

druid, fluid

UIDE
guide \ˈgīd\
see
EYE+*ed*, IDE, Y*+*ed*

guide, misguide

UIL
tranquil \ˈtraŋ-kwəl\
see
IL

jonquil, tranquil

UILD
build \ˈbild\
see
ILD*, ILL+*ed*

build, guild, upbuild

UILE
guile \ˈgī(-ə)l\
see
ILE*, ISLE

beguile, guile

UILL
quill \ˈkwil\
see
ILL

Goose quill, quill, squill

UILT
quilt \ˈkwilt\
see
ILT

Bed quilt, built, guilt, quilt

UIN*
sequin \ˈsē-kwən\
see
IN, UINE

Algonquin, Bedouin, harlequin,
lambrequin, mannequin,
palanquin, penguin, sequin

UIN**   bruin, ruin
ruin \ ˈrü-ən\
see
IN, UINE

UINE*   genuine, sanguine
genuine
\ ˈjen-yə-wən\
see
INE***

UINE**   equine, genuine*
equine \ ˈe-ˌkwīn\
see
IGN, INE*, YNE

UIRE   acquire, esquire, inquire, quire,
squire \ ˈskwī(-ə)r\   require, squire
see
IRE*, Y*+*er*, YRE

UIRT   quirt, squirt
squirt \ ˈskwərt\
see
ERT, IRT, URT

**UISE*   disguise, guise
guise \ ˈgīz\
see
EYE+*s*, IE**+*s*, IGH+*s*,
ISE*, IZE

UISE**   bruise, cruise
bruise \ ˈbrüz\
see
EW*+*s*, IEW+*s*, OE**+*s*,
OO+*s*, OOZE, OSE***,
U+*s*, UE*+*s*, USE**

UISH   anguish, cliquish, distinguish,
languish \ ˈlaŋ-gwish\   extinguish, languish, relinquish,
see   roguish
ISH

UISM
altruism
\ˈal-trü-ˌi-zəm\
see
ISM

altruism, truism, ventriloquism

UIST
altruist \ˈal-trü-ist\
see
ISS+*ed*, IST

altruist, casuist, linguist,
ventriloquist

UIT*
circuit \ˈsər-kət\
see
AIT**, AT***, ATE**,
EDIT, EIT**, ERATE**,
ERIT, ET**, ETTE**,
IATE**, IBIT, ICATE**,
ICIT, ICKET, IDGET,
IGOT, IMATE*,
INATE**, IOT**, IT,
ITE***, OLATE*,
ORATE**, OSET, OT***,
UET***, UGGET,
ULATE**, URATE*

acquit, biscuit, circuit, conduit,
Jesuit, quit, short-circuit

UIT**
fruit \ˈfrüt\
see
EWT, OOT*, UTE

breadfruit, bruit, follow suit,
fruit, grapefruit, lawsuit, pursuit,
recruit, suit, union suit

UITE*
suite \ˈswēt\
see
EAT*, EET, ITE***

mesquite, suite

UITE**
quite \ˈkwīt\
see
EIGHT**, IGHT, ITE*

quite, requite

U SOUNDS

UITY*
annuity \ə-ˈnü-ə-tē\
see
E*, EA*, EE*, I**, IE*,
ITY, Y**

ambiguity, annuity, congruity,
gratuity, incongruity, ingenuity,
perpetuity, perspicuity,
superfluity, tenuity

UITY**
equity \ˈe-kwə-tē\
see
E*, EA*, EE*, ETTY,
I**, IE*, ITTY, ITY, Y**

antiquity, equity, inequity,
iniquity, obliquity, propinquity,
ubiquity

UKE
duke \ˈdük\
see
OOK**

archduke, cuke, duke, fluke,
Mameluke, peruke, rebuke

UL*
awful \ˈȯ-fəl\
see
ULL**

artful, awful, baleful, baneful,
bashful, brimful, careful,
cheerful, consul, cupful,
delightful, distrustful, doleful,
doubtful, Elul, eyeful, faithful,
fateful, fitful, forgetful, fretful,
graceful, grateful, harmful,
heartful, heedful, hurtful, ireful,
karakul, lawful, lustful, masterful,
mindful, mirthful, Mogul,
mournful, mouthful, needful,
pailful, painful, plateful, playful,
powerful, prayerful, proconsul,
purposeful, regretful, remorseful,
reproachful, resentful, restful,
revengeful, rueful, shameful,
shovelful, slothful, sorrowful,
tearful, thankful, thimbleful,
thoughtful, tuneful, unfaithful,
ungrateful, unmirthful, useful,
vengeful, wakeful, watchful,
wilful, wishful, wistful, woeful,
wonderful, worshipful, wrathful,
wrongful, youthful

UL**
annul \ə-'nəl\
see
IFUL, ULL**

annul

ULA
formula \'fôr-myə-lə\
see
A**

calendula, Caligula, campanula,
copula, fibula, formula, hula,
incunabula, nebula, peninsula,
scapula, spatula, spicula, tarantula

ULAR
angular \'aŋ-gyə-lər\
see
AR**, ER*, OR*

angular, binocular, cellular,
circular, corpuscular, funicular,
granular, globular, insular,
irregular, jocular, jugular,
lenticular, lobular, lunular,
molecular, monocular,
muscular, nebular, oracular,
orbicular, particular,
peninsular, perpendicular,
popular, rectangular, regular,
secular, semicircular, singular,
spectacular, triangular, tubular,
unpopular, valvular, vascular,
vehicular, vernacular

ULATE*
insulate
\'in(t)-sə-,lāt\
see
AIGHT, AIT*, ATE*,
EAT**, EIGHT*

articulate**, calculate, circulate,
coagulate, confabulate,
congratulate, ejaculate**,
emulate, expostulate, formulate,
granulate, inoculate, insulate,
manipulate, matriculate,
miscalculate, modulate, osculate,
peculate, perambulate, populate,
postulate**, recapitulate, regulate,
simulate, speculate, stimulate,
stipulate, strangulate, tabulate,
ululate, undulate

ULATE**
inarticulate
\ ˈin-är- ˈti-kyə-lət\
see
AIT**, AT***, ATE**,
EDIT, EIT**, ERATE**,
ERIT, ET**, ETTE**,
IATE**, IBIT, ICATE**,
ICIT, ICKET, IDGET,
IGOT, IMATE*,
INATE**, IOT**, IT,
ITE***, OLATE*,
ORATE**, OSET, OT***,
UET***, UGGET, UIT*,
URATE*

articulate*, consulate, ejaculate*,
immaculate, inarticulate,
postulate, ungulate

ULB
bulb \ ˈbəlb\

bulb

ULCH
mulch \ ˈməlch\

gulch, mulch

ULE*
rule \ ˈrül\
see
OOL*, OUL***, ULLE

ampule, animalcule, capsule**,
cellule, foot rule, globule, Golden
Rule, granule, lobule, minuscule,
misrule, module, molecule, mule,
nodule, overrule, plumb rule,
pule, pustule, reticule, ridicule,
rule, schedule, tule, vestibule,
Yule

ULE**
capsule \ ˈkap-səl\
see
ULL*

capsule*, ferrule

ULENT
opulent \ ˈä-pyə-lənt\
see
ENT**

corpulent, fraudulent, opulent,
succulent, truculent, turbulent,
virulent

ULET
amulet \ˈam-yə-lət\
see
ET

amulet, Capulet, epaulet, rivulet

ULF
gulf \ˈgəlf\

engulf, gulf

ULGAR
vulgar \ˈvəl-gər\
see
AR**, ER*, OR*

bulgar, vulgar

ULGE
bulge \ˈbəlj\

bulge, divulge, indulge

ULGENT
indulgent
\in-ˈdəl-jənt\
see
ENT**

fulgent, effulgent, indulgent,
overindulgent

ULK
bulk \ˈbəlk\

bulk, hulk, skulk, sulk

ULKY
bulky \ˈbəl-kē\
see
E*, EA*, EE*, I**, IE*,
Y**

bulky, sulky

ULL*
bull \ˈbu̇l\
see
OOL**, UL

bull, chock-full, pull

ULL**
dull \ˈdəl\
see
UL

cull, dull, gull, hull, lull, mull,
null, numskull, scull, seagull,
skull

ULLE
tulle \ˈtül\
see
OOL*, ULE

tulle

ULLY*
bully \ˈbu̇-lē\
see
E*, EA*, EE*, I**, IE*,
Y**

bully, carefully, fully, ruefully,
spitefully, sully, truthfully,
untruthfully, willfully

ULLY**
sully \ˈsə-lē\
see
E*, EA*, EE*, I**, IE*,
Y**

dully, gully, sully

ULOUS
fabulous \ˈfa-byə-ləs\
see
OUS*, US

credulous, fabulous, garrulous,
homunculous, incredulous,
meticulous, miraculous,
nebulous, pendulous, populous,
querulous, ridiculous,
scrupulous, tremulous,
unscrupulous

ULP
pulp \ˈpəlp\

gulp, pulp

ULSE
pulse \ˈpəls\

pulse, impulse, repulse

ULT
insult \in-ˈsəlt\

adult, antepenult, catapult,
consult, cult, difficult, exult,
insult, occult, penult, result,
tumult

ULTY
faculty \ˈfa-kəl-tē\
see
E*, EA*, EE*, I**, IE*,
Y**

difficulty, faculty, faulty

ULUS
calculus
\ ˈkal-kyə-ləs\
see
US

calculus, convolvulus, cumulus,
ranunculus, Romulus, stimulus,
tumulus

ULY*
duly \ ˈdü-lē\
see
E*, EA*, EE*, I**, IE*,
Y**

duly, truly, unruly

ULY**
July \jü- ˈlī\ *or*
\jə- ˈlī \
see
AI*, I*, IE**, IGH, UY,
Y*

July

UM
album \ ˈal-bəm\
see
AM**, ANUM, ATUM,
AUM, EUM, ITUM,
IUM, OM*, OME*,
ORUM, UM, UMB, UUM

addendum, adytum, alarum,
album, alum, annum, arboretum,
asylum, bay rum, begum,
bum, bunkum, candelabrum,
capsicum, cerebrum, chewing
gum, chrysanthemum, chum,
colchicum, conundrum,
corrigendum, curriculum, datum,
doldrum, drum, factotum, fe-
fi-fo-fum, fulcrum, glum, gum,
gypsum, harum-scarum, hokum,
hoodlum, hum, humdrum,
interregnum, kettledrum,
labarum, laburnum, laudanum,
lignum, magnum, maximum,
memorandum, minimum,
modicum, momentum, mum,
nostrum, oakum, opossum,
pabulum, panjandrum,
pendulum, peplum, per annum,
platinum, plectrum, plum,

UM

quantum, referendum, regnum, rostrum, rum, sanctum, scrum, scum, scutum, sebum, sedum, serum, simulacrum, sistrum, slum, sorghum, spectrum, strum, sugarplum, sum, sweet alyssum, tantrum, thrum, tintinnabulum, tympanum, tum, unum, vellum, viaticum, wampum, yum

UMA
puma \ˈpü-mə\ *or*
\ˈpyü- mə\
see
A**

Montezuma, Numa, puma, Satsuma, Uma

UMAN
human \ˈhyü-mən\
see
AN**

Hanuman, human, inhuman, superhuman

UMB
dumb \ˈdəm\
see
AM**, OME*, UM

benumb, crumb, dumb, numb, plumb, succumb, thumb, Tom Thumb

UMBER
lumber \ˈləm-bər\
see
AR**, ER*, OR*

cucumber, cumber, encumber, lumber, number, slumber, outnumber

UMBLE
humble \ˈhəm-bəl\
see
EL, LE

bumble, crumble, fumble, grumble, humble, jumble, mumble, rumble, stumble, tumble

UMBO
jumbo \ˈjəm-(ˌ)bō\
see
EAU, EW*, O*, OE*,
OT***, OUGH*, OW*,
OWE

gumbo, jumbo, mumbo jumbo

UMBRA
umbra \ ˈəm-brə\
see
A**

penumbra, umbra

UME
fume \ ˈfyüm\
see
OM**, OMB***, OOM

assume, brume, consume,
costume, exhume, flume, fume,
illume, legume, nom de plume,
perfume, plume, presume,
resume, subsume, volume

UMEN
albumen
\al- ˈbyü-mən\
see
EN**

acumen, albumen, bitumen,
catechumen

UMENT
document
\ ˈdä-kyə-mənt\
see
ENT**

argument, document,
emolument, instrument,
integument, monument

UMID
humid \ ˈhyü-məd\
see
ID, UID**

humid, tumid

UMMER
summer \ ˈsə-mər\
see
ER*, OR*

bummer, drummer, hummer,
Indian summer, midsummer,
mummer, summer

UMMY
dummy \ ˈdə-mē\
see
E*, EA*, EE*, I**, IE*,
Y**

chummy, dummy, gummy,
mummy, thingummy, tummy

UMN
autumn \ ˈȯ-təm\
see
AM**, OME*, UM

autumn, column

UMP
pump \ ˈpəmp\

air pump, bump, chump, clump, dump, frump, hump, jump, lump, mugwump, plump, pump, rump, slump, stump, thump, trump

UMPET
trumpet \ ˈtrəm-pət\
see
ET

crumpet, trumpet, strumpet

UMPH
triumph \ ˈtrī-əm(p)f\

galumph, harrumph, humph, triumph

UMPS
mumps \ ˈməmps\
see
UMP+*s*

dumps, mumps

UN
bun \ ˈbən\
see
ONE***

airgun, begun, Bull Run, bun, dun, fun, gun, homespun, Hun, machine gun, nun, outrun, overrun, pun, rising sun, run, shogun, shotgun, spun, sun, tun

UNA
tuna \ ˈtü-nə\
see
A**

Arjuna, Fortuna, lacuna, luna, tuna, una, Varuna, vicuna

UNC
quidnunc
\ ˈkwid-ˌnəŋk\
see
UNK

quidnunc

UNCE
dunce \ ˈdən(t)s\
see
ONCE*

dunce

UNCH
bunch \ ˈbənch\

bunch, crunch, hunch, lunch, munch, punch, scrunch

UNCT
defunct \di- ˈfəŋkt\
see
UNK+*ed*

adjunct, defunct

UND
fund \ ˈfənd\
see
UN+*ed*

bund, fecund, fund, furibund, gerund, jocund, moribund, orotund, refund, rotund, sinking fund

UNDER
under \ ˈən-dər\
see
AR**, ER*, ONDER**, OR*

asunder, blunder, sunder, thunder, under

UNE*
dune \ ˈdün\
see
EWN*, OON, UGN

commune, demilune, dune, immune, importune, jejune, June, Neptune, opportune, picayune, prune, rune, triune, tune

UNE**
fortune \ ˈför-chən\
see
UN

fortune, good fortune, misfortune

UNG
flung \ ˈfləŋ\
see
ONG**, OUNG

bung, clung, dung, far-flung, flung, high-strung, hung, lung, rung, slung, sprung, strung, stung, sung, swung, underhung, unhung, unstrung, unsung, wide-flung, wrung

UNGE
lunge \ ˈlənj\
see
ONGE

expunge, lunge, plunge

UNION
union \ ˈyün-yən\
see
ION**

communion, nonunion, reunion, union

UNITY
unity \ˈyü-nə-tē\
see
E*, EA*, EE*, I**, IE*,
ITY, Y**

community, immunity, impunity,
opportunity, unity

UNK
junk \ˈjəŋk\
see
ONK**

bunk, chipmunk, chunk, drunk,
dunk, flunk, funk, hunk, gunk,
junk, plunk, punk, shrunk,
skunk, slunk, spunk, stunk, sunk,
tree trunk, trunk

UNNEL
funnel \ˈfə-nᵊl\
see
EL, LE

funnel, runnel, tunnel

UNNY
bunny \ˈbə-nē\
see
E*, EE*, I**, IE*,
ONEY, Y**

bunny, funny, gunny, sunny

UNT
punt \ˈpənt\
see
ONT*

blunt, brunt, hunt, punt, runt,
shunt, stunt

UNY
puny \ˈpyü-nē\
see
E*, EA*, EE*, I**, IE*,
OONEY, Y**

puny

UOUS
virtuous
\ˈvər-chə-wəs\
see
OUS*, US

ambiguous, arduous, congruous,
conspicuous, contemptuous,
contiguous, continuous,
deciduous, disingenuous,
fatuous, flexuous, impetuous,
incestuous, incongruous,
inconspicuous, indeciduous,
ingenuous, insinuous,
mellifluous, presumptuous,

UOUS

promiscuous, sensuous, sinuous, strenuous, sumptuous, superfluous, tempestuous, tumultuous, tenuous, tortuous, unctuous, vacuous, virtuous, voluptuous

UOY
buoy \ ˈbü-ē\
see
E*, EA*, EE*, I**, IE*, Y**

buoy

UP
cup \ ˈkəp\
see
OP**

buttercup, checkup, chirrup, cleanup, close-up, cup, flare-up, frame-up, getup, gold cup, hang-up, het up, hiccup, holdup, hook up, ketchup, keyed-up, larrup, letup, lineup, lockup, makeup, pent up, pick-me-up, pickup, puffed up, pup, roundup, scup, setup, shake-up, shut up, stirrup, stuck-up, sup, syrup, teacup, toss-up, up, up-and-up, windup

UPE
dupe \ ˈdüp\
see
OOP

dupe

UPID
cupid \ ˈkyü-pəd\
see
ID, UID*

cupid, stupid

UPT
erupt \i- ˈrəpt\
see
UP+*ed*

abrupt, bankrupt, corrupt, disrupt, erupt, interrupt

UR
fur \ ˈfər\
see
ER**, ERE***, EUR, IR*, OR*, URE*

augur, chauffeur, concur, cur, demur, fur, incur, King Arthur, larkspur, lemur, murmur, non sequitur, occur, recur, slur, spur, sulphur, Yom Kippur

URA
tempura \ ˈtem-pə-rə\
see
A**

Angostura, Asura, camera
obscura, coloratura, tempura

URAL*
natural \ ˈna-chə-rəl\
see
AL*

augural, conjectural, guttural,
inaugural, natural, preternatural,
scriptural, structural, subnatural,
supernatural, unnatural

URAL**
rural \ ˈrür-əl\
see
AL*

intramural, mural, plural, rural,
Ural

URATE*
accurate \ ˈa-kyə-rət\
see
AIT**, AT***, ATE**,
EDIT, EIT**, ERATE**,
ERIT, ET**, ETTE**,
IATE**, IBIT, ICATE**,
ICIT, ICKET, IDGET,
IGOT, IMATE*, INATE**,
IOT**, IT, ITE***,
OLATE*, ORATE**,
OSET, OT***, UET***,
UGGET, UIT*, ULATE**

accurate, commensurate,
curate**, inaccurate,
incommensurate, obdurate

URATE**
saturate
\ ˈsa-chə-ˌrāt\
see
AIGHT, AIT*, ATE*,
EAT**, EIGHT*

curate*, inaugurate, saturate,
triturate

URB
curb \ ˈkərb\
see
ERB

blurb, curb, disturb, perturb,
suburb, uncurb

URCH
lurch \ ˈlərch\
see
EARCH, ERCH, IRCH

church, lurch

URD
curd \ ˈkərd\
see
EARD*, ERD, IRD,
ORD**, UR+*ed*, URE+*ed*

absurd, curd, Kurd, surd

URDLE
hurdle \ ˈhər-dᵊl\
see
EL, IRDLE, LE

curdle, hurdle

URDY
sturdy \ ˈstər-dē\
see
E*, EA*, EE**, I**, IE*,
IRDY, Y**

hurdy-gurdy, sturdy

URE*
capture \ ˈkap-chər\
see
ASURE, ATURE, ER*,
EUR, ICURE, ITURE,
OOR**, OR*, OSURE

adventure, agriculture, aperture,
capture, censure, cincture,
conjure, culture, debenture,
departure, disfigure, embrasure,
enrapture, failure, figure, fissure,
fixture, floriculture, gesture,
high-pressure, horticulture,
imposture, indenture,
injure, jointure, juncture,
lecture, leisure, low-pressure,
manufacture, misadventure,
mixture, moisture, nurture,
overture, pasture, peradventure,
perjure, picture, posture,
prefecture, prefigure, premature,
pressure, procedure, puncture,
quadrature, rapture, Scripture,
seizure, structure, suture, tenure,
texture, tincture, tonsure,
torture, transfigure, venture,
verdure, vesture, vulture

URE**
sure \ ˈshu̇r\
see
EUR

abjure, allure, assure, azure,
brochure, cocksure, coiffure, cure,
demure, embouchure, endure,
ensure, gravure, impure, insecure,
insure, inure, lure, manure, mind

URE**
cure, mure, obscure, photogravure, procure, pure, reassure, reinsure, secure, sinecure, sure, you're

URER
insurer \in-ˈshur-ər\
see
ER*, OR*

insurer, treasurer, usurer

URF
surf \ˈsərf\
see
ERF

surf, turf

URG
burg \ˈbərg\
see
ERG

burg, Gettysburg, Strasburg, Vicksburg

URGE
urge \ˈərj\
see
ERGE, IRGE

Demiurge, purge, scourge, splurge, spurge, surge, thaumaturge, urge

URGY
liturgy \ˈli-tər-jē\
see
E*, EA*, EE*, I**, IE*, Y**

chemurgy, dramaturgy, liturgy, metallurgy, thaumaturgy, theurgy

URITY
purity \ˈpyur-ə-tē\
see
E*, EA*, EE*, I**, IE*, ITY, Y**

futurity, impurity, insecurity, maturity, obscurity, purity, security, semi-obscurity

URK
murk \ˈmərk\
see
ERK, IRK

lurk, murk, Turk

URL
curl \ˈkər(-ə)l\
see
EARL, IRL, ORL

churl, curl, furl, hurl, purl, unfurl

URLY
curly \ ˈkər-lē\
see
E*, EA*, EE*, I**, IE*, Y**

curly, burly, hurly-burly, surly

URN
burn \ ˈbərn\
see
EARN, ERN*, OURN*

auburn, burn, churn, lecturn, nocturn, overturn, return, Saturn, spurn, sunburn, taciturn, turn, upturn, urn

URNAL
journal \ ˈjər-nᵊl\
see
AL*

diurnal, journal, nocturnal

URNT
burnt \ ˈbərnt\

burnt, sunburnt

URP
burp \ ˈbərp\

burp, usurp

URR
purr \ ˈpər\
see
ER**, IR*, UR

burr, purr

URROW
burrow \ ˈbər-(͵)ō\
see
EW**, O*, OE*, OT***,
OUGH*, OW*, OWE

burrow, furrow

URRY
hurry \ ˈhər-ē\
see
E*, EA*, EE*, I**, IE*, Y*

curry, flurry, furry, hurry, scurry, slurry

URSE
curse \ ˈkərs\
see
EARSE, ERCE

accurse, curse, disburse, nurse, purse, reimburse, wetnurse

URST
burst \ˈbərst\
see
ERSE+*ed*, IRST, URSE+*ed*

bratwurst, burst, cloudburst,
durst, knockwurst, liverwurst,
outburst, sunburst, wurst

URT
curt \ˈkərt\
see
ERT, IRT, UIRT

blurt, curt, Frankfurt, hurt,
spurt, yurt

URTLE
turtle \ˈtər-t°l\
see
EL, IRDLE, LE, URDLE

hurtle, mock turtle, snapping
turtle, turtle

URUS
epicurus
\ˌe-pi-ˈkyu̇r-əs\
see
AURUS, US

Arcturus, Epicurus

URVE
curve \ˈkərv\
see
ERVE

curve, incurve

URY*
perjury \ˈpər-jə-rē\
see
E*, EA*, EE*, I**, IE*,
Y**

augury, Canterbury, century,
conjury, injury, luxury, Mercury,
penury, perjury, treasury, usury

URY**
fury \ˈfyu̇r-ē\
see
E*, EA*, EE*, I**, IE*,
Y**

fury, jury

US
bus \ˈbəs\
see
AGUS, ALUS, AMPUS,
AMUS, ATUS, AURUS,

abacus, acanthus, agnus,
ailanthus, alumnus, amaranthus,
angelus, animus, ankus, arbutus,
Augustus, Bacchus, bacillus,
Belus, bogus, bolus, bonus,

US

EOUS, ERUS, ETUS,
EUS*, INOUS, INUS,
IOUS, ITOUS, ITUS, IUS,
OCUS, OPUS, ORUS,
OUS*, ULOUS, ULUS,
URUS, USS, YLUS, YRUS

Brutus, bus, cactus, Cadmus,
caucus, Celsius, census,
cholera morbus, cirrus, citrus,
colossus, Columbus, consensus,
conspectus, Copernicus,
Coriolanus, corpus, Cronus,
cultus, cyprus, Cyrus, dianthus,
Discobolus, discus, emeritus,
Enceladus, Ephesus, Erasmus,
eucalyptus, exodus, Faunus,
fungus, habeas corpus,
helianthus, hibiscus, humus,
Icarus, ictus, ignis fatuus,
impetus, incubus, isthmus, Janus,
Jesus, litmus, lotus, magnus,
Menelaus, mittimus, modus,
Momus, mucus, narcissus,
nautilus, negus, nimbus,
nonplus, obolus, Oedipus,
Olympus, omnibus, onus, opus,
papyrus, Pegasus, Peloponnesus,
Phoebus, phosphorus, platypus,
plexus, plus, polyanthus,
Polyphemus, Priapus, prospectus,
pus, ruckus, rebus, Remus,
Rhadamanthus, rhombus,
rumpus, sanctus, Silenus,
Silvanus, Sisyphus, solus, status,
stylus, surplus, syllabus, Tacitus,
Tarsus, Tartarus, terminus,
tetanus, thesaurus, thus, thyrsus,
Uranus, Ursus, us, Venus, versus,
virus, walrus

USA
Medusa \mi-ˈdü-sə\
see
A**

Arethusa, Medusa

USAL
refusal \ri-ˈfyü-zəl\
see
AL*

perusal, refusal

USE*
obtuse \äb-ˈtüs\
see
OOSE*, U+s, UICE

abstruse, abuse**, diffuse**,
disuse, Druse, effuse, excuse,
hypotenuse, obtuse, profuse,
recluse, refuse**

USE**
confuse \kən-ˈfyüz\
see
EW+s, IEW+s, OE**+s,
OO+s, OOSE**, OOZE,
U+s, UE*+s

abuse*, accuse, amuse, bemuse,
confuse, diffuse*, enthuse, fuse,
infuse, interfuse, misuse, muse,
peruse, refuse*, ruse, suffuse,
transfuse, use

USH*
crush \ˈkrəsh\

blush, brush, bulrush, crush,
flush, gush, hush, inrush, lush,
mush**, onrush, plush, rush,
scrub brush, slush, thrush,
toothbrush

USH**
push \ˈpu̇sh\

ambush, bush, mush*, push,
sagebrush, tush

USION
fusion \ˈfyü-zhᵊn\
see
ION*

allusion, conclusion, confusion,
delusion, disillusion, exclusion,
fusion, illusion, inclusion, infusion,
intrusion, obtrusion, profusion

USIVE
intrusive \in-ˈtrü-siv\
see
IVE**

conclusive, delusive, elusive,
exclusive, illusive, inclusive,
inobtrusive, intrusive, obtrusive,
unobtrusive, preclusive

USK
tusk \ˈtəsk\
see
USQUE

busk, dusk, husk, mollusk, musk,
rusk, tusk

USP
cusp \ˈkəsp\

cusp

USQUE
brusque \ˈbrəsk\
see
USK

brusque

USS*
fuss \ ˈfəs\
see
US

blunderbuss, buss, cuss, discuss, fuss, muss, percuss, truss

USS**
puss \ ˈpu̇s\

puss, sourpuss

UST
bust \ ˈbəst\
see
US+*ed*, USS+*ed*

adjust, antirust, august, brickdust, bust, combust, crust, disgust, distrust, dust, encrust, entrust, gust, just, locust, lust, mistrust, must, piecrust, readjust, robust, rust, sawdust, stardust, thrust, trust, unjust, wanderlust

USTER
buster \ ˈbəs-tər\
see
AR**, ER*, OR*

adjuster, baluster, bluster, buster, cluster, duster, filibuster, fluster, luster, muster

USTLE
rustle \ ˈrə-səl\
see
EL, LE

bustle, hustle, rustle

USTY
dusty \ ˈdəs-tē\
see
E*, EA*, EE*, I**, IE*,
UST+*y*, Y**

busty, crusty, dusty, fusty, gusty, lusty, musty, rusty, trusty

UT*
cut \ ˈkət\

abut, betel nut, but, butternut, catgut, chestnut, chut, clear-cut, coconut, Connecticut, crosscut, cut, doughnut, gamut, halibut, hut, jut, Lilliput, nut, peanut, rebut, rut, sackbut, scut, shortcut, shut, slut, smut, strut, tut, uncut, walnut, woodcut

UT** brut
brut \ ˈbrüt\
see
OOT*, UIT*, UTE

UT*** debut
debut \ ˈdā- ˌbyü\
see
EW*, IEU, IEW*,
O**, OE**, OO, OU*,
OUGH****, OUS**,
OUT**, OUX, U, UE*

UT**** put, output, shotput
put \ ˈpu̇t\
see
OOT*

UTAL brutal, refutal
brutal \ ˈbrü-tᵊl\
see
AL*

UTCH clutch, crutch, Dutch, hutch,
hutch \ ˈhəch\ smutch
see
UCH*

UTE acute, astute, brute, chute,
cute \ ˈkyüt\ commute, compute, confute,
see cute, dilute, dispute, disrepute,
EWT, OOT*, UIT** electrocute, execute, flute,
hirsute, jute, lute, minute, mute,
parachute, persecute, pollute,
prosecute, refute, repute, salute,
transmute, tribute, Ute

UTH truth, untruth, vermouth
truth \ ˈtrüth\
see
EUTH, OOTH, OUTH*

UTH
bismuth \ˈbiz-məth\
see
ETH, ITH

azimuth, bismuth

UTION
solution
\sə-ˈlü-shən\
see
ION*

ablution, circumlocution,
constitution, contribution,
dissolution, distribution,
elocution, evolution, involution,
locution, persecution, pollution,
prosecution, restitution,
retribution, revolution, solution

UTOR*
contributor
\kən-ˈtri-byə-tər\
see
AR**, ER*, OR*

contributor, distributor,
executor, interlocutor

UTOR**
tutor \ˈtü-tər\
see
AR**, ER*, OR*

persecutor, prosecutor, tutor

UTT
mutt \ˈmət\
see
UT*

butt, mutt, putt

UTTER
butter \ˈbə-tər\
see
AR**, ER*, OR*

butter, clutter, cutter, flutter,
gutter, mutter, peanut butter,
putter, shutter, sputter,
stonecutter, stutter, utter

UTTON
button \ˈbə-tᵊn\
see
ON*

button, glutton, mutton

UTTY nutty, putty, smutty
nutty \ˈnə-tē\
see
E*, EA*, EE*, I**, IE*,
Y**

UTY beauty, duty
duty \ˈdü-tē\
see
E*, EA*, EE*, I**, IE*,
Y**

UUM vacuum
vacuum \ˈva-(ˌ)kyüm\
see
OOM*

UVRE oeuvre, Louvre
oeuvre \ˈə(r)-vrə\

UX afflux, conflux, crux, efflux, flux,
crux \ˈkrəks\ influx, Pollux, reflux, tux
see
UCK+*s*, UCT+*s*

UY buy, guy
buy \ˈbī\
see
EYE, I*, IE**, IGH, Y*

UZ Santa Cruz, Tammuz, Veracruz
Veracruz
\ˌver-ə-ˈkrüz\
see
EW+*s*, IEW+*s*, OE*+*s*,
OO+*s*, OOSE**, OOZE,
OSE**, U+*s*, UE*+*s*,
USE**

UZZLE guzzle, muzzle, nuzzle, puzzle
puzzle \ˈpə-zəl\
see
EL, LE

— Y —
SOUNDS

Y*

cry \ ˈkrī\

see

EFY, EYE, I*, IFY, IGH,
ULY**, UY, YE*

apply, awry, blackfly, blue-sky,
butterfly, by, by and by, cry,
damselfly, dragonfly, dry, espy,
firefly, fly, fry, gadfly, hereby,
housefly, imply, lullaby, mayfly,
misapply, multiply, my, nearby,
occupy, outcry, passerby, ply,
preoccupy, pry, reply, satisfy,
shoofly, shy, sky, sly, small fry,
spry, spy, standby, sty, supply,
thereby, thy, try, whereby, why, wry

Y**

angry \ ˈaŋ-grē\

see

E*, EA*, EE*, EY*, I**,
IE*

abjectly, abruptly, accordingly,
adroitly, Allegheny, amply,
anchovy, angry, anomaly, arcady,
army, aunty, avowedly, baby,
badly, bankruptcy, bel esprit,
belfry, belly, biddy, bigotry,
blackly, blameworthy, blasphemy,
blindly, bloodthirsty, bony,
booby, botany, bossy, brawny,
briskly, buddy, buggy, bunchy,
Burgundy, bury, bushy, busy,
caddy, calumny, canopy, certainly,
certainty, cheeky, chiefly, choosy,
chunky, clingingly, clumsy, cocky,
colony, conspiracy, controversy,
copy, correctly, corruptly,
country, county, coyly, cozy,
crafty, cuppy, curtly, daily, daisy,
darkly, dearly, deftly, deputy,
deucedly, dicky, dinghy, dingy,
directly, dirty, doily, doughy,
doughty, downy, dowry, dreary,
droshky, drowsy, dumpy, early,
easy, eighty, elegy, empty,
entreaty, envy, epilepsy, eurythmy,

Y**

faulty, fifty-fifty, filthy, finicky,
fishy, flaky, flatly, fleshy, flimsy,
flinty, flossy, flunky, foamy,
fogy, foolhardy, forestry, forty,
foundry, frailty, frenzy, freshly,
friendly, frisky, frosty, frowsy,
fusty, fuzzy, gaiety, galaxy,
garden party, gaudy, gawky, gayly,
ghostly, glossy, godly, goodly,
goofy, gossipy, gramercy, greatly,
grimy, grisly, grouchy, grumpy,
guilty, half-empty, haply, happy-
go-lucky, harpy, hazy, heady,
healthy, heathenishly, heavy,
hoity-toity, honestly, hooky,
horny, hostelry, huffy, husbandry,
hypocrisy, idiocy, imperiously,
industry, inly, inquiry, irony,
Italy, ivy, jaunty, jelly, jeopardy,
jewelry, Jewry, jiffy, jointly,
jolly, jumpy, kilty, kindly,
kingly, lanky, larceny, laundry,
leafy, lethargy, liberty, lily,
Lombardy, lousy, lucky, lumpy,
lycanthropy, mammy, meaty,
mercy, mimicry, minstrelsy, miry,
missy, misty, moldy, monopoly,
mostly, mouldy, muchly, muddy,
mumsy, Muscovy, namby-pamby,
narrowly, natty, nearly, neatly,
neighborly, nervy, newly, newsy,
nifty, nightly, nimbly, ninety,
nippy, noisy, noteworthy, novelty,
objectly, oily, oozy, organdy,
orgy, outlawry, overstudy, paddy,
palfry, palsy, paltry, panicky,
panoply, pansy, partly, party,
pastry, patty, pebbly, perfectly,
perfidy, perilously, perky, pesky,
philanthropy, phony, pigmy,
piracy, pithy, pixy, plucky, podgy,
poky, polyandry, poppy, porgy,
porphyry, potbelly, poultry,

Y**

praiseworthy, priestly, priory,
privy, progeny, pudgy, Punch
and Judy, puppy, pussy, rainy,
raspy, ready, regularly, remedy,
revelry, risky, rocky, roughly,
ruby, ruddy, Rugby, rusty, rutty,
sacristy, safety, saintly, saucy,
scaly, scraggy, scratchy, scrawny,
scurvy, seaworthy, secretly, sentry,
shabby, sharply, sharpy, shifty,
shindy, shoddy, sightly, sissy,
sketchy, slangy, slightly, slimy,
smithy, smugly, snoozy, snugly,
softly, softy, solemnly, sooty,
sovereignty, sparingly, speakeasy,
spiffy, spongy, sporty, sprightly,
spunky, squally, steady, stealthy,
stingy, stocky, strategy, study,
subsidy, sultry, sundry, superbly,
surly, suzerainty, swanky, swarthy,
tansy, tantivy, tapestry, tawdry,
tawny, taxidermy, tetchy, theory,
therapy, Thessaly, thinly, third-
party, thirty, thorny, thoroughly,
thrifty, throaty, tidy, timothy,
toady, toby, toddy, tootsy-wootsy,
topsy-turvy, trebly, tricky, twenty,
ugly, understudy, unearthly,
uneasy, unerringly, unfriendly,
ungainly, unknowingly, unlucky,
unsteady, unwieldy, veery, vestry,
villainy, wanly, warranty, waxy,
wealthy, weary, weekly, wheezy,
whimsy, willingly, wily, windy,
wintry, wishy-washy, wooly,
wordy, wormy, worry, worthy,
wrongly, yearly

YAD
dyad \ ˈdī- ˌad\
see
AD*

dryad, dyad, hamadryad

YCH
triptych \ ˈtrip-(ˌ)tik\
see
IC, ICK

triptych

YCLE*
bicycle \ ˈbī-si-kəl\
see
EL, ICKLE, LE

bicycle, tricycle

YCLE**
cycle \ ˈsī-kəl\
see
EL, LE

cycle, recycle, kilocycle,
megacycle, motorcycle

YD
Jamshyd \jam-ˈshēd\
see
EAD**, EDE, EED

Jamshyd

YE*
bye \ ˈbī\
see
I*, IGH, Y*

aye, bye, dye, eye, good-bye, lye,
rye, tye

YE**
ye \ ˈyē\
see
E*, EA*, EE*, I**, IE*, Y**

ye

YKE
tyke \ ˈtīk\
see
IKE

dyke, tyke, Vandyke

YL
idyl \ ˈī-dəl\
see
EL, LE

beryl, dactyl, idyl, methyl, sibyl

YLE
style \ ˈstī(-ə)l\
see
IAL*, ILE*, UILE

argyle, hypostyle, peristyle, style

YLPH
sylph \ ˈsilf\

sylph

YME
rhyme \ ˈrīm\
see
IME*

rhyme, thyme

YMN
hymn \ ˈhim\
see
IM, IMB*, ONYM

hymn

YMPH
nymph \ ˈnim(p)f\

lymph, nymph, wood nymph

YNCH
lynch \ ˈlinch\
see
INCH

lynch

YNE
dyne \ ˈdīn\
see
IGN, INE*, UINE**

anodyne, auld lang syne, dyne, heterodyne, mnemosyne

YNX
lynx \ ˈliŋ(k)s\
see
INK+*s*, INX

larynx, lynx, pharynx

YP
polyp \ ˈpä-ləp\
see
IP

gyp, polyp

YPE
type \ ˈtīp\
see
IPE

archetype, daguerreotype,
linotype, monotype, prototype,
stereotype, tintype, type

YPH
glyph \ ˈglif\
see
IF*, IFF

anaglyph, glyph, hieroglyph,
triglyph

YPSE
apocolypse
\ə-ˈpä-kə-ˌlips\
see
IP+s

apocalypse

YPT
crypt \ ˈkript\
see
IP+ed, IPT

crypt, Egypt

YR
martyr \ ˈmär-tər\
see
AR**, ER*, OR*

martyr, satyr, zephyr

YRE
pyre \ ˈpī(-ə)r\
see
IAR*, IE**+er, IER**,
IGH+er, IRE*, Y*+er

byre, gyre, lyre, pyre, tyre

YRRH
myrrh \ ˈmər\
see
ER**, IR*, OR*, UR,
URR

myrrh

YSM
cataclysm
\ ˈka-tə-ˌkli-zəm\
see
ISM

abysm, cataclysm, paroxysm

Y SOUNDS

YS
chlamys \ ˈkla-məs\
see
ICE**, IS*, ISE****, ISS

chlamys

YSS
abyss \ə- ˈbis\
see
ICE**, IS*, ISE****, ISS

abyss

YST
cyst \ ˈsist\
see
ISS+*ed*

amethyst, analyst, catalyst, cyst, tryst

YTE
acolyte \ ˈa-kə- ˌlīt\
see
IGHT, ITE*

acolyte, gigabyte, neophyte, proselyte, troglodyte

YTH
myth \ ˈmith\
see
ITH

myth

YTHE
scythe \ ˈsī͟th\
see
ITHE

scythe

YTHM
rhythm \ ˈri-͟thəm\
see
IM, ITHM

rhythm

YVE
gyve \ ˈjīv\
see
IVE*

gyve

YX
onyx \ ˈä-niks\
see
IC+*s*, ICK+*s*, IX

onyx, oryx, pyx, sardonyx, Styx